Your Country Needs You

Answering the call, "Your Country Needs You," cadet nurses march
to their Induction Ceremony on May 13, 1944 on the University
of Minnesota campus in Minneapolis. Sixteen schools of nursing
in the Twin Cities area participated in this event. (Courtesy of
Margery Shanafelt Bitter. Bitter is cadet nurse in white cap, outside
in sixth row on right.)

Other books by Thelma M. Robinson
Cadet Nurse Stories/ The Call and Response of Women
During World War II
Co-author, Paulie M. Perry

Nisei Cadet Nurse of World War II/
Patriotism in Spite of Prejudice
Japanese translation by Babel Press,
Tokyo, Japan

For more information:
www.cadetnurse.com

Your Country
Needs You

Nurse Cadets of World War II

Thelma M. Robinson

Thelma M. Robinson

To order additional copies of this book, contact:
Xlibris Corporation
1-888-795-4274
www.Xlibris.com
Orders@Xlibris.com
63412

CONTENTS

Dedicated to Paulie
in remembrance
for her love and devotion for family and friends
and
for her passion in preserving the legacy of the
U. S. Cadet Nurse Corps

ACKNOWLEDGMENTS

M_y sister, Paulie Perry Gilbaugh and I, both cadet nurses during World War II and the post war years, decided that upon retirement we would research and write abut the Cadet Nurse Corps. We launched a nationwide Cadet Nurse Story Telling Project. Together we contacted more than 2,000 women who had served as cadet nurses. Our book, *Cadet Nurse Stories: The Call for and Response of Women During World War II,* was the first book to tell the cadet nurse story. Paulie's cataloguing of stories for more than 380 cadet nurses and significant others is now compiled and available in the Women in Military Service Memorial archives.

The nine nurse authors who participated in that project now tell their stories in full in Part II of this book. They have given us a personal glimpse as to what it was like to come of age during the Great Depression, their desire to be a nurse, and to live in a country involved in a world war. They gave their written permission to share their stories, for which we are grateful. They were participants of a short-lived but significant event in the history of our nation. Each of their stories stands alone and adds to our understanding of the U. S. Cadet Nurse Corps and nursing in the 1940s. In a few instances names in their stories have been changed to protect surviving relatives of those mentioned.

In the final gathering of the U. S. Cadet Nurse Corps archival data I express my appreciation to Alexander M. Lord, Ph. D., Acting Historian of the United States Public Health Service. She welcomed my husband and I to her office to spend as much time as we needed to review and copy pertinent materials. The archivists at the National Archives and Record Administration II in College Park, Maryland, were also helpful and efficient in locating the requested cadet nurse files.

I owe a deep gratitude to my copy editor, Clara Thomas. Her assistance has been indispensable in making this work more readable. Bobby Childer's final review was helpful.

To my amazing children and their spouses, I thank them for their support and love. Dennis and Joan, Mary Louise and Tom, Larry and Sheila, and Bruce and Kathy. I appreciate my eight grandchildren and for their interest regarding the role grandma played in World War II. Most of all, I owe immeasurable gratitude to my incredible husband, Dick, for more than 60 years. His love and his standing by in the archives as my research assistant, has made it possible for me to fulfill my passion in completing and bringing to fruition this last and final offering regarding the U. S. Cadet Nurse Corps.

Thelma M. Robinson

INTRODUCTION

Excitement filled the air in anticipation of the guest of honor. All of us present knew Lucile Petry Leone, but she didn't know us. Fifty years ago she had signed our certificate-of-membership cards designating our induction into the United States Cadet Nurse Corps. In 1994, a small group of cadet nurses of World War II had come together in San Francisco to honor Lucile Petry Leone, Emeritus Director of the U.S. Cadet Nurse Corps. As nurse cadet recruits across the country during the war, we viewed our founding director as an important reason why we continued to share a life-long passion and commitment to nursing.

In the summer of 1941, Surgeon General Dr. Thomas Parran of the U. S. Public Health Service (USPHS) called Petry Leone (then Petry) to Washington, D.C. to work on a program aimed at recruiting more nurses for both civilian and military needs. By 1943 the United States had become deeply embroiled in the World War, and expanding a program for the recruitment of nurses was urgent. The Nurse Training Act of July 1, 1943 created the U. S. Cadet Nurse Corps and was administered by the newly created Division of Nurse Education. Petry was appointed Director and was the first woman to head a division of the United States Public Health Service.[1]

Cadet nurses were the largest group of uniformed women (179,000) and youngest (average age 19) to serve our country during World War II. At the gathering mentioned above, my sister, Paulie Perry, and I were launching our nationwide Cadet Nurse Story Telling Project in preparation for our first book regarding the Corps.[2] We were in San Francisco to meet other cadet nurses as well as to spend time with Petry Leone. This spunky lady of 92 years of age had much to tell us. What a privilege it was to listen to her stories and to hear her tell about her early beginnings in nursing.[3] At the 1994 gathering that included 13 former cadet nurses, Petry Leone recollected:

> I was an only child and grew up in Lewisburg, Ohio. In 1921, I was 19 and moved with my family to Delaware where my father became the new principal of a high school. Earning my own expenses, I enrolled in the State University of Delaware. I had no science in high school so I decided to take science in college and selected chemistry as a major. Physiological chemistry was a revolution for me. I knew I wanted to experience the chemistry in human bodies, not in test tubes. When I told my teacher I was going to pursue nursing, she thought that was a waste of my talents. My father said, "You've never been in a hospital. You've never known a nurse. You had better get some experience."
>
> During my junior and senior year, I went to New York City and worked as a nurse aide in a small hospital and was further challenged to pursue nursing. I graduated from the University of Delaware in three and one/half years with a degree in teaching, but nursing was my goal. My family and advisor were not impressed.
>
> I received a catalog from Johns Hopkins School of Nursing, and a class was starting in February. That settled it, that's where I would go. Hopkins was a wonderful place for me to be, it was then very old-fashioned, very tight, but that didn't bother me. What I saw was blazing new discoveries in medical research every time I walked down the hall. Some doctor had discovered something new. This is what I came for. [Petry received a diploma in nursing in 1927]. I then borrowed money and got my master's degree at Teachers College [Graduating in 1929, Petry ranked first in her class and received a scholarship that entitled her to pursue graduate study in nursing at Teachers College, Columbia University in New York City].

I was lucky to have a teacher there who had graduated from the University of Minnesota (School of Nursing). This school had two firsts: (1) The first school of nursing to offer a bachelor's degree in nursing, and (2) the first school of nursing to leave a hospital and go with a university, leaving what I call an intervening authority. This is what attracted both Katharine Densford and I to this school of nursing.

Katharine J. Densford was an internationally recognized nursing leader who served as the dean of the University of Minnesota School of Nursing (UMSON) from 1930 to 1959. Densford held leadership positions in virtually every national and international nursing organization.[4] Densford, the first dean of a university school of nursing, and her assistant Petry were trail blazers in the course of changing nursing from apprenticeship-type nurse training programs connected with hospitals to university-based nursing education.[5]

Lucile Petry Leone sits by her photograph taken when she was the Director of the U. S. Cadet Nurse Corps (1943—1948). (November 1994, San Francisco. Author's Collection)

> Lucile Petry received a B. A. from the University of Delaware in 1924 and a Diploma in Nursing from Johns Hopkins Hospital School of Nursing in 1927. She received her M. A. from Teachers College at Columbia University in 1929. Petry held teaching positions at the University of Minnesota School of Nursing (UMSON) from 1929 to 1935. In 1936 she returned to Teachers College for graduate study. In 1936 she returned to UMSON, where she was associate professor and assistant dean when called to Washington, D. C. in 1941.

Next at the gathering, it was the audience's turn to share its experiences. Following are some of the amazing stories. Laddie Hughes attended UMSON, which had the largest number of cadet nurses enrolled of any other school of nursing. She joined the Cadet Nurse Corps and graduated in 1946, and she knew both Petry and Densford. This is Hughes' story:

> I am a public speaker and often talk about the Cadet Nurse Corps, and I like to tell my grandchildren who say to me, "Grandma, what did you do in the war?" Of course I am proud to answer that I was a cadet nurse in World War II. I like to share that our government spent a great deal of money educating us through the Corps and it was the first time that this much money was spent on women. I have used my nursing to advance both my political and speaking arenas. Miss Petry and Miss Densford were my role models.

Hughes received an appointment from President George Bush to serve on the USPHS Professional Advisory Committee for Nursing Division in Washington, D.C., and she felt that it had something to do with her being in the Corps. One woman on the staff at the Division of Nursing was also a cadet nurse.

Elizabeth Haglund also graduated from UMSON in 1946, and Densford was also her role model. Haglund said:

> When I was a student nurse, we were not allowed to get married, but because of the war, regulations were relaxed. One of my classmates was to be married in Grand Forks, North Dakota. We were scheduled for an exam, and several of us planned to go to the wedding; however, the hospital where we were training told us that we had to remain to take the exam. We went to see Katharine Densford, and she decided that we should go to the wedding and we could take the exam at another time. Katie D. was a gracious lady.

Petry Leone was reminded of still another story about Katharine Densford. "A wealthy woman gave Katharine $300 to help a student nurse. There was a student nurse who was a good dancer. On thinking that dancing might have something to offer nursing, Katharine gave the money to her. This student became a famous dancer."

Marlo Mason North graduated from Children's Hospital School of Nursing in San Francisco in 1946. Putting in a plug for her school of nursing, she said:

> My school of nursing was the first women's and children's hospital east of the Mississippi. The accelerated program gave me an additional opportunity for the operating room experience which I dearly loved. I continued to work after graduation and became head nurse of that department in charge of instructing students. In 1957, I retired to become a home nurse for my three sons. The Cadet Nurse Corps gave me a wonderful basis, and I'm grateful for that.

Grace Davis graduated from the Stanford University School of Nursing in California and shared this story:

> I started out to be a teacher. It was during my last year in college that I switched to nursing and joined the Cadet Nurse Corps. My last six months were spent serving in military hospitals. We were called third lieutenants and exposed to amazing things that they did in plastic surgery, burns, etc. I enjoyed working with corpsmen and Army nurses. I will never forget an incident one night when I was on duty with an Army nurse lieutenant and one of our patients was terminal. He called out, "Nurse, I'm dying, I'm dying."
>
> I thought we should do something, get the oxygen, get the doctor, but this nurse didn't. The lieutenant went to his bed and held him until he died. What I learned from this woman and the sacred thing about nursing is that we are often with people at a critical time. We need always to listen to our patients. This man knew he was dying.

Davis combined nursing and education and became a nurse educator, teaching at her alma mater then moving on to the University of California School of Nursing San Francisco to teach in the graduate program. She was then appointed assistant dean for student affairs, and that is when she met Lucile Petry Leone in another capacity. Petry Leone coordinated the program for international students and visitors which fell under the department that Davis headed. One day Petry Leone came into her office and said, "I think you are my boss." Davis said that was the time she fell in love with the woman. Petry Leone advised over 100 students from 20 countries. She added that it was the best retirement job one could possibly have.

The circle of stories continued, but the most startling came from two Japanese American cadet nurses, Stella Horita Kato and Ida Sakiohira Kawaguchi. Both had to leave their homes in California and were relocated from the West Coast because of their ancestry during World War II. Furthering their education beyond high school would have been hopeless had it not been for the Cadet Nurse Corps. We were astounded by their stories. Kato was the first to speak:

> My family was uprooted from our home in California and relocated in the Amanche Relocation Center in Colorado, a sage brush forsaken land. I worked in a mess hall for $12 a month then decided to train as a nurse's aide. After working in the camp hospital for a year, the head nurse asked me if I was interested in becoming a nurse, and then she told me about the Cadet Nurse Corps. My head nurse suggested that I apply to the Madison General Hospital School of Nursing, a small school in Wisconsin. I was accepted and joined the U.S. Cadet Nurse Corps. The Corps made it possible for me to become a student nurse with paid tuition, maintenance, books, uniforms, and even a small stipend. I made wonderful friends, and to this day I keep in touch with my former classmates.

Kawaguchi and her family were also incarcerated because of their ancestry. They were escorted under armed guard to the Gila River Relocation Center in Arizona. She, like Kato, volunteered to train as a nurse's aide and worked a year at the relocation hospital. At that time she could become cleared to leave camp if someone would vouch for her and if she could find a way to support herself. For both Kato and Kawaguchi, the Cadet Nurse Corps was their ticket to freedom, a way to prove their loyalty, and an opportunity to serve their country in uniform as well as to earn an education. It was a joyful moment for these women some 50 years later to thank Lucile Petry Leone in person for their opportunity to receive a nursing education.

After fifty years Stella Kato (left) and Ida Kawaguchi (middle) thank
Lucile Petry Leone, Emeritus Chief of the Cadet Nurse Corps for
the opportunity for their education. Both women were interned due
to their Japanese ancestry. The Corps gave the women an opportunity
to leave the relocation camps and train as nurses. (November 1994.
Author's Collection.)

For the next five years following this first exciting gathering,
my sister and I returned to San Francisco each January to celebrate
Petry Leone's birthdays with the cadet nurses living in the San
Francisco area. Each year brought more stories and understanding
of the Cadet Nurse Corps.

Lucile Petry Leone admires the cadet nurse uniform, still in style after
50 years. Paulie Perry models the uniform for the occasion celebrating
Leone's 94th birthday. (January 1996. Author's Collection).

Petry Leone continued to receive honors throughout her
Nonagenarian years. We heard her speak at the 50 Years
Commemorative Cadet Nurse Corps Gala on May 14, 1994, in
Bethesda, Maryland. The following year she traveled to Baltimore,
where she received her tenth honorary doctoral degree from Johns
Hopkins University. At her 95th birthday celebration we read
the following letter, which she had received from Carolyn Beth
Mazzella, Chief Nurse Officer of the Department of Health and
Human Services, with signatures of the nursing staff:

On this occasion of your 95th birthday, the nurses of the Public Health Service want to offer our best wishes and congratulations.

Your leadership of the Cadet Nurse Corps opened new horizons in nursing as a profession, in nursing education, and in service. Your insistence on equality and quality of schools of nursing pioneered integration. And your rise to Assistant Surgeon General created career paths in the uniformed services for women and nurses who followed. We salute you and thank you for your vision and excellence in nursing.

We wish you joy in your many memories of the Public Health Service. We wish for you fresh opportunities to create new memories and to share your legacy of leadership.

Congratulations![6]

The Cadet Nurse Story Telling Project provided Petry Leone the opportunity to share her legacy and she supported our efforts as novice nurse historians. She touched us personally, enabling us to learn from her and to stretch our horizons even at our age. Petry Leone, a nursing witness to history whom I had the pleasure to know, continues to inspire me even after her passing.

In our nationwide Cadet Nurse Story Telling Project conducted during the nineties, my sister and I contacted more than 2,000 women who served as cadet nurses during World War II. To our pleasure 380 women representing 112 schools of nursing from 33 states responded by sharing their stories, photographs, and other memorabilia. Their memories, woven with historical documentation, was the first book to tell the cadet nurse story.[7]

After meeting Kawaguchi and Kato in San Francisco and getting to know them and other Japanese American nurses, I became interested in their plight during World War II. I researched and wrote a second book telling about the Nisei cadet nurses. These Japanese American women in spite of prejudice and internment, proved their patriotism by serving in the Corps. This book is now translated into Japanese. The people living in Japan are interested in learning about what happened to their Japanese American cousins living in the United States during World War II.[8]

While these two publications captured much of the atmosphere and drama of nursing on the Home Front during World War II, there is still more to be told. Much of the operation of the U. S. Cadet Nurse Corps remains hidden away in the tens of thousands of manuscript documents extant in hundreds of file boxes at the National Archives and Records Administration II located in College Park, Maryland. Here one can find an extensive amount of administrative documentation and unpublished internal memoranda supplementing the mammoth quantity of correspondence and reports contained in more than 1,000 school of nursing individual files. Scrapbooks containing pictures and newspaper clippings are also carefully preserved.

My husband, Dick, and I made a third trip to our National Archives II for a final gleaming of cadet nurse archival information. The U.S. Cadet Nurse Corps is one of the best documented nursing events of our time. For those seeking information about a cadet's certificate of membership in U.S. Cadet Nurse Corps during World War II, the information is available. To this location, cadet nurses and their families may request with appropriate information a copy of a cadet's certificate of membership signed by Lucile Petry.[9]

The purpose of this book is to further expound on the legacy of the U. S. Cadet Nurse Corps and to continue to deepen our understanding of this time based on archival information and to read stories told by cadet nurses. As has been requested, a list of each of the 1,125 schools of nursing participating in the Corps program appears in the appendix.

The Maltese Cross that we cadets wore on our sleeves became our badge of courage to speak out against rules and repression that student nurses experienced during this time. My hope is that this final offering, completing a trilogy regarding the U. S. Cadet Nurse Corps, will tell us where we have been and why we went there, as well as to the role the Corps played in the advances made in the schools of nursing that we know today. May we also remember that for cadet nurses of World War II, nursing was a calling and a privilege to be of service in caring for our fellowmen on the Home Front.

PART 1

1

Nursing Preparedness

In Europe in early 1940, one country after another was being swallowed up by dictators—Finland by Stalin's Russia; and Norway, Denmark, Belgium, Luxembourg, Netherlands, and France by Germany. Hitler then turned his full attention to battering Great Britain. Across the Atlantic, Americans were stunned by the war developments. By midsummer the defeat of Great Britain seemed entirely possible. A great debate was going on in the United States between internationalists, who favored rushing material aid to Britain, and the isolationists, who opposed any U.S. involvement in the war.

In September 1940, President Roosevelt signed the Selective Service and Training Act into law, requiring men to register for the first peacetime draft in the history of the country. Men whose number was called would be trained for one year and then remain in an enlisted reserve subject to recall in the event that their country became in peril. As America prepared for war, shortages were in the offing—gas, rubber, steel, coffee, sugar, silk stockings, and most of all, workers.[10]

The defense war boom and building up the armed forces created the mushroom growth of communities in which defense industries and cantonments were located. Serious problems of health and civilian hospitals throughout the country were taxed to capacity. Wage earners, with better-filled pocketbooks could now afford the 3-cents-a-day hospitalization plans (7,500,000 reported subscribers in 1941) that resulted in people seeking health care that had been neglected during leaner times.[11]

The influx of millions of new workers, both men and women, created unprecedented health problems, not only in industrial plants but also in exploding trailer camps and in communities where crowded, unsanitary living quarters menaced the health of workers and their families. War industries more than doubled the number of nurses employed in industrial health work. In addition to the salaried services nurses were rendering in hospitals, defense areas, and communities, nurses were called to teach classes in home nursing and to give volunteer direction to millions of citizens who were eager to be prepared to serve in case of an acute national emergency.

The American Red Cross recruited nurses to serve in the Army but recognized that nurses should be permitted to contribute to the national effort by serving the people in their own community. However, more registered nurses were responding to the popular appeal of joining a military service, which helped create the severe shortage of nurses throughout the country.[12]

Dr. William P. Shepard, a well-known public health physician on the West Coast, outlined the complex and urgent problems and the need for public health nurses on the Home Front:

> Almost overnight great cities of industrial workers have suddenly sprung up where there was little population before. Many small towns have doubled their populations and I can name ten or fifteen that have tripled or quadrupled the population.
>
> Until you see it, you cannot conceive the serious public health problems this entails. In some of these areas, sewer manholes are overflowing into the streets: rat population, always a serious plague menace on this coast, has even outstripped human population increases; sanitation of public eating places has broken down; immunization is being neglected. Hospitalization is at a premium in all places and actually unobtainable in many areas. Remaining physicians are so overworked they are refusing house calls . . . Deliveries are taking place in homes without even a midwife . . .[13]

Dr. Shepard voiced his concern that the war might be lost on the Home Front if trained people were not used where they could do the most good.

Concerns were also mounting over the needs of large numbers of wartime casualties in Europe. Donors were giving blood from which plasma, the liquid component of blood, was removed; it could be more easily preserved and stored than whole blood and used as a substitute. Nurses were needed to assist with the blood donor program. Meanwhile, nurse leaders who had experienced World War I were convinced that the preparation of nurses for the demands of defense and possible war could not follow peacetime ways. In World War I, the Army had had its own School of Nursing. By the advent of World War II, the Army was disinclined to undertake again the training of nurses. Therefore, the responsibility of supplying military as well as civilian nursing needs rested with nursing organizations and health authorities.[14]

While nurses of the first World War had learned that emergency training did work, they also knew that too great of an expansion in the profession could leave a peacetime nation with large numbers of nurses unemployed, which had occurred during the Great Depression. On July 29, 1940, the American Nurses' Association sponsored a meeting in New York City to discuss the actual role of nursing in national defense. The deliberations resulted in the formation of the Nursing Council of National Defense. The representatives from six national nursing organizations, the American Red Cross, and the federal agencies involved in nursing were present.[15]

As demands for civilian and military nursing service increased, the Council concentrated on two projects: (1) a survey of national nursing resources, and (2) a plan to secure federal funds to expand educational opportunities for nurses. In 1940, for the first time, registered nurses were classified as professional workers by the U. S. Census Bureau. The census data, however, was of little value as the Census Bureau did not differentiate between graduate nurses and nursing students.[16]

The national inventory identified 100,000 nurses who were eligible for military duty, providing they could pass the physical examination. The Council also surveyed nursing school resources and discovered that most schools were not equipped to expand their instructional and housing facilities. The Council then proposed an appropriation of federal funds for nursing education.[17]

Isabel Maitland Stewart (1878-1963) was America's most influential spokeswoman in the area of nursing education at this time. Stewart, born in Ontario, Canada, was one of nine children, all of whom were encouraged to engage in educational pursuits. Beginning her career as a school teacher, she turned to nursing and graduated from Winnipeg General Hospital School of Nursing in 1903. She continued to further her education at Teachers College, earned several degrees at Columbia University in New York City, and became a professor in that institution. She studied history and believed that women and nurses could not measure up to the demands of a vocation or profession without education and knowledge of the social conditions and needs of their day.[18]

As Director of the Division of Nursing Education, Stewart believed that a period of crisis was also a period of opportunity. She said, "We shall lose some parts of the old system, but there will be a chance to try out new ideas and methods." Stewart's reputation as a curriculum expert was well-established, and in later years she became known as "Miss Curriculum." Regarding the past and future of nursing, she said in 1940:

> Nursing inherits certain monastic, military, and medical traditions that tend strongly toward authoritarianism and repression. These different strains in our blood are constantly in conflict . . . By helping to defend democracy we may help also bring about our own professional emancipation, achieve our full professional maturity, and win for our educational system the measure of support it has a right to ask from society which we serve.

No one will question the fact that nurses are essential to national defense and to social welfare and safety at any time. No one will question the need for funds to support a proper system of education for nurses. At the present time, however, the government is pouring out funds for the training of military and naval officers and men, for airplane pilots and mechanics, industrial workers of many varieties—but there seems to be no money in any of Uncle Sam's many pockets for the basic training of nurses. Yet nurses must be ready to care for all these men when they are sick; they must be ready to ride in the flying ambulances, to go into the front line trenches—wherever the battle against disease is being fought.[19]

In February 1941, Stewart was ready with a "proposal to expand the present nursing education program for nurses to provide for national defense needs," which she presented to Dr. W. Studebaker, U. S. Commissioner of Education. The proposal included financial aid of $12,000,000 to selected schools of nursing.

As the result of Stewart's leadership, the Appropriation Act for 1942 (effective July 1, 1941) became the first federal support of nursing education. However, the proposed expenditure was reduced to $1,200,000. The act—Training for Nurses, National Defense—provided for three types of training: (1) Refresher courses for inactive registered nurses; (2) postgraduate education in special fields for graduate nurses; and (3) increased student enrollment in basic nursing school. The surgeon general of the Public Health Service was empowered to establish regulations for the administration and allotment of funds. These were issued, reviewed, and approved, by the nursing education advisors to the program. Thus, two years before the creation of the U. S. Cadet Nurse Corps, a method of federal grants to nursing education was established.[20]

Congress passed the Labor-Security Agency Appropriation Act of 1942 allocating $1,200,000 to selected nursing schools. This poster symbolizing Uncle Sam capping a student nurse assisted in the recruitment of 6,000 women to train as nurses. (National Library of Medicine.)

In May 1941, on the eve of United States involvement in World War II, Stewart read an address on "National Preparedness" at a session of the 47th Annual Convention of the National League of Nursing Education, in Detroit, Michigan:

> If war comes, the cry of nurse shortage will become louder. Reactionary movements will flare up again—indeed they have already begun. All kinds of short cuts will be tried and we shall be told that patriotism demands the sacrifice of many of our hard-won standards. Some compromises may be required, but let us not forget that a period of crisis is also a period of opportunity.[21]

Stewart had asked an old colleague, M. Adelaide Nutting, to review her speech. In 1907, Nutting became the first professor of nursing in the world at Teachers College at Columbia University in New York City. Stewart became an assistant to Prof. Nutting. In 1925 Nutting retired and Stewart succeeded her as director of the college's Division of Nursing Education.

Stewart received an answer back in strong, bold handwriting that was remarkably vigorous for a frail lady of nearly 83 years. Nutting reminded Stewart that "the past is the present and the present is the future." Stewart then said that "we shall remind ourselves often of that truth in the crucial days ahead—that we are not only meeting an emergency, but building the future of nursing by the actions we take or fail to take today and that our successors will some day read the record and appraise it.[22]

With the bombing of Pearl Harbor, the nurse shortage became more critical and the need to expand the enrollment of young women in schools of nursing was evident. On the opening page of the January 1942 issue of the *American Journal of Nursing*, Editor Mary Roberts emphasized that a state of war existed and appealed to nurses to come to the defense of their flag by volunteering for the Army Nurse Corps, Navy Nurse Corps, and the American Red Cross.[23]

Julia C. Stimson, the President of the American Nurses' Association, announced to nurses in that same issue:

> This is our hour—the hour toward which everything in our past lives has been leading. Perhaps we have been complacent and indifferent to life's need for us. But now in this time of real danger the future depends on you and me. We cannot deny the fact that the war can be lost. If we and others refuse to believe this and remain careless of our country's danger, the fate of other unprepared peoples can be ours. But now the time of excuses and delays is past. The destruction of the lives and homes of our countrymen has occurred and our liberties are being imperiled.

We know we shall win, but victory won't be gained because of shock, horror, and grief. We shall have to earn it every day by doing more than our best—giving more than our all. We nurses are working together with all our might, but our might each day is going to be mightier. Nurses are leaders. Each must lead herself to greater giving of self, greater willingness to seek and find more ways to add her strength to that of others.

This is our hour. Our hour today of utmost giving will be our hour in God's good time, of victory and content because we have not failed.[24]

The Nurse Training Recruitment Program, initiated as part of the National Defense health activities, was successful within the limitations imposed by law. Appropriations during the fiscal years 1941 and 1942 aided 12,000 student nurses in 309 schools of nursing. Equipment and supplies for libraries and laboratories and salaries for instructors were also provided. About 3,800 inactive nurses were given refresher courses, and some 4,800 graduate nurses received postgraduate training in special fields essential for the war effort. In 1941, 41,397 women were admitted to schools of nursing, which was an increase of 3,284 over those recruited the previous year. Enrollment, however, was still not high enough to alleviate the nurse shortage.

Graduate nurses continued to respond in large numbers to the call of the armed forces, leaving staffs of hospitals, health and welfare agencies, schools of nursing, and institutions depleted. Nurses were constantly leaving to get married at a time when hospitals were reluctant to hire married women with children. By the end of 1942, student nurse enrollment reached 47,500, but continued to fall short of the national need for nurses. It became evident that nurses could not be trained fast enough to meet the rapidly increasing demands of both the military and civilian populations. The need for more substantial government aid in the recruitment of nurses became apparent when the Army and Navy issued a call for 2,500 nurses each month during 1943 in addition to the 35,000 already in military service.[25]

In 1942, the National Council on National Defense was renamed National Nursing Council for War Service and summarized the problem this way: (1) Some civilians continued to demand special private duty nurses and luxury services; (2) As opportunities for well-paid jobs in industry increased, many nurses were leaving their profession for higher salaries; (3) State boards of nurse examiners were loathe to modify hard-won nurse practice regulations, and nurses whose licenses had expired found reentry into their profession tangled with red tape; (4) The military forces had recruited nurses in anticipation of action in the various theaters, and these waiting nurses wrote home discouraging letters about the Army Nurse Corps; (5) Professional nurses in the Army lacked permanent status; (6) Negro nurses were not admitted by the military on an equal basis with white nurses and frequently not at all; (7) Local, state and even national recruiting councils had no official status for the recruitment of nurses.[26]

The Subcommittee on Nursing and other advisors to the nurse training programs reevaluated the Nation's nursing needs and recommended Federal Aid for basic nursing education be doubled for fiscal year 1943. Representative Frances P. Bolton, of Ohio, a champion of nurses since World War I, was a strong advocate for increasing the federal aid and supported the increase. She reported to Congress that still further expansion of schools of nursing might be required the following year.

As the war progressed and employment increased, competition for woman power also increased. The number of nurses in training was climbing steadily, however, enrollment lagged behind. Maintaining a necessary balance of civilian and military nursing service had not been solved.[27]

2

Creation of the Corps

President Franklin D. Roosevelt addressed the nation on January 1, 1942 saying, "The new year calls for courage and the resolution of old and young to help win a world struggle in order that we may preserve all we hold dear. We are confident in our devotion to our country, in our love for freedom, in our inheritance of courage. But our strength, as the strength of all men everywhere is of greater avail as God upholds us."

The President set aside the first day of the year as a national day of prayer. During the twelve months following Pearl Harbor, the nation buckled down to the immense task of arming itself to combat aggression around the world. President Roosevelt's charge was to hasten the nation's military and economic preparation for war.[28]

As the war progressed, the demand for nurses both (civilian and military) heightened to the extent that leaders in nursing and hospital fields consulted federal agencies to see what could be done. The fact was emphasized that the nurse training program in operation was insufficient to meet the requirements of the armed forces and, at the same time, maintain essential civilian services. Broadening the scope of the nurse education program was urgent.[29]

Out of the deliberations of many groups concerned with the problem of nursing service grew first the conceptions of a "Victory Nurse Corps." On January 9, 1943, the Subcommittee on Nursing called a meeting of representatives of the National Nursing Council for War Service, the Public Health Service, the Subcommittee on Hospitals, and several nursing schools. These representatives appointed a committee to work out the details of a student nurse corps (see endnote).[30]

Before this committee was a proposal to admit 65,000 new students in the fall of 1943. The number of students admitted in 1942 was 47,500. The rationale for requesting 10 times the amount of the already appropriated moneys of $65,000,000 was as follows:

1. The competition for woman power was becoming acute. The women's auxiliaries of the military forces and war industries were attracting many women who would ordinarily enter schools of nursing.
2. Under the competition of lucrative wartime job offerings, girls who would normally have been willing to pay for nurse training would be attracted to other fields.
3. The pre-Corps plan for nursing training was based on the incentive principle that schools would receive assistance in training nurses in excess of the prewar enrollment. A new approach was necessary.
4. Student nurses were contributing two-thirds of the nursing care in hospitals with schools, and it was essential to increase the number of student nurses so services would not fall to a dangerously low level.

Supporters of a Victory Nurse Corps held further that: (1) Uniforms and insignia would appeal to young women; (2) payment of a small stipend would cover personal expenses; (3) acceleration of the traditional 36 month's course to 30 would attract additional students; (4) provision for full maintenance would offset high salaries paid by industry; (5) the plan made it possible to receive a lifetime education; (6) and reimbursement of hospitals for partial costs of maintaining all students for nine months would provide schools an incentive to increase enrollment.[31]

Some nurse leaders present at the meeting were shocked to hear that the government was proposing the classroom instruction be reduced to a 24 month minimum, and that student nurses be retained throughout the remaining year for general staff duty. The laws that required the nurse to attend school for three years would be fulfilled, but the exploitation of the nurse by the hospital (long a blot on the traditional system of nursing education) would be increased. This amounted to the use of indentured labor and was a throwback to the dark ages of nursing. Although no decisive action was taken, there was no question that every person present was profoundly impressed by the increasing urgency to prepare nurses as rapidly as possible.[32]

Out of the deliberations grew the legislation introduced in the House (H.R. 2326) on March 29, 1943 by Mrs. Francis P. Bolton, Ohio Congresswoman. Bolton had been a friend to nursing since World War I. As wife of Representative Chester Bolton, she had supported the Army School of Nursing, which was the answer to the nurse shortage at that time. She also contributed to nursing education by endowing, in 1923, the Frances Payne Bolton School of Nursing of Western Reserve (now Case Western) University in Cleveland, Ohio.

Bolton was drawn into active politics in 1932 when she took part in the campaign of reelection of her husband. In campaigning, she exhibited a flair for reducing complex issues to simple terms and for getting across a woman's point of view. Upon the death of her husband in 1939, she was asked to fulfill his term. Congress gave her a check for $10,000 as a widow which she returned as she said it was excessive.[33]

The bill that Bolton introduced would provide for the training of nurses for the armed forces, governmental and civilian hospitals, health agencies, and war industries through grants to the institutions providing training. The Senate companion bill, introduced by Senator Josiah W. Bailey of North Carolina, added an amendment that barred discrimination against race, creed, or color.[34]

Hearings were held by committees of the House and the Senate on May 7-8, 1943. Surgeon General Dr. Thomas Parran of U. S. Public Health Service said, "The nurse training bill has been drafted after much care and deliberation and extended consultation with the nurse-training institutions of the country and their associations, and with hospital groups in the country. In fact, I should like to say for the record that there has been the closest possible cooperation between the Public Health Service and the professional groups who are concerned equally with us in this important problem."

Dr. Claude W. Munger of the American Hospital Association testified before the committee that "the shortage of nursing personnel is serious . . . In some places desperate." He pointed out that 90 percent of the nursing schools were owned or controlled by hospitals, and if they could increase enrollments there would be replacement of graduate nurses entering the armed forces.

Katherine Faville, Chairwoman of the National Nursing Council Recruitment Committee, in presenting why students should receive a personal allowance from the government stated, "Nursing is the only woman's war job at the present time in which the trainee has to pay her way while she is training, and that is certainly a handicap in recruiting."

One of the most forceful statements was made by Marion W. Sheahan, who represented both private and government agencies—the National Council for War Service and the Subcommittee on Nursing . . . She summarized the consideration that lead to the Corps plan, testifying in the Senate hearings as follows:

> We in the [nursing] profession feel we have done all that we can. We are competing with all of the other spectacular and dramatic appeals to women of the country . . . We do feel that in order to compete with all of the other attractions for young women, through industry paying large salaries, through the other women's activities of the Government—the WAAC's and the WAVES and the SPARS that there must be some evidence that the Government considers . . . that nursing is essential.

> . . . we feel that opening up the government hospitals
> and the hospitals under the Army and Navy will provide
> extra clinical facilities so that students can actually be
> given reasonably sound nursing education. We have come
> to the point where we feel justified in asking for this aid,
> because without it we just don't see that we could do the
> job.[35]

Congress accepted the reasoning that if thousands more nurses entered training, they would help replace graduate nurses enlisting for military service. Congress also heard with interest that after nine months of training, three students could replace two graduate nurses. The supporters of the legislation expressed no fear that subsidizing of nurse education would bring an overabundance of nurses when peace came. They predicted that peacetime America would need to employ more nurses in the care of veterans and in larger public health programs, as a result of expanding health insurance. Francis Payne Bolton, cosponsor of the legislation said:

> As I look into the future I believe that nursing
> will be one of the most important activities requiring
> an almost unlimited number of nurses; not only will
> military, naval, and veterans' hospitals be carrying
> probably the greatest load in history, but the effects of
> total war will take on an unpredictable toll here, and
> our rehabilitation program will require highly skilled
> nurses: nor can we stop at our own frontiers—all the
> world will need the consecrated intelligent care that
> only the professional nurse is equipped to give.[36]

On May 12, 1943, Bill H.R. 2664 was passed by the House of Representatives. This bill referred to the Senate on May 24, was passed on June 4 without a dissenting vote. The Nurse Training Act was ready on June 15, for the signature of the President. On July 1, 1943, the act became Public Law No. 74, which would be referred to in the future as the Bolton Act.

President Roosevelt signs into law the bill that created the Nurse Training Act which later became known as the Bolton Act. Sugeon General Dr. Thomas Parron looked on. (National Archives and Records Administration.)

Proposed names for the newly established nurse corps were "Victory Nurse Corps" or "Student War Nursing Reserve." These were discarded, and the training program for student nurses became the United States Cadet Nurse Corps.

Surgeon General Dr. Thomas Parran immediately sent a long telegram to 1,300 schools of nursing in the states and territory of Puerto Rico describing the program, followed up with an application form and instructions by mail. The two schools of nursing in Hawaii could not participate as they were in the war zone, and there were no schools of nursing in Alaska at that time.

Briefly, the Bolton Act provided for a uniformed Cadet Nurse Corps and for grants for postgraduate training. All state accredited schools of basic nursing were eligible to apply for funds in the program. The three-year program provided basic training accelerated to 30 months as well as a six-month period of student service for senior cadets to serve in a federal or nonfederal hospital or other health agency. In return, the federal government paid the schools for tuition and fees, as well as for the maintenance of students for the first nine months of training. These funds enabled the schools to increase enrollments and to meet their added costs. As for the cadets, any young woman who was a high school graduate and who could meet the admission requirements of an approved school of nursing participating in the program could join the Cadet Nurse Corps. Out of government funds, the school then transmitted to the cadet a complete scholarship and a monthly stipend as her personal allowance. In return, cadets agreed to remain in essential nursing service, military or civilian, for the duration of the war.[37]

After the passage of the Bolton Act, a Division of Nurse Education was established in the office of the Surgeon General of the U. S. Public Health Service, Federal Security Agency. Miss Lucile Petry (later Leone) was appointed director, becoming the first woman to direct a division in the U. S. Public Health Service. She had been on the nurse education staff of the Public Health Service for the past two years and had recently been appointed Dean of Cornell University, New York Hospital School of Nursing, in New York City. She was granted leave of absence from this position to take up her duties as director of the new division.[38]

As provided by law, an Advisory Committee of nursing and related professional groups was appointed by the federal security administrator to assist in guiding the nurse-training programs. Drawn from various sections of the country, the members of the committee were:

Isabel M Stewart, Director of Nursing Education, Teachers College, Columbia University, New York City.

Anna D. Wolf, Director, School of Nursing and Nursing Service, Johns Hopkins Hospital, Baltimore, MD.

Marion G. Howell, Director, Frances Payne Bolton School of Nursing, Western Reserve University, Cleveland, OH.

Estelle Massey Riddle, Executive Secretary, Committee on Negro Nursing, National Council of War Service, New York City.

Margaret Tracy, Director, School of Nursing, University of California, Berkeley, CA.

Sister Helen Jarrell, Dean, Loyola University School of Nursing, Chicago, IL.

James A. Hamilton, President, American Hospital Association, Chicago, IL.

Dr. Oliver C. Carmichael, President, Vanderbilt University.

Dr. Hyrum Leo Marshall, Professor of Public Health, University of Utah, Salt Lake City, UT.

Rev. Alphonse M. Schwitalla, S.J., Dean, School of Medicine, St. Louis University, St. Louis, MO.[39]

On June 25, 1943, in Washington D.C., the advisory committee held its first meeting with government administrators. It was the beginning of a series of conferences that were to continue throughout the war. Representing the government were the Surgeon General Dr. Thomas Parran of the U.S. Public Health Service, Director of the Cadet Nurse Corps Lucile Petry, and Mary Switzer representing the Federal Security Administration and the War Manpower Commission. This group considered the initial task of formulating regulations to carry out the purposes of the Nurse Training Act. The excitement of charting an untried course pervaded the meeting.

Schools of nursing, hospitals, and public health services were flooded with questions about the new U.S. Cadet Nurse Corps. To answer these questions the three administrators of the new program—Dr. Parran, Petry, and Associate Director, Mrs. Eugenia K. Spalding, made a nationwide tour during July and August. At meetings scheduled in seventeen key cities, they discussed practical questions about the types of programs offered, the uniform, the eligibility of married students, the obligation of the Corps members, and the relationship of the government to schools participating in the program. Dr. Parran emphasized that the Corps was not a federally standardized program. The Corps members could attend any of the 1,300 accredited nursing schools that met the requirements of the Corps. Parran added, "In my opinion, the Bolton Act, which authorizes the Corps, is the most important piece of war legislation for the protection of public health, both civilian and military."[40]

The newly formed Division of Nurse Education's Memorandum No. 1 to nursing schools, hospitals, nursing councils, and state Boards of Nurse Examiners set forth the details and principles of the Cadet Nurse Corps. Much of the work was decentralized to six Public Health Districts with headquarters in Richmond, Virginia, San Francisco, New York City, Kansas City, Missouri, New Orleans, and Chicago. These offices were directly responsible to the Washington D.C. headquarters.[41]

With an initial appropriation of $65,000,000 for the year beginning July 1943, the nurse training program was under way. Only a few weeks after appropriations were available, the first school was approved for participation in the Corps program. Uncle Sam had called for 65,000 new nurses, and recruits were in line waiting to join the Corps.[42]

3

Charting the Course

Lucile Petry, Director of the Cadet Nurse Corps, lost no time in taking up her charge after being appointed in 1943. At that time she said, "So vital is the nation's need for woman power in nursing that the seventy-eighth Congress has appropriated sufficient funds to give assistance to every nurse to prepare herself for this work. Through the Bolton Act, health on the home front and healing on the battlefront are thus accorded their rightful place in the total effort of a nation at war." [43]

The regulations governing the eligibility of nursing schools for participating in the program followed the standards of the National League of Nursing Education. The school of nursing had to be approved by the nurse examining board in the state or territory in which the school was located. The school also had to be affiliated with a hospital approved by the American College of Surgeons.[44]

In 1942, the Committee on Educational Problems in Wartime of the National League of Nursing Education had been drawing plans for shorter basic nursing programs to fit war needs, while at the same time maintain educational standards. The earlier federal nurse training program did not require acceleration. Many schools, balked at the numerous problems involved and resisted acceleration of their programs. In the past, a student's clinical experience had often been based on the hospital's need for nursing service on the wards, rather than on the student's well–rounded educational experience.[45]

The acceleration of training for cadet nurses, a key feature of the Cadet Nurse Corps, was required of participating schools by Public

Law 74. The reason behind acceleration was to get more students out faster, to distribute their service among other hospitals, and to free living quarters and educational facilities in schools for incoming recruits. During the first nine months, the cadet was protected by Corps regulations from serving more than an average of 24 hours a week on the wards. No longer scrubbing of floors or endless hours of cleaning on the wards was acceptable as part of the training for beginning student nurses. Regulations stated that the junior cadet now had a 44-48 hour week, including classes. Previously, this was a time when students were assigned a six day week of eight hours of night duty and were still required to attend their daytime classes. A senior cadet, free of classes, could now request assignment outside her school for a specialized practice of her interest.[46]

Acceleration of training proved to be one of the thorniest problems in administration of the Nurse Training Act of 1943. University schools of nursing with five-year programs were eligible to participate, but they could only receive Corps scholarships after the student had completed two years of pre-nursing courses. The Corps scholarship covered a 30-month period. Since most states required 36 months of training for graduation and to earn a diploma in nursing, it was not possible to cut six months from the educational program. It was agreed, therefore, as a compromise plan, to design a Pre-Cadet and Junior Cadet period to take 30 months as well as a Senior Cadet period of six months' full service preliminary to graduation. All State Boards of Nursing cooperated with the plan.[47]

The school would provide units of instruction in conformance with accepted present practice in basic nursing education as well as with adequate clinical experience in the four basic services—medicine, surgery, obstetrics, and pediatrics. The educational staff had to carry out a well-balanced schedule of organized instruction, clinical experience, and study. Well-equipped classrooms, laboratories, libraries, and other facilities that were adequate for the proposed enrollment had to be provided. Schools would be checked for satisfactory living facilities and adequate student health service. The federally sponsored program was voluntary; however, the school of nursing that wished to survive had a strong incentive to participate since prospective students sought admission to schools where they would benefit from the Bolton Act funds.[48]

The majority of schools had not applied for accreditation by one of the national professional nursing organizations, and a visit from a nurse education consultant from the U.S. Public Health service was an unprecedented experience. The consultant's role was to help institutions develop satisfactory educational standards for participation in the Corps. Further, the nurse educational consultant worked with state boards of nurse examiners, nursing councils, hospital associations, procurement and assignment committees, and other organizations in her district.[49]

Lucile Petry Leone gave full credit to the 25 nurse education consultants for assisting schools of nursing to dramatically increase their enrollments as well as to improve nurse education standards at the same time. In 1994, she said, "These committed professional nurses worked hard and put in long hours. In addition to their weekly scheduled visits, they conducted Saturday morning workshops and invited nurse educators in the area to participate. During these sessions they discussed new and better ways to teach the nursing student."[50]

One consultant reported on her assignment. She said that before visiting a school of nursing she first went over the application, noting especially the financial part. She invited the state board's director to meet with her emphasizing the importance of federal and state agencies to work together. The standards of state boards varied greatly which was a concern for the consultants. With the accelerated program of the Corps, graduating cadets, still had to meet the requirements of their licensing agency.

The consultants emphasized education for the students knowing that for the hospital, staffing by cadets was the priority. However, the consultants helped nurse directors visualize the path nursing would need to take after the war. They used their influence with the hospital administrators to push for needed improvements in the school of nursing programs. Often these problems of deficiencies ignored by hospital administrators were the ones the nursing directors recognized, but did not have the power to change.[51]

The strong incentive was for the weak nursing schools to improve to the point in which they could participate in the program. Although the Cadet Nurse Corps program was established primarily to expand the quantity of nursing service personnel, it also became a force in improving nursing education and nursing service throughout the country.

In each Public Health District, recruitment and public relations officers supervised local recruitment, organized community groups, carried on programs for mass communication, and consulted with the central office on policy matters and recruitment techniques. Auditors assigned to district offices were responsible for auditing the accounts of participating schools for accuracy and compliance with federal requirements. They also surveyed fiscal and accounting practices of schools which requested such assistance.

Surgeon General Dr. Thomas Parran, in addressing hospital administrators said in 1943 that all communication would be sent directly to the nurse directors of the schools of nursing. He said that each nursing school would need its own budget for audit purposes. This was a drastic change for many schools of nursing during the 1940s. Budgets often lay buried within hospital expenditures controlled by hospital board of directors.[52]

The Rev. Alphonse M. Schwitalla (S.J.), member of the Advisory Board to the Surgeon General, sent out an appeal to Catholic hospitals and schools of nursing to fully participate in the Corps. He noted that Catholic schools were educating approximately one third of the nurses in the country and emphasized the importance for the new program to be successful and to achieve the intended results. One Sister superintendent expressed concern of a financial burden with the loss of the third-year student's services just at the time when they were most helpful to the hospital. The Reverend stressed that Catholic schools would gain influence in the future if they showed full strength in meeting the national emergency. He said, "We are called upon to participate in the education of student nurses for a life of intensified usefulness and self-sacrifice . . . This fact alone is the challenge. We must accept it."[53]

Nurse leaders of the day were determined to maintain the essentials of good preparation for nursing and at the same time aid in meeting the increased demands for wartime nursing services. Stella Goostray, RN, President of the National League of Education, presented her views at the American Hospital Association's second War Conference in Buffalo, New York in 1943. She said:

> We have accepted the principle of acceleration for the period of the war. We are in good company for most of the other types of educational institutions have done likewise . . . It is necessary to see that the pruning shears are used judiciously where there is overlapping and repetition . . . We accept the principle that our first responsibility is to supply the military with the nurses needed . . . We are asking 65,000 young women to enter our schools at a time when the world is theirs. Neither the glamour of the uniform, nor the attraction of all expenses paid, nor the jingle of money in the change purse, nor the appeal to patriotic motives is going to attract the kind of young women we want in our schools . . . these young women will have to be assured that in a nursing school they are getting something more, and that "something more" is a sound preparation in nursing.[54]

Anna Wolf, Director of the Johns Hopkins School of Nursing, also expressed her concern during an advisory committee meeting in 1943. She added:

> The national picture is not altogether pleasing. A large number of our 1,300 nursing schools are not training skilled nurses and haven't [been] for the past 40 to 50 years. The main reason is the small school with its plea to be left unchanged . . . There must be some solution to

this which doesn't penalize the whole country, and every student who goes to these poor schools."[55]

As the regulations were tested against actual conditions, the "reasonable standards" did not seem possible of attainment by some schools. These borderline schools produced only a small percentage of the total Cadet Nurse Corps force, but they were trouble spots for the administration. Some of them were given provisional approval and allowed three months in which to improve their educational goals. During this period the schools received help from the educational nursing consultants.[56]

Nationwide scarcity of nurses in the past had often been due to insufficient educational teaching staff and facilities. Here Corps Director Lucile Petry and her administration advised taking advantage of the junior college and universities for the subcontracting of instructors in the teaching of basic preparatory nurse courses. The use of non-nurse instructors would be used when appropriate, and the nurse teacher would be relieved of non-teaching functions.[57]

The hiring of married women was recommended, and they were welcomed by overworked colleagues. The married nurses, like other professional women, were proving that they could continue with their careers and at the same time keep the home fires burning. In order to take more students, schools of nursing were encouraged to expand into clinical specialties such as psychiatric and public health, thus enriching and broadening the experience for the student nurse. Postgraduate traineeships were a part of the Corps program.

As waves of patriotism swept the country, nurses volunteered for military services in large numbers and continued to create a shortage of nurse instructors. As the war progressed the need for more nurses with advanced preparation continued to grow. Administrators were fearful that the new and larger cadet classes would be without teachers. At the end of 1943, the Procurement and Assignment Service of the War Manpower Commission classified nurses enrolled in postgraduate study as essential; that is, they would not be released to join a military service. Colonel Florence A. Blanchfield, Superintendent of the Army Nurse Corps, reported to the Advisory Committee in June 1944:

> Our efforts last year concentrated on all groups of nurses. From now on, we will turn our efforts to individual contacts with nurses who have been declared available, instead of trying to build up a large spirit and eagerness for service among nurses in general. We don't want to overstimulate those nurses who are already in essential positions.[58]

But the postgraduate plan was not meeting the wartime need and Surgeon General Dr. Thomas Parran called a meeting. It was decided that the way to deal with this situation was to devise on-the-job training for those nurses in greatest need of special training but who were unable to leave their posts. The Nurse Training Act of 1943 was amended to permit federal subsidy of intensive on-the-job courses and emergency university courses. With that impetus, this gap in the training program was rapidly narrowed.[59]

Many conferences and workshops for teachers and directors were held throughout the country dealing with curriculum problems. A large proportion of the schools were benefiting from these opportunities to learn and to share ideas. Motivation ran high, for the spirit of helping the war effort as well as the desire to assist student nurses in earning an education.[60]

Nurse Historians, Beatrice J. Kalisch and Phillip A. Kalisch noted, "Until World War II, the federal government had ignored conditions in the nurse training schools. Now a combination of circumstances was responsible for an abrupt shift. Federal aid to the nursing education program had an enormous impact on conditions in the hospital wards and the classrooms. The administrators, faculties, students, and patients all experienced direct benefits from the Corps program and would affect future standards."[61]

4

Style Right

By 1943, Surgeon General Dr. Thomas Parran announced that the way had been cleared to undertake the cooperative program for the Cadet Nurse Corps. Plans were moving rapidly to meet the acute shortage of nursing services through the provision of the Bolton Act (passed by the 78th congress and signed into law by President Roosevelt on June 15, 1943).

Describing this "partnership job" Dr. Parran said:

> The task of the U. S. Cadet Nurse Corps is to enroll 65,000 additional students in basic schools of nursing during the present fiscal year; to make the students available for full-time nursing duty under supervision at an earlier date than was possible under the former plan; and to maintain a continuous supply of graduate nurses pledged to serve in essential nursing positions for the duration of the war. Whether we accomplish this vital war objective depends upon the teamwork which all of us apply to our specific tasks in the program.
>
> The U. S. Cadet Nurse Corps offers benefits to the individual student, to the schools of nursing, and to the hospitals and agencies that avail themselves of the senior cadets' services. But this broad program with its generous provisions also lays definite responsibilities upon all those who participate. This is a partnership job between the U. S. Public Health Service, the institutions, and the students. I am confident that through continued

teamwork we shall achieve the goal which means so much to the health of our country.[62]

On July 14, 1943, the New York Times headlined that 100,000 were expected to enroll in the new U. S. Cadet Nurse Corps. It explained that this was an accelerated program, and the student would be required to meet the admission, scholastic, and graduation requirements of the particular school of nursing in which she was enrolled. All cadets would be provided with a distinctive street uniform which would identify them as members of the Corps. The article further noted that the uniform design was not yet available, although it would be "pretty and feminine" rather than military-style.[63]

On August 16, 1943, the National Nursing Council for War Service invited dignitaries to a fashion show and a luncheon held at the Waldorf-Astoria in New York City. (See endnotes for list of dignified guests present at the luncheon.)[64]

Dr. Parran brought word from Paul V. McNutt, chairman of the War Manpower Commission, that the WMC was giving the same priorities to women in essential industries (such as agriculture and war manufacturing), could transfer to the Cadet Nurse Corps like the recruits who wanted to transfer to the WACS, WAVES, SPARS and Women Marines.[65]

A jury of 32 fashion editors were present to choose an official uniform for the Cadet Nurse Corps from three designs selected from a group submitted by outstanding designers. Francis P. Bolton, Representative from Ohio who introduced the bill that created the corps, congratulated the designers. She said, "We are here today on a joyous spirit. We want our students to feel themselves at once a part of the great military strength of this country. Nothing could do this as adequately as putting them into uniform. It is our business to make this uniform style-right . . . and as charming as humanly possible."

Molley Parnus designed the winning uniform to be worn with the beret modeled by Sally Victor, well-known New York millinery designer, after that of Great Britain's General Montgomery. The basic color was a soft dark gray with scarlet button-on epaulets which gave a military air to the softly tailored garments.[66]

The National Nursing Council for War Service sent the following release describing the official cadet nurse uniform:

> The summer uniform, a jacket suit of gray and white striped cotton, is accented with red epaulets and big pockets. It is worn with a plain round-neck white blouse. The skirt is simple and gored.
>
> For winter, a guard's coat of gray velour, fitted and belted in back, with convertible collar, side pockets, and set-in sleeves will identify the Corps members. It also features the red epaulets on the shoulder and is worn over the jacket suit of gray wool. The fitted jacket, single breasted with pockets fastened with button flaps, will match the skirt, five gored for action. The U. S. Public Health Service insignia will be worn on the jacket lapels and the Corps insignia of the Maltese on the upper left sleeve.
>
> The raincoat is of gray paratroops satin twill, water repellant with an officers collar, large patch pockets, red epaulets of the same material and a wide belt. It is single breasted and fastened with the official U. S. Public Health Service official insignia silver buttons.
>
> The gray Montgomery beret carries the official U. S. Public Health Service insignia beneath the spread eagle and American Shield. The official button of the Cadet Nurse Corps is silver, bearing the official U. S. Public Health Service insignia of a horizontal fouled anchor with a winged caduceus upright in the center of the shank. The fouled anchor represents the seaman in difficulty. The caduceus is the staff of Mercury, the messenger of the Gods, and is the ancient symbol of the physician. This insignia dates back to the earliest response of the Public Health Service, the medical care of sick and injured seamen.[67]

The winter topcoat, with trim guard's-coat lines, is of gray wool. Like the uniform, it has red epaulets and sleeve insignia. Silver buttons are marked with the corps device of the U. S. Public Health Service.

This attractive two-piece suit is of gray wool contrasted by regimental red epaulets, silver insignia buttons, and the Cadet Nurse sleeve insignia—a silver Maltese Cross on a red ground. The cocky Montgomery beret matches the uniform.

In addition to the uniform and topcoat shown above, a summer suit, raincoat, summer beret, and specified accessories will be issued without charge to all members of the U. S. Cadet Nurse Corps. From models submitted by prominent designers and stylists, a jury of New York fashion editors chose the coat and suit originated by Molly Parnis and the beret designed by Sally Victor. Wearing of the uniform is optional with students except on special occasions which will be designated by the school of nursing.

The cadet nurse uniform, heralded as the most attractive for all women who served in uniform during World War II, provided a strong incentive for your women to join the Corps. (National Archives and Records Administration)

The Maltese cross became the insignia of the Cadet Nurse Corps and was worn on the left shoulder of both the outdoor uniform and the student nurse uniform of her school of nursing. The Maltese cross, once worn by the Knights of St. John and a survivor of the crusades, became the insignia of many groups caring for the sick. The eight points of the cross signified the beatitudes that the knights symbolized in their works of charity. These declarations of blessedness made by Jesus in the Sermon on the Mount included the following:

Spiritual joy
To live without malice
To weep over thy sins
To humble thyself to those who injure them
To love justice
To be merciful
To be sincere and pure of heart
To suffer persecution[67]

The outdoor uniform of the Cadet Nurse Corps was considered a masterpiece of uniform design. The recruitment slogan of the Council of War Service was "Join a Proud Profession," and the uniform fit the slogan.

The school of nursing in which the cadet was enrolled supplied the outdoor uniforms with the exception of blouse, gloves, shoes, and stockings. Cadets provided these items at their own expense. As shoes were rationed, cadet nurses used their shoe ration coupons to purchase their shoes. Every individual in the country during World War II was entitled to two pairs of wearable or repairable shoes. Lucile Petry sent a memo out to schools of nursing advising them that if a cadet had only one pair of wearable or repairable shoes, it was possible for her to obtain a special ration coupon from her local Office of Price Administration Office. The wearing of the uniform was optional, except for occasions when the school designated the wearing of the uniform mandatory.[68]

The National Nursing Council for War Service, along with their communication about the Cadet Nurse Corps uniform, noted that production and distribution were being worked out and information would be released as soon as possible. The Council approved a mail-order house geared for wide distribution which could handle the uniform contract most efficiently. J. C. Penney Co., one of three bidders, was selected. Since the Corps had no military status, there were difficulties in securing materials under priority controls of the War Production Board, and the newly enlisted cadets would wait many months for their uniforms. The wardrobe would cost the government $100 per cadet.[69]

The cadet would wear the student uniform of her own school of nursing with the Maltese patch on her left sleeve while on duty in the hospital. Each school of nursing in the 1940s took pride in their distinctive uniform, cap, and cape. The impressive capping ceremony that took place after the probationary period was a time of joy and accomplishment for the student. Her cap was the symbol of nursing.

Historically, the white starched indoor nurse uniform and cap for both students and graduates were worn only in the hospital, a practice that continued into the 1970s. A quote from an American Journal of Nursing in December 1944, read as follows:

> I can't imagine a well-bred as well as a properly trained nurse being willing to "exhibit" herself in uniform either in a hotel dining room or in any other public place. I consider the uniform sacred to the sick room and the hospital . . . Let us be known by our deeds and not by our uniform.[70]

Exceptions to the wearing of the all-white uniform outside of the hospital took place when a special nurse event occurred such as capping, graduation, or community recognition. The "nurse in white uniform" caught the attention of the public when 3,500 graduate nurses were honored at a merit award ceremony in New York's City Hall on October, 14, 1944. Twenty-five registered nurses received pins for outstanding performance while merit certificates were presented to nurses representing the staffs of the city's twenty-eight hospitals. Edward M. Bernecker, M.D., Commissioner of Hospitals, told the nurses present:

> The graduate nurses of the municipal hospitals of this city, for almost three years now, have done a magnificent job in caring for the sick despite serious shortages of personnel and material. Their ranks have been depleted

from a normal complement of 6,200 to 3,500, but still they carry on, unselfishly and devotedly ministering to the sick.

The ceremony paid tribute to the Home Front Army of Nurses in the New York City municipal hospitals.[71]

The nurse cadet uniform was heralded as the dressiest of any design for women in war service. On September 5, 1943, Lucile Petry was photographed in the striking gray uniform when she visited the White House. Her purpose was to explain the purpose of the Corps to the visiting Mrs. Winston Churchill and her daughter Mary Churchill, who was wearing the uniform as member of the British Auxiliary Territorial Service.[72]

Much to the disappointment of the cadets, the Corps would reach a strength of 95,000 in more than a thousand schools of nursing before the uniform was available. The few uniforms available would be worn by models recruiting for the Corps. The first time the cadets appeared en masse in uniform was on May 6, 1944, at the dedication of residence halls for nurses at Adelphi College, Garden City, New York.[73]

5

Enlist In A Proud Profession

According to the Nursing Council for War Service, unless 65,000 new students were recruited by schools of nursing by the end of 1943, the country would have been unable to maintain civilian health on the Home Front. The quota represented almost twice the number of students admitted to schools of nursing during former peace-time years. The challenge was to present a better image of nursing and to improve public relations for schools of nursing in order to increase the enrollment of student nurses.[74]

Jean Henderson, Chief of Recruitment and Public Relations for the Corps, said that urgency of securing recruits as rapidly as possible made it impossible to conduct a study to determine all of the prejudices and misconceptions regarding nursing. All that was needed was to verify the prevalent attitudes about nursing that were roadblocks in the recruitment of cadets. To convince young women, as well as their families, friends, and counselors, the first year would focus on nursing as a proud profession.

Henderson emphasized that the nursing school should be considered an institution for higher learning and reeducation would be required in that student nurses could no longer be considered as chattels of service. The cadet nurse should now realize that it was her responsibility to prove that nursing was a proud, honorable, and distinguished profession. Henderson would take every means to publicize the vital wartime contribution of cadet nurses.[75]

The National Nursing Council for War Service had been in operation since 1941 and served as the official clearing house for nurses who wanted information as to how they could serve their country in uniform. The Box 88 in New York City was established as a national Information center and handled 80,000 inquiries during the first year. It was there, to Box 88, that young women wrote for information about nursing opportunities regarding the Corps.[76]

First year recruitment poster presented nursing in a positive light. Complex attitudes about nursing had to be overcome in order to conduct a successful recruiting campaign. (Photo courtesy—Program Support Services, Department of Health and Human Services)

The American Hospital Association responded by establishing recruiting centers in all member hospitals operating nursing schools—1,295 of the approximately 6,500 hospitals in America. Recruitment booths in these hospitals offered information to potential candidates for the Cadet Nurse Corps. Recruiting materials were supplied by Washington headquarters, but the work was carried on by volunteers.[77]

Another great boost in promoting the Cadet Nurse Corps came from the War Advertising Council working through the federal Office of War Information (OWI). The OWI listed some of the specific problems that were inherent to the nursing profession:

(1) Nursing was more than a job; it was a demanding profession. To be a nurse required personal sacrifice and unselfish dedication which only the finest type of woman was capable.

(2) The competition for woman power was at a premium. Most jobs in war plants required less training but paid very well from the onset. The women's branches of the armed services offered quick and glamorous participation in the war and were making strong appeals to women.

(3) A longer training period was needed to become a nurse. There would need to be a sincerity of purpose that went beyond a mere desire to "get into the war."

(4) The high standards to serve humanity reduced the number of women eligible to be student nurses.

(5) Parental objection was standing in the way because of misconceptions about nursing as a career. Misunderstandings would need to be overcome by emphasizing the many opportunities for nurses with proper training.[78]

Previously the national recruitment drive had to rely almost exclusively on patriotism for its persuasive appeals. Many women became discouraged when they had to pay for years of long training. Others wanted to be quickly identified with a war activity and were more attracted to the military auxiliary services. Now the Cadet Nurse Corps could offer a more equitable position in the growing competition for women war workers with substantial inducements. In return for benefits received, members of the Corps would agree to remain in nursing, either in military or essential civilian positions, for the duration of the war.[79]

A brief summary of what the Cadet Nurse Corps offered recruits follows:

(1) **Training for a Career:** Of all war work open to women, nursing was one of the few professions. A nursing career was well paid and respected in civilian life. No work could better prepare a woman for marriage and motherhood.

(2) **Paid Training Period:** Entrance requirements varied with schools of nursing but in general, a recruit must have been in good health and have graduated from a high school in good standing. Tuition from date of registration until graduation would be paid. Living expenses would include room, board, laundry, textbooks, health, and laboratory fees. The smart new outdoor uniform would be provided without cost to the student. A monthly allowance would start for pre-cadets at $15 a month. Junior cadets would receive $20 a month, and the senior cadet in supervised practice would receive no less than $30 a month.

(3) **An Accelerated Period of Training:** Under the provisions of the Corps, the Cadet would receive complete preparation through speedup courses. Even though the course was accelerated, a student would receive the same complete education that she would have received before the curriculum was addressed.

(4) **Completion of Training Assured:** It was pointed out that the education program would not come to a sudden halt when the war ended. Any member of the Corps enrolled 90 days prior to the end of the war would complete her training with full benefits of the U. S. Cadet Nurse Corps plan.

(5) **Privilege of Wearing the Outdoor Uniform:** Students would not be required to wear the uniform but would wear it when they chose and on all occasions specified by the school. The indoor uniform remained property of the school of nursing in which the student was enrolled along with the insignia of the United States Cadet Nurse Corps.[80]

On another topic, in the use of media presenting information to the public, OWI suggested several themes. OWI noted that nursing would have a vast range of emotional and dramatic appeal that could be used effectively. Four themes with a suggested brief approach follows:

(1) **Learn a Proud Profession—Free:** Nursing is a woman's highest calling in the service of humanity. It commands the respect of everyone. As a profession it demands a sincerity of purpose and depth of understanding unmatched in any professional field open to women.

(2) **Nursing Assures Financial Independence:** There will be a great demand for nurses in the postwar world, for the United States will be relatively well equipped to help handle the vast problems of disease, malnutrition, and war shock.

(3) **Nursing Develops the Individual:** A nurse's hands are trained to be quick, sure, and gentle. Her eyes, ears, and touch are trained to be alert to the slightest changes. Her mind is trained to relate cause to effect. She learns the science for health coupled with the art of human kindness.

(4) **Nursing Is Woman's Foremost War Work:** As soon as she enrolls, the student nurse becomes an important figure in a busy hospital and helps send a graduate nurse to the Front…a nurse who may take care of her own brother on some remote battlefield. Since every school of nursing is connected with a hospital, the nursing she does in a hospital makes it possible for the hospital to get along with fewer graduate nurses.[81]

There were 6,000,000 women in the country over 20 years of age who were not in essential industry, (examples of essential industry included war production and agriculture) and the military services were directing appeals to them. The only opportunity for the 17 or 18-year-old girl to get into uniform was by joining the Cadet Nurse Corps. The guidelines for advertising were established. Now the task was to persuade thousands of firms and individuals to donate time and space for publicity that received governmental backing.[82]

The War Advertising Council, a voluntary organization, assigned a special task force for the recruitment of student nurses. The service of the well-known J. Walter Thompson Advertising Agency became available to the Cadet Nurse Corps.[83] Now nursing, with the expertise from Madison Avenue along with $13,000,000 worth of donated service, set out to attract unprecedented numbers of new students within the shortest possible time by utilizing all available media. The nursing profession had never received so much public attention. Few outlets, for the Corps' message were overlooked.[84]

Radio appeals were heard by 700 million listeners. National radio broadcasts at both the network and local station level were effective in reaching possible recruits. A cadet nurse was added to the popular radio serial "One Man's Family." Cadet nurses and Surgeon General Dr. Thomas Parran appeared on a nationwide favorite program, "We the People." Cadets were asked to participate at the local radio station to describe their uniform and what the Corps had to offer. [85]

To capitalize on record numbers of movie attendees, news clips were shown in theaters of President Roosevelt signing the Bolton Act and another of the modeling of the new Cadet Nurse Corps uniform at a fashion show at the Waldorf Astoria in New York. Appealing to teenage audiences, a film was produced starring Cadet Nurse Peggy Adams. This film, entitled "Reward Unlimited," received awards for the best recruitment film in 1944 and was shown in 16,000 theaters.[86]

The ten minute recruitment film "Reward Unlimited" starring Dorothy McQuire as Cadet Nurse Peggy Adams was distributed to 16,000 theatres and viewed by an estimated audience of 90 million. (Natioinal Library of Medicine)

Another effective medium was short dramatizations written about the Corps and presented by theatrical groups by women's clubs, high schools, and colleges throughout the country. One of these sketches, entitled "This Is Our War," revealed the inner conflicts of a young carefree girl who eventually recognized her responsibility to her nation and joined the Corps. This short presentation received recognition as one of the best special purpose plays written for the war effort.

During the first year of recruitment, some three million posters were distributed presenting the cadet in such locations as theater lobbies, women's shoe stores, beauty salons, high schools, YWCA's, public libraries and churches. Cadets smiled attractively from covers of magazines as well as from billboards on streets and highways.

Pamphlets and leaflets were placed in high schools, physician's offices, schools of nursing, and drugstores as well as on buses and street cars. Teenage girls were captivated by a color recruitment publication, "Enlist in a Proud Profession." This 16-page brochure contained photos of cadets in winter and summer uniforms with messages from Dr. Parran and Lucile Petry, Director of the Corps. Qualities needed for entering a school and the immediate and long-range benefit of membership were emphasized. Up to this time in history, most nursing school catalogs had been poor and unappealing. One of the requirements for schools of nursing to participate in the national program was to publish an attractive and appealing catalog. The results were beyond expectations.

The printed word with publicity connected with the Corps was abundant during the first two years, 1943-1944. The Division of Nurse Education publicists sent out scores of publicity releases about cadets and encouraged the publicity in their own communities. Articles about the Corps appeared in popular magazines such as *Mademoiselle, Charm, Tomorrow, Cosmopolitan, Coronet,* and a host of others totaling 100 pages in the first year. Various hospital, medical, and nursing journals promoted the Corps, and *The American Journal of Nursing* faithfully recorded the monthly activities of the Corps with editorial support.

In spite of the war, magazine advertising reached a new high of $888,000,000 worth of business, and the Cadet Nurse Corps reaped its share. The Eastman-Kodak Company, in cooperation with the War Advertising Council, sponsored a series of full-page color ads that were placed in 15 of the nation's leading magazines with a combined circulation of about 12 million. Each ad contained a coupon that the reader could send to the National Nursing Counsel for War Service, Box 88 in New York City for additional information. In February of 1944, some 33,000 inquiries were received.

Manufacturing took advantage of marketing to the Corps members. A cosmetic company created a special kit of lipstick and rouge to match the trim of the Cadet uniform and named it "Rocket Red." The cosmetics were packaged in a gray plastic case with an eight-point Maltese cross in red as the motif. Occasionally a magazine or newspaper slipped in an advertisement by a cigarette or liquor company, much to the disapproval of the Division of Nurse Education.[87]

Lucile Petry shared this story at the Cadet Nurse Corps 50th anniversary in Bethesda, Maryland in 1994. She said:

> The surgeon general's office received word that the U.S. Cadet Nurse Corps had a cooperative advertisement with Southern Comfort and Dr. Parran asked me to check it out. I called the publicist in that region, who confessed that she didn't know that Southern Comfort was a whiskey; she thought it was a mattress.[88]

Some individuals complained that there was too much emphasis on "free education with pay" and not enough regarding "if you qualify." Traditional nurses complained that there was too much glamour and cadets were pictured wearing rings and that their hair touched their collar which was unacceptable. One advertising company responded to such complaints by stating that perhaps they should say that nursing was poorly paid, working conditions were terrible, and perhaps the recruit might consider a second-rate nursing school and live in the most uncomfortable surroundings.

Numerous letters were sent out to publicize the Cadet Nurse Corps and urge membership. For example, 5 million mailings of dependency checks to servicemen's families carried inserts about the Corps, in the fall of 1943. Lucile Petry wrote to selected applicants who had asked information about the Corps making sure all questions had been answered. To one applicant she wrote:

> Dear Miss Brown:
>
> This is a rather personal letter. I thought I would write you myself to see if we had answered all of your questions about the U. S. Cadet Nurse Corps, when we were last in touch with you. I remember when I became a nurse: at first, there were a few doubts in my mind

which made me hesitate. But when those questions were answered—well I wondered why I had questioned at all. Perhaps you have some questions like that in your mind. If you do, I hope you will let me know what they are . . .

Lucile Petry[89]

Although it was the high school graduate who was the main target of the advertising drive, college girls were sought as candidates, too. In 1943, the National Nursing Council selected 35 nurses to appeal to nursing students on university and college campuses. By March 1944 they had visited more than 600 senior and junior colleges. While the number of college girls entering nursing schools was increased slightly, the spectacular increase came from high school graduates.

The goal of 65,000 new student nurses for the first year was exceeded by 521. Appeals to the young women shifted for the second year of the Cadet Nurse Corps. The program had acclaimed success in numbers, and the appeal for patriotic service and free education gave way to describing the desirability of nursing as a career. "Girls with a Future" on posters pictured nursing as a worthwhile career for professional or homemaking girls. The nurse was portrayed as a leading force in her community, and the need for adequate nursing service was emphasized.[90]

Nurse historians, Kalisch and Kalisch reported that in the end, the cost of recruiting each Cadet came to a total of $92, of which $87 represented donated space, time and service. They said, "Given the magnitude of the task and the competing forces present at that time, it was a remarkably low amount with an impressively high return.

In the months before victory, the Cadet Nurse Corps continued to push the recruitment of student nurses. The second year's goal of 60,000 was exceeded by 1,471 enrollments. The machinery of the Corps recruitment had built up great momentum when the war ended. The Japanese surrender promptly halted recruitment plans. Releases, speeches, and new publications were canceled. The 30,000 young women recruited by August 1945 were admitted to schools before October 19. These young women would be the last to join the Cadet Nurse Corps.

6

In the Limelight

From a historical standpoint, nursing has had its greatest recognition and advancements during times of war. Federal support of nursing and nursing education was significant during World War II. Nurse historians, Beatrice. J. Kalisch and Phillip A. Kalisch noted:

> Before the Cadet Corps, nursing received little attention from the general public. Like medicine and certain other professions, nursing shied away from publicity, viewing it as unprofessional, undesirable, unethical, and undignified. In addition to this fear, nurses lacked the skills necessary to present themselves and their cause effectively. But the U. S. Cadet Nurse Corps, established by Congress on June 15, 1943 (the Bolton Act) as an emergency program to provide an adequate supply of nurses at home and for the military, was to change all that.[91]

Every opportunity was seized to focus national attention on the women who joined the U.S. Cadet Nurse Corps through traditional and special events. When the beginning student nurse finished the probation or preclinical period, a capping ceremony took place. At this time she was granted the full-fledged status of student nurse. Receiving the nursing cap of her particular school of nursing took on a patriotic emphasis during World War II. In some schools of nursing student nurses who had joined the Corps not only received their nursing cap but repeated the cadet nurse pledge as well. Two capping ceremonies were described in the January 1944 issue of *The American Journal of Nursing*:[92]

(1)Keuka College of Nursing, Keuka Park, New York

Following the pledge of the allegiance to the flag and singing of the national anthem in which the audience participated, Dr. Henry E. Allen, president of the College, spoke briefly of the significance of the Corps and the service rendered by the student nurses in the hospitals. All the nurses in the school arose to give the pledge:

> As a member of the United States Cadet Nurse Corps, I promised to apply myself with diligence to my studies and to seek to perfect myself in the skills appertaining to nursing: and I gladly pledge myself, health permitting to remain active in nursing so long as my country shall be at war.

The capping ceremony was simple, with the nurses standing to receive and accept the charge and them coming to the platform to be capped by the Director and the Nursing Arts Instructor. The impressiveness of the ceremony lay in the significance of the words incorporated in the charge and in the sincerity of their expression. The Director of Nurses said:

> I charge each of you that you shall be faithful in the performance of your duties, seeking always the welfare of the patient, serving all without favoritism or prejudice, failing not in patience nor in gentleness; that you shall give loyalty to whom loyalty is due, working with your associates without pettiness or ill will, and that you shall be discreet in speech, careful of confidences and reverent toward the solemnities of life and of death; and that finally, you shall hold honesty and honor in high regard, and conduct the course of your life in correspondence thereto.

To the question, "Do you accept this charge?" The students replied: "I accept this charge, and wearing my cap promise to regard it as a pledge thereof."

The ceremony closed with a brief prayer and singing of the college Alma Mater.

(2)Iowa Methodist School of Nursing, Des Moines

Thirty-nine freshmen nurses, designated as the Victory Class, received their caps. Exercises took place in the dining room at 6:30 a.m. Due to the time of day and to limited space, few invitations were extended to friends and relatives; then too, it was more of a family occasion.

The candle-lighted dining room with a table at the front of the room was decorated with red, white, and blue streamers, flags, and lighted candles. On the table were thirty-nine candles arranged in a V; each candle had a ring of red, white, and blue fluted paper at its base. Beautiful red roses, (a gift to the class) decorated the piano, and on a nearby table thirty-nine freshly starched caps were attractively arranged . . .

The Director sat at one end of the table and at the other a Red Cross nurse in full uniform. After the presentation talk, the Director presented each nurse with her cap and pinned a red, white, and blue bow of ribbon on her left shoulder. The Red Cross nurse placed the cap on her head and gave her one of the candles from the table. The student nurse then passed out into the corridor. As the last one went out, members of the Glee Club sang "Angels of Mercy."

At the close of the song the class came in again in a double line. Each was wearing a red, white, and blue corsage which had been pinned on her right shoulder by her big sister and carried her lighted candle in her right hand. They came to the center of the room, where they stood and repeated the pledge. The program closed with prayer.[93]

Rituals played an important part in the regimented schedule of the student nurse. This was "Capping Day" for Pauline Morey (left) when her "big sister" Thelma Morey (author) pinned on her nurses cap signifying that she was no longer a probation nurse. Their parents were present for this important occasion. (1945. Author's collection)

Induction Ceremonies

Cadet Nurse Corps induction ceremonies received nationwide attention. On April 5, 1944, Lucile Petry, Director of the Corps, sent a memorandum to each director of a school of nursing in the country. She announced that a National U. S. Cadet Nurse Corps Induction would be broadcast nationwide from Constitution Hall in Washington, D. C. over the National Broadcasting Company (NBC) network on Saturday, May 13.

Petry further explained that government officials and stars of stage, screen, and radio were cooperating with the Division of Nurse Education and the National Nursing Council for War Service in staging the program in our nation's capitol and on the air. First Lady Eleanor Roosevelt had consented to speak along with the Honorable Paul V. McNutt, Administrator of the Federal Security Agency and Mrs. Frances P. Bolton, who sponsored the Bolton Act establishing the Corps.

The Induction Ceremony would be conducted over the air by Dr. Thomas Parran, Surgeon General of the U. S. Public Health Service, with cadet nurses repeating the pledge in unison. Every Cadet Nurse in the country would have a part of the ceremony. The Washington ceremony would provide the nucleus in a way that would strengthen the spirit of the organization among the more than 90,000 members of the Corps. It would recognize and pay tribute throughout the nation to the newest women's uniformed service.

Every school of nursing was urged to participate. A plan to combine a city-wide induction ceremony was encouraged to take place in cities where there were several schools of nursing. Directors of schools of nursing were reminded to invite civilian and military officials, community leaders, educators, and parents.[94]

Later in the month, a general news release to the public from Jean Henderson, Recruitment and Public Relations Officer, announced that the nationwide induction ceremonies would be conducted simultaneously on May 13. The keynote induction service would be broadcast over the NBC network from 4:30 to 5 p.m. Eastern War Time. The ceremonies throughout the country would bring 96,000 student nurses officially into the Cadet Nurse Corps. Approximately 46,000 of these were new student nurses (three-fourth's of the nation's June 30th quota). Dr. Parran would administer the induction pledge to 750 uniformed cadet nurses in Washington, D. C. from nine schools of nursing, while others assembled in listening groups while the country stood at attention.

Helen Hayes would appear on the program in a dramatic script paying tribute to the service of nurses in time of war. The new U. S. Cadet Nurse Corps March would be introduced by the U. S. Navy Symphony Orchestra.[95]

In preparation for the formal induction, a temporary military note was introduced into Washington's schools of nursing. The innovation of the military drill for the cadet nurses in the District of Columbia was in line with programs of other schools of nursing throughout the country. Dr. Parran said:

> Although the U. S. Cadet Nurse Corps is *not* a military organization, knowledge of military carriage and the significance of wearing a uniform with pride and distinction will be a valuable asset to its members. By improving posture, so important to a nurse who must be on her feet many hours of the day, this military drill should help cadet nurses in their work.

Through the cooperation of Brig. Gen. John E. Lewis, Commander of the Military District of Washington, instructors in "foot and squad drill" were furnished to nine schools of nursing in the vicinity of Washington.

Directors of schools reported that the cadet nurses responded with enthusiasm to the drill instruction. Officers of the 703 Military Police Battalion commended their feminine "rookies" and expressed confidence in their ability to present a trim, smart appearance in the guardsmen gray and red uniform of the Cadet Nurse Corps. Lucile Petry reviewed the cadet nurses as they practiced on the Georgetown University campus drill field prior to the day of induction.[96]

The following article, titled "National Induction as Seen by a Cadet Nurse" appeared in the August 1944 issue of the *American Journal of Nursing* :

> Today I stood in the midst of 750 cadet nurses at Constitution Hall in Washington, D. C. and repeated our inductive pledge as administered by Dr. Thomas Parran, Surgeon General of the U. S. Public Health Service.
>
> I have been enrolled in the Corps about six months but I have been too busy to stop and think about things. I chose to be a cadet nurse because I wanted to continue my education and still be of help in the crisis that faces my country.

When I entered Constitution Hall on May 13 in the opening processional for the national induction of cadet nurses, some feeling started deep inside me as well as at the end of the ceremony as I sang the stirring new corps march. I had a deep feeling of thankfulness and pride in my profession.

On the stage forty-eight of our cadet nurses stood before the flags of the different states. A cadet nurse guarded the impressive flag of the Surgeon General of the U. S. Public Health Service—blue, with caduceus and anchor—and another cadet nurse stood watch over the brave new banner of our Corps, gray field with silver Maltese cross blazing in a center of red. After we were seated Captain Burgess Meredith, USAAF, more familiar to us as a motion picture star, described the beautiful scene, the huge flag of the United States rippled down from the ceiling and came to rest above our heads.

Mrs. Roosevelt painted an interesting picture of nursing as she has witnessed it on the actual battle fields of the world, and she commended us for our work on the home front. She told us that many a man will come out of this war owing his life not only to the doctor who may have operated on him but to the nurse who watched over him.

When the voice of Bing Crosby came through from Hollywood singing a song dedicated especially for us, a wave of approval swept over our grey-suited ranks; and when Helen Hayes stepped to the center of the stage and gave us a story, "Remember Tomorrow," a warm and moving picture of the gift the cadet nurses are bringing to suffering people in our country, I glanced rapidly about me and all eyes were misty. I hope you heard her, too, because misty eyes are good for you when your feelings have been deeply stirred.

Congressman Frances P. Bolton, who sponsored the Act that made our Corps a reality on June 15, 1943, praised the work we are doing to relieve the critical shortage of nurses for both armed services and hospitals caused by wartime demands, and she explained to the vast audience the functions of the Corps to assure a continuous flow of graduate nurses pledged to essential nursing for the duration.

All these words of praise made you proud of the gray suit you were wearing, its red epaulets, and sparkling silver insignia. It made the long hours of work behind you seem like a mere nothing and the hours to come a privilege to be anticipated.

I realized for the first time the vast scope of the Cadet Nurse Corps membership of approximately 96,000 when our dynamic leader, Miss Lucile Petry, Director of the Corps, extended a cordial welcome to us and to the young women in a thousand schools of nursing over the nation. She expressed my feeling about the Corps when she said, "In taking unto yourselves the task of ministering to the wounded and the sick on the battle fronts or wherever you are called, you are carrying on a tradition which represents the finest in American womanhood."

Dr. Parran reminded us that this was a great moment in our lives, one we would treasure in years to come, and he said that it was also a great moment for him as Chief of the Service that administers our Corps to stand before us and hear our induction pledge:

> I am solemnly aware of the obligations I assume toward my country and toward my chosen profession;
>
> I will follow faithfully the teachings of my instructors and the guidance of the physicians with whom I work;
>
> I will hold in trust the finest traditions of nursing and the spirit of the Corps;

I will keep my body strong, my mind alert, and my
    heart steadfast;
I will be kind, tolerant, and understanding;
Above all, I will dedicate myself now and forever to
    the triumph of life over death.
As a Cadet Nurse, I pledge to my country my service
    in essential nursing for the duration of the war.

In unison we affirmed our awareness of our obligation toward our country and profession. Then the music began:

The Maltese cross is marching again
To answer the call, a new Crusade . . .

I joined my fellow cadet nurses in singing the rousing new Corps march. I thought of the thousands of cadet nurses who were listening in wards and in small hospitals, taking a little time to receive the commendation, but not much because there was work to be done, the job of guarding our country's strength and might from coast to coast.

It is hard to describe the thrills I received from the first national induction program. I suppose I can sum it up by saying that I am determined to keep the lamp of personal interest in my profession ever burning to help preserve a world where free men live.[97]

Throughout the country, 250 local induction ceremonies with one in every state tied into the National Induction.

One of the largest mass induction ceremonies took place in New York City, where 1,300 Cadet Nurses were inducted into the Corps by Mayor La Guardia. The colorful ceremony was attended by 3,000 spectators while 2,446 cadets remained on duty in 47 hospitals listening to radios and joined in reciting the pledge at the appropriate moment.

The cadet nurses, some garbed in the smart gray uniform of the Corps and others wearing distinctive uniforms of the hospitals in which they were serving, marched into City Hall Plaza to the music of the Corps played by the Department of Sanitation Band. A color guard from the Army post at Fort Jay led the procession. A chorus of eighty WAVES (U.S. Navy) from the Hunter College training station sang the national anthem and joined with the audience in singing "God Bless America."[98]

The first National Induction Ceremony had an estimated radio listening audience of over 2,000,000 people, higher than any other Saturday afternoon program. In addition, a wealth of publicity over the ceremony was generated at the state and local levels. In Atlanta, Georgia, a special feature of a program was recognition of high school pledges to the Cadet Nurse Corps. Publicity included cooperation from the Chamber of Commerce for promoting an effective program and signs in streetcars announcing the program. North Dakota had a statewide plan for the Cadet Nurse Corps Induction with the state governor making a proclamation and giving the pledge to cadet nurses. In Massachusetts, cadet nurses paraded from the State House to Boston Common for the ceremony.[99]

A year later, announcement was made that the second National Induction (planned for mid-May 1945) would highlight the cadet nurse's vital wartime service to her country. The second issue of the *Cadet Nurse Corps News* reported the event:

> On the National hookup, Miss Petry's message gave us all the proud feeling of working side-by side, while the pledge administered by Dr. Parran brought the same feeling of unity.
>
> We know, too, that you laughed at the humor of Edgar Bergen and Charlie McCarthy, were proud of the tribute paid by actress Jane Cowl, enjoyed the singing of Ginny Simms and the music of Mitchell Ayres and his orchestra, with interpolations by MC Jim Ameche.
>
> Induction was wonderful. The pledge of 112,000 patriotic young women represents a tremendous force of woman power, ready to fill one of America's vital needs. It also looks toward a better, healthier America after V-Day.[100]

Cadet Nurse Corps Anniversaries

On June 3, 1944, Director Lucile Petry sent a memorandum to the directors of schools of nursing announcing that July 1 had been designated as the official birthday of the U. S. Cadet Nurse Corps and to make the occasion a memorable and significant occasion. This became another highly publicized event. Petry wrote:

> Because you contributed so splendidly to the success of the National Induction Ceremony on May 13, we do not feel we should call upon you again so soon for extensive cooperation. Therefore, arrangements are being made from Washington for a series of Birthday "Picture Events." These will be held in six or eight key cities.[101]

Highlights of the first anniversary included the following events:

(1) On June 30th, uniformed cadets from seven schools of nursing in New York City attended a tea honoring Petry that was sponsored by the National Nursing Council for War Service. High points of the occasion were the cutting of a very large birthday cake and Miss Stella Goostray announcement that the quota of 65,000 new students for 1943-1944 had been more than met.

(2) The new official flag of Corps was unfurled and formally presented to the Corps in a special first anniversary ceremony July 1, 1944, by Surgeon General Dr. Parran on the steps of the Public Health Service building on Constitution Avenue, Washington, D. C. The Surgeon General noted that victorious battle flags of the United Nations were flying in far corners of the earth, adding, "We know what these banners mean to the men who fight and die for them. We look to them as our symbol of united strength, loyalty, honor and heroic sacrifice. What is a more fitting tribute to a vital and patriotic organization than its first battle flag be added to those now flying in the vanguard of the Allied cause."

Lucile Petry accepted the white, silver, and scarlet banner emblazoned with the Maltese cross on behalf of the Corps. In response, Petry declared that the flag represented the desire of every cadet nurse to be of service to her country.[102]

A stirring flag presentation ceremony, marking the first birthday of the U. S. Cadet Nurse Corps, was held on the steps of the U. S. PHS Building. Left to right: Frances P. Bolton, Color Guards of Cadet Nurses holding the flags, Dr. Parran and Miss Petry. (National Archives and Records Administration II)

The American Journal of Nursing reported that the Corps commemorated the second birthday (July 1, 1945) with church services, mass meetings, window displays, and radio programs throughout the country and wished the Corps Godspeed in the coming third year of its service to the country. Some of the events reported included the following:

(1) In Independence, Missouri, President Truman reviewed plans for the Corps coming year and Mrs. Truman cut the Corps birthday cake at Independence Sanitarium.

(2) In Philadelphia, Pennsylvania, cadets had their "day" at the Army Nurse in War Exhibit where a cake three feet high contributed by the Bakers' Union graced the festivities. Katharine J. Densford, President, American Nurse' Association, and Captain Mary Haggerty, Army Nurse Corps, were among the speakers.

(3) In New York City, 600 cadets gathered in Times Square to take part in a war bond drive.

(4) Governor Tobin took part in the Boston celebration, as did Miss Petry, Benny Goodman, and Helen Hayes. More than 5,000 people attended the activities. Cadet Nurse Beatrice Graham Whitney, a graduate of the Massachusetts Memorial, Boston, was given the Avon Award as typical cadet nurse in America.

(5) On Los Angeles, Mary Pickford's little daughter, Roxanne, sang "Happy birthday, dear nurses" when Miss Pickford entertained cadets at Pickfair.

(6) In Wichita, Kansas, where the second anniversary of the first production-model B-29 flight coincided with that of the Cadet Nurse Corps, a B-29 was christened and named for the Corps. Cadet nurses from the Wesley Hospital School of Nursing were there and helped speed the war bird on its way.[103]

The second Corps birthday anniversary fell on a Sunday and in appropriate observation of the day, cadet nurses went to church. A line of gray, flecked with scarlet, marked the pews where they sat. A hymn written especially for the Corps was introduced—sometimes sung by a cadet nurse choir. The music was written by R. Deane Shure, a noted composer of church music, and the words composed by a member of the staff of the Division of Nurse Education.

Cadet nurses from Freedmen's Hospital School of Nursing, in Washington, D. C., found a warm reception at the Third Baptist Church. The pastor held up his usual punctual services to pose for a picture with them, based his sermon on service to mankind—using the Cadet Nurse Corps as an illustration, then called upon the cadets to sing their new hymn. Founded in 1894, Freedmen's was one of America's oldest and largest Schools of Nursing for Black girls.[104]

Cadet Nurse Corps News

The *Cadet Nurse Corps News* first issue was printed in April 1945. The purpose of the News was to provide a common bond for cadet nurses across the country. In the first issue, Dr. Parran addressed the cadets:

> We of the United States Public Health Service appreciate the splendid record you have made. I know your parents share our feeling of pride in your accomplishments and in your daily expression of the spirit of nursing. I know that you will meet your future obligations with equal enthusiasm and success.[105]

Cadet nurses throughout the country continued to make headlines as reported by the *Cadet Nurse Corps News*. Some of these special events reported included the following:

(1) Launched by Corps members, the S. S. Coastal Nomad slid down the ways July 9, 1945 in Wilmington, California. Arriving in Los Angeles its sponsors: Cadet Nurses Alyce Valandry, a Sioux Indian; and Rowena Pentewa, a Hopi; and Chief Richard Davis Thunderbird. Both cadet nurses were from Sage Memorial Hospital School of Nursing in Granada, Arizona.

(2) A nurse first, a full-fledged American next, Cadet Nurse Gerda Furth, a student of the California Hospital School of Nursing in Los Angeles, became a citizen of the United

States. Fleeing Nazi-held Vienna, Austria, she arrived in this country in 1939 and joined the Corps four years later.[106]

(3) From Butler County Memorial Hospital in Pennsylvania came the news that a total of $2,550 worth of Victory war bonds have sold in the hospital . . . due to the efforts of the cadet nurses.

(4) Cadet nurses of the Elizabeth General Hospital School of Nursing in New Jersey, received a full military salute from Admiral Halsey when he returned to Elizabeth on November 7, 1946 . . . a fitting reward for a faithful group of girls who practiced military drill under the guidance of the New Jersey State Guard.[107]

(5) If the patients at Santa Rosa Hospital, in San Antonio, Texas can almost hear a song in the hearts of the students, it could have been because of the influence of the excellent musical organizations of the School of Nursing. Music plays an important part in the lives of the cadet nurses, and weekly rehearsals are held for both the band and the chorus. Objectives of the musical groups are to promote culture, recreation, morale, and appreciation of good music.[108]

(6) Memories of her coronation as Queen of Newport News and an entertaining trip to Hollywood were still with Cadet Nurse Dorothy Hudson as she went about her activities as a student nurse at the Elizabeth Buxton Hospital School of Nursing in Newport News, Virginia. Cadet Nurse Hudson was chosen over 40 other young women of Newport News, winning a majority of approximately 700,000 votes.[109]

(7) Three cadet nurses in the Sacred Heart School of Nursing, in Havre, Montana, were mighty hard to distinguish from one another. They are the Tommcrup triplets, Myrtle, Margaret, and Minnie . . . Following graduation they planned to specialize in their favorite fields of surgery and obstetrics.[110]

Cadet nurses in the limelight—did they always appear slim and trim in the gray and scarlet, the uniform so often pronounced the handsomest of all women in the service of their country? The first issue of the *Cadet Nurse Corps News* announced a posture manual written especially for cadet nurses with a twofold purpose. The edition included troubleshooting exercises aimed at poor posture, caused by long hours of standing, lifting, and bending as well as the damage done to the sacroiliac when slumping half-mast in class. Cadet nurses were asked, "Why not check front and back with your full-length mirror now to see where you'll start equating you with your uniform—figuratively speaking?"[111]

The second issue of the *News* again appealed to cadets. ". . . wear it proudly. But do you wear it right? There's a slim margin between the grooming that attracts admiring glances and the one that gathers puzzled or disapproving stares. The uniform of the Cadet Nurse Corps is a badge of distinguished service to your country."

A detailed description of how to appropriately wear each piece of the uniform, including the insignia, was included along with its significance and proper placement. For example, the summer uniform was designed as a suit-dress, to be worn with or without a blouse. A word of caution included when no blouse was worn, the jacket must be trimly buttoned at all times. The cadet furnished her own blouse, gloves, shoes, and stockings. Regulations still applied. Decorated stockings, ankle socks, and leg make-up were out! The wearing of the cadet nurse uniform was summarized as follows:

> In uniform, everyone recognizes you as a young woman dedicated to a vital war service; in uniform you are the Corps best recruiter. Wearing it is a responsibility—so wear it proudly, wear it right![112]

Some cadets took action and appointed sergeants-at-arms to monitor cadets who assumed they were not under strict military regulations and neglected a trim appearance. The Cadet Police were sharp-eyed girls who didn't miss an untidy hairdo, too-red nails, or a rumpled blouse. The first violation carried a one dollar fine, and the second the same. Third-time offenders lost the privilege of wearing gray and scarlet for an entire month.[113]

Cadet nurses, not their supervisors, resolved the issue of an unkempt appearance in uniform. The following item appeared in the fourth issue of the News:

> Parading Cadet Nurses everywhere have distinguished themselves for their trim military bearing. On Flag Day, Brooklyn and Manhattan students drew admiration from a parade-wise New York City alderman. "Never," he said, "in 19 years, have I seen a smartly group." (One reason: the Cadets voted to bar four girls wearing hit-or-miss uniforms.)[114]

7

Race, Creed, Color and
the Married Nurse

The Married Student

The Bolton Act set a precedent by stating that there would be no discrimination in the administration of benefits . . . on account of race, creed, or color. What about the married nurse in being accepted into the Corps? Married women were not accepted in a military service during World War II. In the past, the majority of schools of nursing did not admit a married women nor maintain a student nurse once she married. Before the war the trend had been slow in increasing the employment of married women in both industry and the professional world. Now the war effort was calling for all available man and woman power regardless of marital status.[115]

A tradition among schools of nursing prevailed. Women who married while students faced dismissal, left on their own accord, or kept their marital status secret. In the past, whether married women should or should not be admitted to schools of nursing had not been questioned. There was sufficient number of unmarried women to fill the classes. Now with the war on, the question was raised due to an acute shortage of nurses and as attitudes and practices began to change.

An editorial in the August 1942 issue of *The American Journal of Nursing* asked, "Does marital status in itself have any bearing on a woman's acceptability as a student nurse?" A story about a young married woman was told. She had applied for admission to a school of nursing and was told, "No good school in this state admits married students."

The article further stated:

> The National Nursing Council for War Service recommends that, for the duration, an effort be made to encourage young married women who are otherwise eligible to enter schools of nursing and that schools be urged to retain students to marry during the course . . .
>
> It is not our purpose here to urge that married women be generally admitted to schools of nursing without due consideration, or that a general policy be adopted permitting students to marry while in the school, without viewing the total situation. It does seem timely, however, to point out what seems to be the trend and to raise certain questions. We need nurses—students and graduates—in increasing numbers.
>
> Marriage rates always rise in war time. Student nurses and brides are drawn from the same age groups. Young married women without children whose husbands are in service are eager to serve their country too. If we limit those admitted to schools of nursing to the group of unmarried young women, are we excluding some very desirable applicants?[116]

A few schools of nursing were beginning to admit married nurses with strict expectations that they were to be free of home responsibilities. War widows who had no children and women whose husbands were serving in the armed forces were beginning to be accepted into certain schools of nursing. One school of nursing reported that they had eighteen married students enrolled, fourteen whom lived outside the dormitory. The school regulation required that a student contemplating marriage confer with the director before her marriage. At this time the director pointed out that the new responsibilities which she would assume with matrimony must not interfere with her school and clinical work in the hospital. In many schools, unmarried as well as married students could live at home but must have lived within walking distance to the hospital and were required to have a telephone. When on call for the operating room or for delivery room, they slept at the hospital's call rooms as did the residents.

The *American Journal of Nursing* made this patriotic appeal in regard to married nurses:

> Our married nurses, we believe, will gladly *nurse for victory* when they realize that the importunities of those directly responsible for the care of patients in civilian hospitals should be heeded because the care of these patients is such an extremely important part of the gigantic task of winning the war.[117]

Black Cadets

The National Nursing Council took the first step to integrate the activities of Black nurses into the total war program Before the war, the Council had formed a Black unit to provide a better and wider use of the Black nurse. Financed by the General Education Board of the Rockefeller Foundation, with supplementary aid from the Kellogg Foundation, the unit was directed by Estelle Massey Riddle, of the National Association for Colored Graduate Nurses. This mutual cooperation of Black and White nurse leaders was a step toward better understanding and fuller utilization of all nurse power, regardless of race.[118]

During the first year of the cadet nurse program, Riddle traveled thousands of miles, visiting schools of nursing and hospitals, and giving counsel on all types of nursing education and service problems that affected Black nurses (both students and graduates). Born in Texas, Riddle was a teacher in a rural school at the age of 16. An older brother, Doctor E. O. Massey who practiced dentistry in St. Louis, Missouri, encouraged his sister to further her education. She entered the St. Louis Hospital School of

Nursing and graduated in 1923. She was immediately placed in a head nurse position of a large unit of the hospital. Later she served as a special teacher in nursing arts and hygiene at a high school in Kansas City, Missouri.

Cadet nurses in a Florida school of nursing ready for their special capping service. (National Archives Record Administration)

Riddle became intensely interested in nurse education and received a scholarship to attend Teachers College at Columbia University. In 1930 she received her bachelor degree and was awarded a masters a year later from Columbia. She completed a year on her doctorate before she was called back into nursing administration. Riddle was superintendent of nurses at the Homer G. Phillips Hospital School of Nursing in St. Louis when she accepted the appointment as Consultant with the National Nursing Council for War Service. Riddle was delighted to be invited to serve on the Council. She saw it as occupying a strategic position from which to provide leadership and to improve racial relations within the profession and the country at large.[119]

The late Dr. Mary Elizabeth Carnegie, educator, editor and historian, described the situation for Blacks that was prevalent during World War II in her book, "The Path We Tread:"

> In the South, a typical pattern emerged: the dual system, in keeping with the doctrine of "separate but equal" as an outcome of the Plessy vs. Ferguson Supreme Court Decision of 1896. This decision supported the constitutionality of a Louisiana law requiring separate but equal facilities for whites and blacks in railroad cars. As a result, schools of nursing were established in all-black institutions—hospitals and colleges. Some white hospitals conducted two programs—one for whites and one for blacks. Theory was usually given by the same white faculty in separate classrooms; practice was also gained separately—for black students in separate buildings, wings, or wards for black patients. Separate, yes but in no way equal![120]

Recruitment of Black women for the Corps remained an ongoing effort until the end of the war. This special release regarding a Black cadet nurse from the Office of War Information went out to all of the Black presses throughout the country:

> "There will be a big job for me after the war, helping soldiers readjust themselves to life," says Cadet Nurse Annie G. Banks, young Negro student at Hampton Institute, Hampton, Virginia. When Annie first decided to become a nurse, she didn't know that a war would provide the opportunity. She was a young child when her father was injured in an automobile accident. Anxious to help, Annie sat for hours by his bed. She watched as nurses cared for her father, determined that someday she would be a nurse.

Firm in her purpose, she worked as a mother's helper, store clerk, summer camp counselor, and finally as a gun part inspector in a defense plant for her tuition. By 1941 Annie enrolled in Hampton Institute and began the two and a half years prerequisite courses necessary for nurses education. Having completed her preliminary instruction, she attended a lecture about the opportunities the U. S. Cadet Nurse Corps had to offer. Annie enlisted and had this to say, "It seemed to afford a great opportunity towards the attainment of my goal and also gave me a chance to help in the war effort."

Her enlistment, however, is more than a patriotic wartime gesture. Following the emergency, she intends to remain on active duty as a Public Health Nurse . . . Mr. and Mrs. Gus Banks of Hartford, Connecticut, are justly proud of their only daughter and happy that she has chosen a career which will insure her future in the postwar world.[121]

In May 1945, Surgeon General Dr. Thomas Parran requested a survey regarding Black nursing. The first National report of Black nursing schools and nurses was completed by Estelle Massey Riddle. She observed:

> In 1943, there were 32 schools listed by the National League of Nursing Education admitting 1,918 Negro students. This number represents a 21 percent increase in Negro students in the same number of schools over 1942. The number of schools admitting Negroes into mixed student enrollment has increased . . . The State Council in California has stated that 10 more schools have set policies which admit the Negro student . . .

Riddle's report brought national attention to the many problems troubling Black members of the nursing profession. The report pointed out the inadequate number of schools to train Black nurses, poor clinical facilities, poorly trained instructors, and inadequate housing for student nurses. There was lack of employment opportunity for Black nurses in hospitals and agencies, including the Army and Navy.[122]

In order to qualify for the Bolton Act windfall, some schools of nursing abandoned their discriminatory policies. Boston City Hospital became one of the first northern institutions to admit a group of Black Senior Cadets from Tuskegee Institute School of Nursing for affiliation. By 1945 approximately 2,600 Black students had been trained during the Corps program, a significant increase from previous years. By the end of the war, 49 schools of nursing with Black and mixed enrollments had admitted Black students compared to 29 in 1941. One of the indirect benefits was that Black nurses were better able to secure employment after graduation in institutions previously closed to them.[123]

The Japanese American Cadet

Japanese American student nurses, along with 2500 American-born Japanese (Nisei) college and university students living on the West Coast, became victims of World War II. They were part of a mass evacuation from a proscribed area of 120,000 persons of Japanese ancestry, 80,000 of whom were American citizens. These young men and women were not "aliens" but American citizens, brought up in American schools. They were eager to demonstrate their loyalty to American ideals, and to get on with their education in preparation for useful service and still fuller assimilation into national life. In all, about 75 students, including a few student nurses, found their way east in those first frantic days before internment in March and April 1942.[124]

Nursing leaders were deluged by questions from directors and superintendents regarding the acceptance of the Japanese American students into their schools of nursing. A letter was read at a national nurse conference, and the emotional response reflected the times. Nurse leaders expressed doubt that any school of nursing would be willing to take them and they could complete their education after the war.

Back in California, Margaret Tracy, Director of the University of California School of Nursing fumed. She said:

> It seems to me that denying these young women an opportunity to complete their nursing work until after the war is not only an injustice to loyal American citizens, but it is also a tremendous waste of nursing power when we are so badly in need of graduate registered nurses.[125]

On May 29, 1942, in Chicago, the National Japanese American Student Relocation Council was born under the sponsorship of the American Friends Service Committee. Its membership included college presidents and deans, officers of college associations, representatives of leading Protestant churches, Jews, Catholics, Quakers, and the Student YMCA and YWCA. The cost of operation had been met by generous grants from the church boards and two philanthropic foundations. Government procedures for clearing colleges and schools of nursing was cumbersome, and not until 1943 was there any great flow of students from internment camps to schools of higher learning.

In the early days of Japanese relocation from the West Coast, it was difficult for a Japanese American girl who wished to become a nurse find her acceptance in a reputable school of nursing. Hospitals in the East and Midwest were afraid of unhappy patient reaction. Young women wishing to enter schools of nursing encountered resistance not met by ordinary university students. A suggestion was made that schools of nursing be established in the Japanese relocation center hospitals. Nurse educators discounted this idea in that the distribution of clinical material and staff in these hospitals was not such to provide an adequate experience for the nurse student.

The War Relocation Authority and the National Nursing Council, cooperating with the Student Relocation Council, located a few schools of nursing willing to pioneer and find out by actual experience just how their patients would react. Several large hospital schools of nursing in Philadelphia, New York, and Chicago began taking the Japanese American young women into their training programs and discovered that the Nisei student nurses were cheerful, reliable, and good students. Patient reaction proved excellent. Instead of fearing the Nisei's services, the patients begged to have that "lovely Nisei girl" assigned to them. Word began to spread to other hospitals. Articles were being published in nursing journals. Information circulated at hospital conventions.

By November of 1943 schools of nursing began to open up for the Nisei student. The U. S. Cadet Nurse Corps had just been implemented and would provide full scholarships for those who could meet the school of nursing requirements. Financing an education had been a problem for the Japanese American who wanted to study nursing. Family finances were frozen, and wages for those who worked in the relocation camps was $19/ month or less.

The Japanese-American Student Relocation sent out a plea, "Don't let them down," with this statement:

> A great deal is at stake in this job of relocating Nisei students. Their belief in American democracy, which they have been taught as American citizens, and in good faith of the nation of which they are a part is at stake. The morale of the entire Japanese-American community can be boosted if we give these young people a chance. These students will be our strongest allies in helping to keep that community loyal to this country.[126]

More than 400 young Nisei students benefited with an opportunity to gain an education in nursing when more than 70 schools of nursing opened their enrollment to Japanese American women. Without exception, they joined the Cadet Nurse Corps and took advantage of this once-in-a-lifetime-opportunity. Other young women from minority groups benefited from the Corps as well.[127]

Other Minority Groups

Located in the heart of the Navajo Reservation, the Sage Memorial Hospital School of Nursing in Ganado, Arizona trained

Native American women to become nurses. The hospital, built and operated by the Presbyterian USA Missions was the largest in the Southwest and well-equipped. The purpose of the school was to provide Native American young women an opportunity to secure through training in the art and science of nursing, a much-needed service for the people of their own tribes.

Native American Cadet Nurses from Sage Memorial Hospital School of Nursing stand at attention ready for their induction ceremony May, 1944. At this time the hospital was the largest center to provide health care to Native Americans. (National Archives and Records Administration)

In 1945, 40 young women were enrolled in the Sage Hospital School of Nursing, representing 25 tribes from 12 states. Almost all of these young women joined the U. S. Cadet Nurse Corps. They proudly wore their uniforms, and their stipends made them relatively rich in an area that was desperately poor.[128]

The Corps also helped Hispanics achieve their nursing goals. In one case, despite her excellent grades, Sarah Gomez encountered discrimination. She, like other Hispanics, could not find a job after graduating from high school in Southern California. The San Bernardino Country Hospital School of Nursing offered the Corps program, and according to regulations, had no ethnic barriers. This made it possible for Gomez to achieve her dream of becoming a nurse. After the Corps she served 34 years in the U. S. Army Nurse Corps, retiring as a full colonel. Gomez continued to work and made significant contributions in migrant health in her home state of California.[129]

Training opportunities for men in nursing in 1940 had improved over the past 25 years. There were four accredited schools of nursing in the United States that admitted only men students and 70 schools of nursing that admitted both men and women. Eight hundred men were enrolled in schools of nursing at the onset of the war. However, there was discrimination when it came to serving in the armed services. The American Red Cross enrolled qualified men nurses who, if needed by the Army or Navy, would serve not as members of the Army or Navy Nurse Corps (which under basic law was limited to women nurses) but as technologists for service auxiliary to the Army and Navy Corps. While meeting the same requirements as women recruits, men nurses served as noncommissioned officers in the Army and as petty officers in the Navy.[130]

Jacob Rose RN, a recent graduate of the prestigious Bellevue School of Nursing, when inducted into military service, requested that his three years of training apply where the need was the greatest. Instead of using his nursing skills, he found himself assigned to driving a truck followed by learning to drive a 12-ton bulldozer in the Pacific war theater in India. This was his complaint:

> They cried for nurses, spent huge sums in advertising that urged nurses to volunteer, but a registered male nurse didn't merit recognition in the medical department. Instead, we continued to hear lectures from a non-medical officer on first-aid whose lectures made little sense.[131]

Several nursing groups attempted to obtain rank for men nurses. These moves reappeared in the War Department from time to time and consistently were opposed by the Army and Navy Nurse Corps. The result was that men nurses who were employed in military service had no official status. The effect of the war and Selective Service wiped out most of the enrollment of men in schools of nursing and contributed to the later shortages of men nurses.[132]

A few young men, however, made it in the Corps. Emanuel Goldberg, a student nurse at the Creedmoor State Hospital School of Nursing in Queens Village, New York, wrote this letter to the editor of the *New York Times*. He said:

> A news item in your issue of July 2 pertaining to the Cadet Nurse Corps states that "the recruits are all young women." The Cadet Nurse Corps is open to young men as well, proof of which is that I am a member of the corps, having entered Feb. 1, 1944.[133]

With credit to the discriminatory clause in the Bolton Act and the shortage of women in the work force, World War II had an effect of enhancing opportunities for minorities and married women. In the case of most men who aspired toward nurse training along with the unfortunate situation of the male nurse in the armed services, a real movement for fair treatment and equality never got off the ground. General public sentiment adhered to the view that the man's place was on the battlefield and that nursing was the exclusive role of women.

8

Nurses for a Nation at War

In a news release on November 19, 1944, Surgeon General Dr. Thomas Parran of the U. S. Public Health Service reported that 30,000 new student nurses had been enrolled in the U.S. Cadet Nurse Corps. This was in addition to the 65,321 new student nurses admitted to the nation's nursing schools during the Corps' first year, which ended June 30,1944.

Director of the Cadet Nurse Corps Lucile Petry pointed out that Corps members served while they learned. "Cadet nurses are now carrying a large proportion of the civilian patients load at home, thereby helping release graduates for essential military or civilian nursing here and abroad, she said."

Dr. Parran added, "That we have reached the halfway goal in the 1944-45" recruitment by November is due to the wholehearted response of the patriotic young women of America and to the recruiting efforts of all cooperating groups."[134]

The fact that cadet nurses were carrying the large proportion of nursing care in the civilian population was attributed to two factors: (1) acceleration, and (2) the Senior Cadet Nurse program.

During World War II, America's leading educators re-examined the question as to how long it takes to train personnel of various types. In the military, servicemen had to master technical skills in shorter periods and those slated for officers were trained in "90-day wonder programs." Doctors were graduating from medical schools in accelerated programs. Nursing education found itself faced with the same issues.

The earlier Federal Nurse Training Program did not require acceleration. To help nursing schools put a shortened program into practice, the Committee on Educational problems prepared a bulletin, "Nursing Education in Wartime" which outlined adjustments in curricula for shorter programs. Many schools balked at the cumbersome problems involved and resisted acceleration of their programs.

Acceleration of training, a key feature of the Cadet Nurse Corps, was required of participating schools by Public Law 74. Once a school of nursing was approved to participate in the Cadet Nurse Corps program, assurance of implementation and continued operation of an accelerated curricula were required in order to receive federal funds. The school had to provide for the student the four basic clinical experiences of medical, surgical, obstetrical, and pediatric requirements in 30 months instead of the traditional 36.

Six months before graduation, the senior cadet served under the control of her school, rendering full-time service equivalent to that of a graduate nurse in either a federal or civilian hospital or service. As a senior cadet, free of classes, she devoted herself to full-time practice under supervision.[135]

Maximum benefit in relieving the nurse shortage relied on the distribution of a portion of senior cadets to appointments outside the home hospital. Lucile Petry outlined a "good" senior cadet nurse assignment. The experience would: (1) round out the previous experiences of the student, (2) assist the student to develop a line of special interest, and (3) make a contribution in meeting the acute needs for nursing service throughout the country. Petry informed directors of schools of nursing that the plan for senior cadets in either their own institution or other institutions required the approval of the State Board of Nurse Examiners.[136]

The Division of Nurse Education assured that no more than 50% of the senior cadets should be appointed to an outside service. By allowing a senior cadet to leave who was now qualified to give the same service as a registered nurse would be a financial loss to the hospital. Directors and administrators of schools of nursing demurred prompting Petry to write the following letter:

July 14, 1944

    We must depend on the school directors to realize that other hospitals need Senior Cadets. By assigning Senior Cadets elsewhere, schools have more facilities for expanding their own enrollments, and they are making a fine contribution in the war effort.[137]

In 1944, 12,000 such students became senior cadets; a year later 25,000 were ready for assignment. As a senior cadet, they were eligible to apply for any hospital or service approved for the program. However, 73 percent remained in the same hospital in which they received their training. Sometimes the school had not advised the senior cadet of their choices. As a whole senior cadet tried to serve where they were most needed and were widely commended for their service.[138]

Senior cadet stipends were not provided by the federal government. Federal funds went only to the pre-cadets and junior cadets. The law stated that during the six-month senior cadetship, the hospital receiving the service would pay maintenance costs and a minimum of $30 monthly to senior cadets. The rate established by a subsequent legislation for federal service was $60 a month.[139]

In June 1945, the *Cadet Nurse Corps News* announced that 4,178 senior cadets from every State in the United States had been assigned to Army hospitals and 3,000 were currently serving. The *News* reported that the Army had high praise for the senior cadets and found their enthusiasm had inspired the entire staff of every hospital to which they had served. The article asked preclinical and junior cadets to consider serving as seniors in an Army hospital. The senior cadet who planned to serve with the Army was told what she could expect:

> Your 48-hour work week will include the ward-teaching program of instructing enlisted men who were serving as technicians and had received minimal hospital training. Your full course will consist of ward clinics, demonstrations, seminars, and military training.

Many fields such as surgery, psychiatry, and treatment of medical and communicable diseases will be covered. You will see wonderful new methods of treating injuries and diseases of a global war—plastic work, bone repair, improved types of splinting. Under the supervision of skilled Army doctors and nurses, you will be privileged to watch some of these methods developed, or even help to apply them.

The Army nurses had this to say in regard to the assigned senior cadets:

Our nursing staff was cut terrifically low in order to help fill the overseas quota of nurses. By the time the cadets arrived, they were welcomed with open arms. Their arrival seemed to provide a blood transfusion for the majority of Army nurses . . .

At present, if it were not for the senior cadets in our hospitals, we would be unable to give the amount of nursing care which our patients deserve, and the type of care we are determined they shall have.[140]

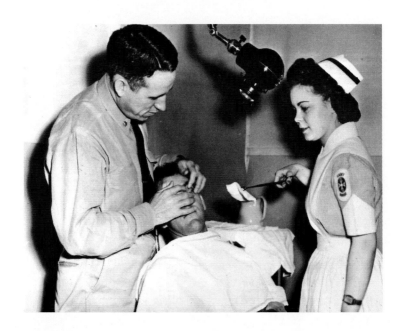

A senior cadet assists a Navy commander physician in the treatment of this serviceman's battle injury. More than 7,000 cadet nurses spent their last six months serving in military hospitals. (National Archives and Records Administration)

Other federal assignments for senior cadets included the Navy, Marine, Veteran's Hospitals, and Indian Health Services. The latter offered a rare opportunity for the student to become familiar with the culture pattern of one of America's most interesting and colorful minority groups. Although most Indian Reservations were in rural areas, senior cadets found that there were advantages that compensated for the lack of social recreational facilities to be found in cities. Nurse Historians, Philip Kalisch and Beatrice Kalisch further explained:

> Important among these was the opportunity to know personally the interesting groups descended from the original owners of America, especially in the many scenic areas where much of the romance, color, and pageantry of the old days was preserved. Cadet nurses assigned to

the Indian Service had an incomparable opportunity to acquire understanding and appreciation of early American history as related to Indians.[141]

The senior cadets were extremely valuable as one-third of all of the nursing positions in the Indian Health Service were vacant. Cadet Nurse Dorothy Gerdan from Detroit, who spent her senior cadet period at Navajo Medical Center in Fort Defiance, Arizona, wrote about her experiences:

> It's just wonderful out here. The fort is surrounded by a high mesa which sort of isolates us, but also makes it kind of cozy. It is like a little village ... The hospital is very modern. It has 150 beds. All of the Indians are of Navajo blood, except for one or two government employees. The patients are just super! Where I am working most of the patients are ambulatory and make their own beds ... The nearest town is Gallup, New Mexico, thirty miles away. The only way to get into town is to beg a ride with someone going in. We have a big barn fixed over with bowling alleys and a gym for basket ball games and dances. We have at least one dance every week, and a movie at the fort every Friday night.[142]

Civilian hospitals benefitted as well. An emergency call for nurses during the poliomyelitis epidemic in Minnesota resulted in many senior cadet nurses volunteering for a two-week experience that had been approved by the State Board of Nurse Examiners. The cadets learned how to care for patients in iron lungs and to apply Kenny hot packs. The year 1944 was the second worst polio epidemic in U.S. history, with 18,500 cases of infantile paralysis reported.[143]

In Philadelphia, New York City, and other large cities, programs in public health training and practice were offered to broaden the senior cadet's knowledge and practice in family health in the community. In this environment she became adept in applying nursing knowledge and teaching skill to the family in the home. Senior cadets discovered some health conditions occurred more frequently in the home than in the hospitals, such as expectant mothers, well children in need of immunizations, and convalescent and chronic patients. This was a unique opportunity to gain the confidence and respect of families and subsequently to learn a great deal about home and neighborhood.[144]

Other assignments supplementing the experience of the senior cadet included psychiatric institutions where they learned a new aspect of mental health nursing. The University of Minnesota School of Nursing and a few other schools assigned senior cadets to rural hospitals where they contributed invaluable services.

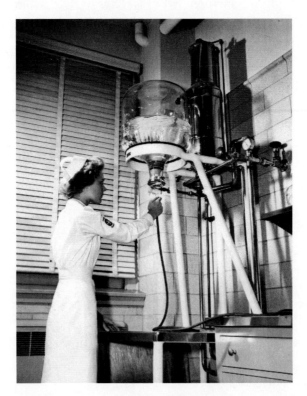

A cadet nurse turns off the distilled water which has been flowing through intravenous tubing as the last step in the cleaning before it goes into the autoclave for sterilization. Cadet nurses provided 80% of the nursing service in participating hospitals during World War II and postwar years.(NARA II)

In February 1945, Dr. Parran testified before the House Committee of Military Affairs. He reported:

> The U. S. Cadet Nurse Corps has been highly successful; in fact, it has been recognized as the most successful recruitment effort of the war. More than 1,100 out of a total 1,300 nurse training schools are participating. A quota of new admissions to all schools was set at 65,000 for the first fiscal year. The actual admissions was 65, 521 . . . .
>
> Our best estimates are that students now are giving 80 percent of nursing care in their associated hospitals. By replacing graduate nurses who already have gone into the military, the U.S. Cadet Nurse Corps has prevented a collapse of nursing care in hospitals.

Cadet nurses had been criticized because not all of them had applied for military service after graduation. Dr. Parran explained that the law passed by Congress did not impose this obligation on them. The Surgeon General noted:

> Of the approximately 10,500 nurses who have graduated from the Cadet Nurse Corps during its first eighteen months existence [that] ended Jan. 1, 1945, 40 percent have applied or have actually been accepted by the military services, and this record was made during the time when the public believed the war about to end. They have responded in much greater proportion than have their classmates who were not in the corps.

Dr. Parran concluded:

> As the war progresses, the major civilian health problems are still ahead of us. We shall see the cumulative effects of fatigue, long hours of work, worry, anxiety and grief.[145]

The shortage of nurses with advanced and specialized training continued to be acute, threatening the quality and stability of America's nursing service. Nurse administrators, teachers, supervisors, and public health and other specialists joined the Armed Forces, while on the home front the demand for these services grew steadily.

The Nurse Training Act of 1943, which created the Cadet Nurse Corps, also provided for the postgraduate and refresher training of graduate nurses that was administered by the Division of Education of the Public Health Service. While some graduate nurses enrolled and completed advanced nursing courses, many who were qualified continued to enlist in the military services. As the war progressed, the need for more nurses with advanced preparation continued to grow. Administrators were fearful that new, larger cadet classes would be without teachers.

By the end of 1943, the Procurement and Assignment Service of the War Manpower Commission had classified nurses enrolled for postgraduate study as essential. They were now ineligible to join a military service. Col. Florence A. Blanchfield, Superintendent of the Army Nurse Corps, said:

> Our efforts last year were concentrated on all groups of nurses. From now on, we will turn our efforts to individual contacts with nurses who have been declared available, instead of trying to build up a large spirit and eagerness for service among nurses in general. We don't want to over stimulate those nurses who are already in essential positions.[146]

In the Summer of 1944, the Division of Nurse Education reported to the Advisory Committee that the postgraduate plan was not meeting the wartime need. The surgeon general called a meeting of university representatives to consider the problem. The solution was to devise on-the-job courses for those nurses in greatest need of special training but who were unable to leave their posts. Lucile Petry said, "If nurses can't take the time to go to the universities to study, then we will get trainers to give the advance preparation."

The Nurse Training Act was amended to permit federal subsidy of intensive on-the-job courses and emergency university courses. With that impetus, this gap in the training program was rapidly narrowed. A total of 6,516 graduate nurses took on-the-job courses.

Civilian hospitals relied largely on student nurses and volunteer nurses' aides for patient care. The American Red Cross, under the able leadership of Mrs. Walter Lippman, trained more than 181,000 nurses' aides nationwide. The Red Cross nurses' aides cared for the hospital patients when the cadets were attending classes. Thanks to the nurse aides and the cadets in training, a nursing crisis in the civilian hospitals was averted.

On the advent of war, the Army grew overnight and so did the demand for Army nurses. The Army advised the War Manpower Commission that 50,000 Army nurses were needed, then a year later lowered the quota to 40,000. The Army justified the reduction on the basis of the use of airplanes for quick evacuation of wounded men and convalescence was shortened with the advent of penicillin and sulfa drugs. With the success of the Normandy Invasion, General Eisenhower and others predicted that the war would be over by the end of 1944.

The Army discharged 10,000 nurses, most of them on the basis of marriage. Other inconsistencies included the role of Black nurses. Only 330 Black nurses out of 9,000 were recruited and serving in the Army. There was also rank discrimination for 3,000 male nurses, although they had the same training as female nurses. According to Surgeon General of the Army Norman T. Kirk, male nurses were not utilized in a nursing capacity because:

> The situation concerning male nurses is not at all parallel to that of female nurses, who are appointed for a single specific type of duty for which they are peculiarly qualified by reason of their sex . . .

Although there was considerable criticism of the practice of not using the skills of male nurses, the Army was persistent in its argument that the performance of certain nursing tasks would ruin an officer's usefulness in the eyes of enlisted men.[147]

Just as victory appeared to be in sight, in December 1944, the Germans launched a fierce offensive in Belgium called the Battle of the Bulge by the Americans. Allied casualties totaled 60,000 with a rate of 1,750 per day. Thousands and thousands of the Army's seriously wounded and sick were flowing back to the United States each month. The Army's 60 general hospitals were filling up. The question was asked, "What can be done for them now—for the men with mutilated faces and legs and minds?"

On December 19, 1944, newspapers throughout the country carried an editorial by the nationally syndicated columnist, Walter Lippman who wrote the editorial, "American Women and Our Wounded Men." Lippman charged the Army with gross neglect of wounded soldiers by not providing an adequate number of nurses for their care. He said:

> The last thing our people will put up with is that sick and wounded American soldiers should suffer because the Army cannot find enough women to nurse them. Yet I am reporting only the stark truth, which is well known to the Army and to the leaders of the medical profession, when I say that in military hospitals at home and abroad our men are not receiving the nursing care they must have, and that with casualties increasing in number and in seriousness, this will mean for many of the men brought in from the battlefields that their recovery is delayed, and even jeopardized . . .[148]

The public was outraged that such a plight should exist. Secretary of War Henry L. Stimson demanded an explanation from the Surgeon General of the Army Norman T. Kirk who admitted that the situation was nearly hopeless. Stimson received an approval for a drastic solution from President Franklin D. Roosevelt—a draft of female nurses.

On January 6, 1945, the President of the United States shocked the nation in his State of the Union address to Congress when he requested a draft of women nurses. President Franklin D. Roosevelt concluded that volunteering had not produced the number of nurses needed. Between January and June 1945, Congress became enmeshed in a controversial proposal to draft women nurses. The U. S. Government, for the first and only time in history, was asking for a draft that discriminated in respect to an occupational category. The adequate nurse supply for the military had become a prime consideration.

The bill to draft nurses, H.R. 2277, was passed by the House on March 7, 1945. It provided that graduate registered nurses and new graduates of state accredited nursing schools between the ages of 20 and 45 would be subject to induction into the Armed Forces of the United States. The bill did not apply to women with dependent children or to women married before March 15, 1945. It exempted certain religious groups and provided against discrimination for race, color, or creed.

Surgeon General Dr. Thomas Parran called on Corps members who had completed their training for help. He said:

> We are confident that you realize the seriousness of the situation in the military nursing services, particularly the Army. It is here that you, as graduate nurses, will have your opportunity to serve where you are most needed. If you as individuals and the Public Health Service can help meet the present emergency, we shall have fulfilled our greatest service to the Nation.

Sixty percent of the graduating cadets responded by applying for military service. Brought to the floor of the Senate on April 9, 1945, the draft bill was "passed over." A month later the Germans surrendered. With the changing circumstances there was no longer a need for the pending bill to draft nurses.[149]

Despite all the complications, voluntary mobilization of nurse power served the Nation in a time of war crisis. Nursing services provided for both the civilian population and military to an extent that exceeded all previous records. The Nurse Training Act made possible the rapid preparation of graduate nurses to replace the teachers and specialists drawn from the civilian supply by the military. Young women joined the U. S. Cadet Nurse Corps in unprecedented numbers. As students, these young women filled the depleted ranks of civilian nurses and gave a high proportion of nursing services in hospitals and other health agencies throughout the country. As graduates they continued to serve during the latter years of the war and met the increasing health needs of the postwar period. On both the home and war fronts, nursing came through with honor.

9

V–J Day and After

Lucile Petry Leone, Emeritus Director of the Cadet Nurse Corps said she would always remember the late afternoon of August 6, 1945. She was riding a commuter train from Bryn Mawr, Pennsylvania, to Philadelphia where she would transfer to a "Pennsy" fast train to Washington, D.C. She had attended a meeting at Bryn Mawr College and was now on a train that stopped every three to eight minutes to take on and discharge passengers. As the train drew into the last station before her transfer, she saw people on the platform yelling, jumping up and down, hugging, and slapping each other's backs; they were exultant. Several newsboys had arrived with wagons loaded with extra news editions that were selling like hot cakes! A boy held up a paper so those on the commuter train could see tall red letters that read, "Bomb Dropped," "Hiroshima Bombed."

Petry Leone said she was soon on the transfer train and found herself with a small group that had boarded in New York City (its only previous stop). They thought the ink on her paper which had been printed in Philadelphia was wetter than theirs, indicating more up-to-date news. What conversations!

"Was the war over?" "Is there another kind of atom to split?" "Who had won?" "The democracies?" "What would that mean to nations everywhere?" "Could nations unite?" "And bring peace." "The war over, how long peace?"[150]

The White House issued a release stating that an atomic bomb had been used against the Japanese and America was now waiting for them to accept the terms of the allies. When there was no response from Tokyo, on August 9th, a second bomb was dropped on Nagasaki. The atomic age had begun with a vengeance. On August 15, millions of Japanese listened to the sacred voice of their emperor. Hirohito told his people to accept their fate and said because the war situation had not developed to their advantage . . . the unendurable must be endured.

Word of Japan's surrender touched off jubilant celebrations across the Nation. People cheered and rejoiced for the soldiers who would be coming home and wept for those who would not. Perhaps no one felt greater joy and relief than the servicemen who were scheduled to take part in the final assault against Japan. The young men were already training in the Philippines and on Okinawa, and the thousands who awaited transfer from the European theaters to the Pacific were relieved in the thought of their deliverance from the threat of death or maiming.[151]

Hundreds of radio stations across the nation were broadcasting appeals to young women to join the Cadet Nurse Corps when suddenly, on August 14, 1945, all broadcasts were interrupted to announce that Japan had surrendered. The tightly wound spring of war mobilization was released. Recruitment to the Cadet Nurse Corps was terminated at once, but the vast nurse-training program could not close with the news of peace. Still in training under the federal subsidy were 116,498 cadets. Student nurses were supplying 80 percent of the nursing care in more than 1,000 civilian hospitals.[152]

President Truman announced the status of the Cadet Nurse Corps and set October 5, 1945 as the final date for new admissions to the Corps. This action, the White House said, permitted "orderly termination of an important wartime activity." It added:

> The U.S. Cadet Nurse Corps has contributed greatly to meeting the needs of the Nation for nurses . . . military and civilian. The Corps has made a substantial contribution to health in wartime. Its graduates will continue in the days of peace to serve the health needs of our veterans and civilian population.

The President's action meant that the 30,000 cadet nurses recruited by August 20 for Fall classes would receive federal aid to graduation.[153]

Cadet nurses had pledged to be available for military or other federal governmental or essential services for the duration of the war. The pledge was purely honorary, and the inability or failure to fulfill it involved no break of legal obligations. In the following issue of the *Cadet Nurse Corps News*, Lucile Petry urged cadets to continue their vital contribution and to continue serving where they were most needed. Petry reminded cadets that they were still needed to help the nation maintain a solid health front.[154]

The *News* also announced to new cadets that those who were admitted on or after June 30, 1945 would receive one washable sleeve patch to be worn on the indoor uniform that would identify them as members of the U. S. Cadet Nurse Corps. The fact that the popular uniform was no longer issued was a disappointment to many of the new cadet nurses. The uniform, designed to give national recognition for a vital wartime service, had won instant acclaim for its smart good looks.

President Truman and a cadet nurse reviewed plans for the U. S. Cadet Nurse Corps. When the War ended in August 1945, the President authorized a gradual phase out of the Corps. (Program Support Center, Department of Health and Human Services)

With victory, Congress requested all war-created agencies to cut down expenses immediately. After careful review of expenditures necessary to continue the Cadet Nurse Corps program, the Division of Nurse Education decided that the first step should be the cancellation of the uniform contract. This decision was based on the fact that uniforms were not essential to the education scholarships. All other regulation benefits would be available to all students alike. The Division of Nurse Education expressed regrets to the new recruits, explaining that when expenditure curtailments became necessary, the uniform had to be the first to go.[155]

In January 1946, Surgeon General Dr. Thomas Parran sent the following message to members of the Corps:

> The Cadet Nurse Corps has reached the halfway mark. For two and one/half years the loyalty and inspired enthusiasm of the Corps members has set an unparalleled war record. In another two and one/half years the last Cadet Nurse will graduate. The full peacetime value of work begun under pressure and stress of war has now been determined. America depends on Cadet Nurses to continue the prevailing high standard of essential service in hospitals where the situation remains critical.
>
> Today we stand on the threshold of a New Year . . . before us a new world where peace, gained at high cost must be maintained. Your youth, energy, spirit and knowledge are needed to help cement this peace . . . We must think in terms of one world, and fight prejudice, hatred and disease, along with all other enemies of peace . . .
>
> May we all resolve to work together for world happiness and world peace.[156]

Petry's memo in the *News* reminded cadets that with the rapid demobilization of women in the armed services, the national spotlight no longer focused on uniforms. She advised that rather than assigning the cadet nurse uniform to mothballs—and oblivion—to make them over into attractive civilian suits with minimum effort and expense. A noted fashion editor suggested removing the epaulets, pocket tabs, and changing the buttons. If more variation was desired, the editor suggested to remove the collar and lapels, the cadet would then have a good looking cardigan suit. The epaulets could also be removed from the reefer, and a fur collar could be added. Also, all three pieces could be dyed in an exciting new color.

The Army and Navy paid tributes to senior cadets who had served in military hospitals. Vice Admiral Ross T. Mintier, Chief of the Navy's Bureau of Medicine and Surgery, wrote the following:

> It is with regret that we write the last set of orders for a Cadet Nurse to proceed to a naval hospital for her Senior Cadet Nurse period. However, this feeling is mixed with a great deal of gratitude because we do not have the hundreds of sick and wounded pouring into our hospitals and requiring the nursing care that the Senior Cadet Nurse can give.
>
> Since April 1, 1944, nearly 1,100 Cadet Nurses from schools of nursing in 40 States and the District of Columbia have been assigned to naval hospitals for their Senior Cadet Nurse period. They have given expert nursing care to critically ill patients and assisted the members of the Nurse Corps in the administration of the wards and the instruction of the members of the Hospital Corps.
>
> The enthusiasm, desire for knowledge and never-flagging interest of these student nurses has undoubtedly acted as a stimulus to all connected with the naval hospitals. In this way, as well as through the many hours of nursing care, they have contributed to the recovery of our men.
>
> May we take this opportunity to thank the members of the United States Nurse Corps, those who served

in naval hospitals and those who remained at home to release Senior Cadets and graduate nurses for service.[157]

In grateful appreciation for more than 6,000 senior cadets who served in Army hospitals, Major General Norman T. Kirk, Surgeon General of the Army, added these words:

> Now that the great national emergency has come to an end, I should like to take this opportunity to thank you and the members of your organization for the magnificent contribution of the Cadet Nurse Corps to the Medical Department of the Army. I do not need to repeat the many nice things that you already know about your grand Corps, but two outstanding contributions they have made to this country come readily to mind: 1. They have stabilized the civilian home front nursing service at a time when the military demands would have disrupted a less efficient organization. 2. They assumed nursing responsibilities in Army hospitals second only to our own Army nurses. By doing so they endeared themselves not only to the professional personnel of our hospitals, but to the patients over whom they so carefully watched.

The Surgeon General of the Army concluded that "It was a job well done."[158]

In March 1946, Lucile Petry received an appointment as Chief of the newly formed Division of Nursing of the United States Public Health Service. The creation of the Division was in recognition of the great importance of nursing activities of the Public Health Service. The responsibilities of the Division fell under three main groups: Public Health Nursing, Hospital Nursing, and Nurse Education. The administration of the Corps program was absorbed by the new Division. Of the five original leaders of the women's uniformed organizations serving their country, Petry was the only one still active in the same capacity.[159]

Soon after the war, it became evident that America was more health conscious than ever before. A survey by the American Hospital Association reported that the shortage of civilian hospital personnel was even more serious than it had been during the war. Senior cadets continued to be in demand for civilian hospitals, federal hospitals, and public health agencies. In 1946, a large number of senior cadets had hoped to "serve those who had served us" and asked for assignments in the Veterans' Administration but were rejected due to the impact of the housing shortage. By July the construction plans for housing cadets had been materialized. A call for 600 senior cadet nurses was sounded by Dr. Paul Haley, Chief Medical Director of the Veterans Administration. In a direct plea to cadet nurses, Dr. Haley urged to "help us provide the best in nursing service for the discharged soldier who still has a battle to win."[160]

From 1945 to 1948, Veterans Administration (VA) hospitals were understaffed to the danger point. More than 7,000 senior cadets responded to the call by serving in VA hospitals.

The senior cadet period eventually provided a more equitable distribution of nursing service throughout the nation during the post-war period of 1946 through 1948. A supervised experience during the senior cadet period could be one or more of the following clinical services: medical, surgical, obstetric, pediatric, psychiatric, tuberculosis, communicable disease, as well as in an outpatient department or a public health agency. Such experiences might also include assistance to instructors, head nurses, or supervisors. Senior cadets in civilian hospitals and institutions received at least $30 a month; by presidential order, those in federal services received $60. The senior cadet period afforded an opportunity for a student nurse to try out a field of nursing in which she might later elect to serve.[161]

Excellent plans for the use of senior cadets was set up by several public health nursing agencies. The senior cadet assigned to public health agencies wore the beret and top coat of the U. S. Cadet Nurse Corps uniform and the standard blue washable uniform dress of the agency. The agency furnished her bag and field equipment and made suitable arrangement for her transportation. After orientation, her experience might have included participation in maternal and child health conferences, as well as in venereal disease and tuberculosis clinics. She would assist in immunization clinics and make home visits, giving bedside nursing care, and teaching personal hygiene and family health. More than 2,000 senior cadets served in public health agencies.

With the emphasis rapidly shifting from the traditional courses consisting of training in four basic services—medical, surgical, obstetric, and pediatric—to a type of preparation stressing the broad social functions and social needs for nursing, the importance of experience in such services as psychiatric and communicable disease came to be considered basic. In 1947, a total of 57,000 senior cadets rendered valuable nursing service and won public recognition by their work during the polio epidemic. Between 1939 and 1943, there was very little change in the number of schools providing experience or their students in the so-called nursing specialties. On the other hand, there were marked differences between 1943 to 1948 (the cadet nurse years).

There were relatively few nurses trained in psychiatry in civilian life in 1940. Few states at that time listed psychiatric nursing experience as a prerequisite for licensere as a nurse. Mental disorders were the leading cause of rejection for military service in World War II. This fact was especially significant as these men were in a period of life when they should have possessed the greatest health and vigor. In the year following the end of the war, Congress debated and passed the National Health Act. This legislation provided for a broad program of mental health services to be conducted by the Public Health Service.

The operation of the Senior Cadet Program was not without its cumbersome aspects. The Division of Nurse Education repeatedly urged a wider distribution of senior cadet services. "We must depend on the school directors to realize that other hospitals need Senior Cadets," wrote Lucile Petry to one hospital administrator. Each school of nursing director was instructed to give every prospective senior cadet the opportunity to choose a

Federal Nursing Service. This was required by law. As might be expected, the senior cadet experience in some schools remained below standard. It was emphasized that the senior cadet period was to be a supervised practice and students at this stage of the program could not be held responsible for tremendous work loads. However it was not uncommon for student nurses to serve alone at night on large wards of 25 patients or more with a supervisor only on call in the event of an emergency.

One cadet nurse filled out an application to serve with a public health agency only to be informed by the director of nursing that she had been too busy to submit the request. Instead she was assigned duty in the central supply where she would be cleaning, repackaging and sterilizing used hospital equipment and supplies for six months. All hospital supplies such as syringes, needles, and tubing of all types were recycled in the 1940s.

Seventy-three percent of all senior cadets served in the hospitals where they were trained. The fact that the great majority of students remained in their home hospitals was due, in some instances, to the fact that their schools failed to advise them of the opportunity to choose another learning experience. As one nursing director expressed, "The government is asking us to give up our students at a time when their service is most helpful to our hospital." As a whole, senior cadets themselves tried to serve where they were most needed and were widely commended for their services.[162]

On July 1, 1946, health leaders congratulated cadet nurses on the Corps' third birthday. On behalf of the American Hospital Association, President Peter D. Ward, M.D., said that cadet nurses had written a glorious record of achievement during the war years. He continued to say that Corps members and graduates would bring credit to their country as they entered a professional career bright with opportunity.[163]

Katharine J. Densford, President of the American Nurses Association, congratulated the "Cadet Nurse of today . . . the graduate professional nurse of tomorrow!" She said that never before had there been so many opportunities in the nursing profession. Densford, Dean of the University of Minnesota School of Nursing, was a great supporter of the Cadet Nurse Program. Her school of nursing trained 1,640 cadet nurses, more than any other school of nursing in the country.

Roger I. Lee, M.D., President of the American Medical Association, added that cadets had chosen a distinguished career; one which would bring self-satisfaction gained from helping fellow man. He added, "In peace, as in war, this is a noble achievement."[164]

In summing up, Lucile Petry said that one of the most lasting beneficial effects of the Corps was that a greater public than ever before was now informed of the needs and uses of nursing. She further said:

> We shall not realize the total impact of the Corps program for several years until Corps graduates have matured professionally and have accepted their rightful place in the profession, but the shadow of coming events is growing longer and stronger. From young cadet nurses, educated during the war and in these golden days of peace, I expect to see the finest leadership the nursing profession has ever seen.[165]

When the war was over, two facts stood out: (1) The great majority of American nurses served where they were most needed; and (2) The persons responsible for training and supplying nurses had carried through a difficult task.

10

Historical Perspectives

Tradition, which is often a barrier to change, held high priority in nursing education with strict obedience to authority and dedication to duty continued to prevail early 1940s. Nurses considered their service a calling that required hard work with minimal compensation. These ideals had been emphasized by military and religious traditions. Modern nursing, inspired by Florence Nightingale, was born during the Crimean War (1854-1856).

By the turn of the 20th century, new developments in surgery and sanitary science had led to a tremendous expansion of hospitals. It soon became apparent that a school of nursing was critical in saving costs in operating a hospital. Hospitals throughout the country established their own schools of nursing on an independent basis. Most hospital training schools were opened not for the purpose of educating nurses but for the sole objective of providing care for the hospitalized sick. Not only did nursing students provide and improve the nursing service to patients and but saved hospitals money with low staffing costs. The students worked grueling long hours caring for the patients in payment for the training they received.[166]

These new frontiers appealed to women who wanted an opportunity to be of service to their fellow man and to obtain a respectable position in society. Visionary nursing leaders of the day became concerned that student nurses were long on practice and short on education. They began to organize in the effort to control their own educational standards and to attack the chaos that had been created with the multitude of independent schools of nursing, each with a different set of standards and ideals.[167]

In 1923, Mary Adelaide Nutting, the first nursing professor in the world, wrote about the discrepancies between the education of nurses and the education of other professionals:

> Nursing is our art in which we must unfailingly excel. To do this we need apply our very highest energies, striving constantly to gain a truer understanding of our work and toward fairer and sounder methods in it. There does not seem to me to be any reason why a nurse with real command of her work should not become as distinguished in her own field, as are eminent teachers in other fields. Our schools should be noted for their gifted and inspiring teachers, as for their able administrators.[168]

"The national picture is not altogether pleasing," Anna Wolf, who served on the Corps Advisory Committee, said. "A large number of our 1,300 nursing schools are not training skilled nurses, and haven't for the past 40 or 50 years. The main reason is the small school with its plea to be left unchanged. And so we must keep our standards low enough to allow them to get through, and thus we have held back nursing education all these years."[169]

In 1909, the University of Minnesota offered a full course of nursing and is recognized as the pioneer in this new type of educational affiliation. This was largely due to the efforts of Dr. Richard Olding Beard, who had always been sympathetic with nurses in their educational objectives. The school of the university hospital was put on a university basis under the direction of Louise Posell. By 1938 approximately one hundred colleges and universities in the United States had established schools of nursing.[170]

In the 1940s a few more than ten percent of the schools of nursing were university programs with great variations in regard to requirements and standards. A war measure and to take advantage of the grants provided by in the U. S. Cadet Nurse Corps, collegiate programs offered the choice of a diploma and at the end of the three years, the baccalaureate degree at the end of an additional year which would be paid for by the student.

While the wartime contribution of the Cadet Nurse Corps was tremendous in providing a great reservoir of nurse power for the military and preventing the collapse of civilian nursing service on the Home Front, certain long-range benefits stood out. Surgeon General Dr. Thomas Parran of the U. S. Public Health Service enjoyed the strong backing of President Roosevelt and key congressional leaders and gave full support to the Division of Nurse Education (DNE). The DNE staff, under the direction of Lucile Petry, emphasized accountability. The weaker schools of nursing had to be concerned with meeting the Bolton Act requirements so they could receive federal funds, thus the poor and marginal schools of nursing were challenged to reform or disband.

A marked shift in the preparation of nurses was spearheaded. In accelerating programs, schools of nursing had to eliminate repetition and nonessentials in the basic curriculum. Schools found that they were able to purchase a great deal of instruction, especially in the sciences from junior and senior colleges, and that by planning cooperatively, they could take advantage of the vast instructional facilities available in their own or neighboring communities.[171]

In 1944, the National Nursing Council for War Service conducted a survey to determine the number of colleges and universities offering an undergraduate program that led to both a diploma in nursing and a degree. The Council reported that 150 schools of nursing, or 13 percent of all schools, had such a program. However, there was great variation in regard to requirements, length, and standards. Students were advised to give careful consideration in the selection of a good college and university program. Ninety-six percent of all collegiate schools of nursing participated in the Corps program.[172]

Forty-four percent of faculties of more than 980 Corps hospital schools of nursing had received no college experience. In most of these schools, physicians taught the lecture courses, and the follow-up lessons were taught by nurse-instructors or head nurses or supervisors. The instructors did not follow the progress of students on the wards and were cut off from students' experience in practice.

A far-reaching change that took place during World War II was the introduction of nurse instructors in lectures on disease. An adjustment recommended for wartime conditions was efficiency in using the busy physician's time by supplementing the doctor's lectures to a greater degree by nurse instructors. Thus, a greater emphasis was placed on the nursing aspect, which changed the focus for students to become nursing experts rather than clinicians. Funds for postgraduate courses were also available under the Bolton Act, and more than 10,000 graduate nurses took advantage of the opportunity.[173]

The Division of Nurse Education could claim credit for encouraging and assisting curricular change, the development of better instruction, and other efforts to make better use of time, space, and personnel in the schools. It also pressed for student health, a more humane institutional environment, expanded libraries, and heightened pride for nurses.

The public relations campaign of the Bolton Act presented nursing as a challenging and satisfying career for intelligent young women. Qualified young women who could not afford to enter a program could now do so and successfully complete their preparation for nursing.[174]

When World War II ended, Americans began to focus on domestic problems. Larger and better systems of higher education and health care were on the list. The impact of the favorable image of the Cadet Nurse Corps brought about the need for a more vigorous nursing workforce in postwar planning for health. Nurses began to see themselves as part of a vital professional role in the care of patients, which required more than a perfect execution of a series of procedures. "Become a nurse. Your country needs you" again became the call of the 1960s when the second Nurse Training Act of 1964 was signed by President Linden Johnson. The war against poverty required better preparation of nurses which was central to the nation's health agenda. The federal government's response to more and better educated nurses complimented the broad intervention programs in civil rights, poverty, and social welfare.[175]

Bonnie Bullough found new opportunities in nursing when she took advantage of both Nurse Training Acts. She became a major nurse researcher, a pioneer nurse practitioner, an activist in bringing change in the nurse practice acts, a historian of nursing, an influential researcher into human sexuality, a college administrator, and an expert on alienation and the health profession in general. Here is her story:

Bonnie Bullough was born in 1927 in Delta, Utah. When Bonnie was not quite four, she was badly burned when a Halloween Jack O' Lantern which she was carrying caught her clothes on fire. She suffered first-, second-, and third-degree burns on her legs and part of her face and lost most of one ear. She survived, but was badly scarred, and her mouth was twisted out of shape. Fortunately, a heavy coat protected much of her body.

The full effects of the depression of the 1930s hit Bonnie's unemployed parents and the family struggled to survive. It was not until after the passage of the Social Security Act of 1935, with its provisions for crippled children, that Bonnie could enter into a long-term program to repair some of the damages done to her face, mouth, ears, and legs. Since the hospital was in Salt Lake City, 100 miles away, and her surgery had to be done in stages, she spent much of the summers for the next four years in the hospital alone and away from her family. It was here she became committed to nursing.

In the summer of 1944, after graduating from high school Bonnie, enlisted in the U. S. Cadet Nurse Corps under the joint auspices of the University of Utah and Salt Lake General Hospital. Bonnie opted for the diploma program in order to marry her husband, Vern L. Bullough, in 1947, who was still in the Army. Combining parenthood and a nursing career, she continued to pursue her nursing education. When her family moved to Ohio, she took advantage of the Youngstown University where she received her bachelor's degree. She joined the faculty as a part-time lecturer in the required health class. Here she discovered her talent for speaking to large audiences.

When her family moved to Los Angeles, she entered the University of California where she would receive her M.S. in nursing. She went on to earn a M.A. in sociology in 1965 and a Ph.D. in 1968. While in the doctoral program, she received an appointment as a Fulbright lecturer at the University of Cairo in Egypt. In Egypt, her eldest son was killed in an accident and after her return to Los Angeles, the Bulloughs adopted their fifth child. Later in her career she was appointed dean and professor at State University of New York in Buffalo.[176]

Bonnie Bullough, who may have never had a distinguished career in nursing without the Cadet Nurse Corps, added her historical perspective. She wrote:

> Since the Corps forbad discrimination on the basis of race or marital status and set minimum educational standards, it was a significant factor in improving the educational system. The federal assistance set a precedent for governmental cooperation in nursing and, although [in] the postwar years that assistance varied with administrations and national conditions, the funds that were granted helped the schools as they moved into the mainstream of American education. Federal funds gave educators stronger bargaining power within colleges as they sought affiliations for nursing schools . . .

Bonnie concluded, "Paradoxically, the Cadet Nurse Corps which used students as workers, set precedents for federal aid to nursing education which later helped the schools escape from the apprenticeship system."[177]

ENDNOTES

1. U. S. Federal Security Agency, Public Health Service. (1950). **The United States Cadet Nurse Corps, 1943-1948.** (PHS Publication No. 38, p.20) Washington, D.C.: Government Printing Office.

2. Robinson, T. & Perry, P. (1993-1995). Cadet Nurse Story Telling Project. Boulder, CO.

3. The occasion was a coffee honoring Emeritus Director Lucile Petry Leone at the Sequoias, San Francisco sponsored by Paulie Perry and her sister Thelma Robinson on November 12, 1994. The former cadet nurses continued to meet each year, 1994 through 1999, to celebrate Petry Leone's birthdays and to share stories. Lucile Petry Leone was born on January 23, 1902 in Lewisburg, Ohio and died November 25, 1999 in San Francisco.

4. (Lucile P. Leone—Curriculum Vitae, 10/14/1996).

5. Disch, J. (1984). Nursing: Something for Everyone, **Minnesota Medicine**, 84 (2001): 4.

6. Letter addressed to ASG Lucile Petry Leon USPHS (Ret.) from Office of the Chief Nurse, Parklawn Building, Room 11-05, Rockville MD dated 1/17/1997 and signed by RADM Carolyn Beth Mazzerlla, Chief Nurse Officer and 24 members of the USPHS Professional Advisory Committee for Nursing.

7. The first book by the author and Paulie M Perry, **Cadet Nurse Stories—The Call For and Response of Women During World War II** was published by Center Nursing Publishing, 550 West North Street, Indianapolis, Indiana 46202 in 2001.

8. Robinson, T. (2005). **Nisei Cadet Nurse of World War II—Patriotism in Spite of Prejudice** was published by the Black Swan Mill Press, 2525 Arapahoe Ave., Suite E4, PMB, 534, Boulder, Colorado 80302 in 2004. The Nisei Cadet Nurse Telling Project received the 2002 Cadet Nurse Award from the American Association for the History of Nursing. The Japanese translation is available through Babel Press, Tokyo.

9.   To request a copy a cadet nurse Certificate of Membership of the U. S. Cadet Nurse Corps, write to: National Archives and Records Administration II, Textual Records, 8601 Adelphi Rd., Suite 2600, College Park, MD 20740. Include the following information: Full name when a cadet, birth date, school of nursing, city, state, and first year of service. There is no charge.

10. Luce, H. R. (1968). Editor's note. **Time capsule 1940: A History of the year.** (p. 8). New York: Time/Life Books.

11. Amidon, B. (1941). Better nursing for America. (Public Affairs Pamphlet, No. 10). (RG 90). College Park, Maryland: National Archives and Record Administration II.

12. Ibid. (Here after cited as NARA.)

13. When does the home front have priority? (1943). **Public Health Nursing,** 35: (1), 77-78.

14. Federal Security Agency, Public Health Service. (1950). The U.S. Cadet Nurse Corps, 1943-1948. (Public Health Service Publication No. 38, p.8). Washington, D.C.: Government Printing Office: 7. (Hereafter cited as PHS No. 38).

15. Members of the National Nursing Council on National Defense organized July 1940. The group was reorganized as the National Nursing Council for War Service, Inc., July 1942.: Name changed to National Nursing Council, Inc., November 1945. Members included the following:

      American Nurse's Association
      National League of Nursing Education
      National Organization for Public Health
      National Association of Colored Graduate Nurses
      Association of Collegiate Schools of Nursing
      American Red Cross Nursing Service
      Division of Nursing Education of United States Public Health Service
      Federal Nursing Council
      American Hospital Association
      American Medical Association
      International Council of Nurses
      American Association of Industrial Nurses
      National Association of Practical Nurse Education
      Members at large
      Office of Civilian Defense
      Procurement and Assignment Service of War Manpower Commission
      Subcommittee on Nursing of Health and Medical Committee,

Office of Defense Health and Welfare

Ex officio members were representatives of the following:

Federal Nursing Services:

U.S. Army Nurse Corps

U.S. Navy Nurse Corps

U.S. Public Health Services

U.S. Veterans' Administration

U.S. Office of Indian Affairs

U.S. Children's Bureau

American Journal of Nursing

Public Health Nursing

Nursing Information Bureau

Chairmen:

Julia C. Stimson (served July 1940-Jan. 1943).

Stella Goostray (served Jan. 1943-March 1946).

Sophie C. Nelson (served March 1947 to Oct. 1948).

Executives Secretaries:

Elmira B. Wickenden (served Oct. 1941-Jan. 1947).

Marjorie B. Davis (served Jan. 1947-Oct. 1948).

16. Flanagan, L. (1976). **One Strong Voice—The Story of the American Nurses Association.** (pp. 112-114). Kansas City, Missouri: Lowell Press.

17. PHS No. 38: 4-6.

18. Donahue, M. (1996). **Nursing the Finest Art—an Illustrated History,** 2nd Ed. (pp. 342-4). St. Louis, Missouri: Mosby.

19. Stewart, I. M. (1940). Nursing education and national defense. **The American Journal of Nursing,40.** (12), 1376-1385. (Here after cited as AJN.)

20. PHS No. 38: 11-12.

21. Stewart, I. M. (1941). Nursing Preparedness: Some lessons from World War I. **AJN 41** (7), 804-815.

22. Donahue. 333-4. M. Adelaide Nutting developed the first preliminary course for nursing at Johns Hopkins School of Nursing in 1907. The preparatory course was six months long and offered basic sciences as well as nursing principles and practice, with the later experience in the wards. The purpose of the ward experience was for the purpose of education, not service. Nutting advocated lectures from the

university, high school graduation, and the eight hour day for the student nurse. These standards became the requirement for a school of nursing participating in the Cadet Nurse Corps.

23. Stimpson, J. C. (1942). Our hour. **AJN, 42** (2),108-9.

24. Ibid.

25. PHS No. 38: 11-12.

26. PHS No. 38: 9-10.

27. Ibid.

28. Luce, H. R. (Ed.) (1968). The presidency. **Time capsule/1942: A history of the year**. (pp. 8-9). New York: Time-Life Books.

29. U.S. Federal Security Agency, Public Health Service, Division of Education. (No date). **U. S. cadet nurse corps: origin and plan of operation.** (Document from Cadet Nurse File). Bethesda. MD: National Library of Medicine.

30. Committee to Study Proposals for a Student Nurse Corps. (January, 1943). Members were: Anna D. Wolf of John Hopkins Hospital School of Nursing; Isabel N. Stewart of Columbia University and the National League of Nursing Education; Mary Beard of the American Red Cross; Katherine Faville of the Henry Street Visiting Nurse Service of New York and the National Nursing Council, Dr. Winford Smith of Johns Hopkins Hospital, Dr. Claude W. Munger of St. Lukes's Hospital in New York represented the American Hospital Association. Ex officio members were Elmira Wickenden of the National Nursing Council, Pearl McIver of the U. S. Public Health Service, and Alma C. Haupt of the Subcommittee of Nursing.

31. PHS No. 38: 12-14.

32. Kalisch P. A. and Kalisch B. J. (1974). **From training to education: The impact of federal aid on schools of nursing in the United States during the 1940's.** (Vol. 1 of Final Report of NIH Grant NU 00443, p.176).

33. Ibid. 28 & 79.

34. PHS No. 38:15.

35. Ibid. 16.

36. Ibid. 18.

37. Ibid.

38. Federal Security Agency, Public Health Service, Division of Education. (October 1944) **U.S cadet nurse corps: Its history and background.** (Document from Cadet Nurse File). Bethesda, MD: Army Medical Library.

39. PHS No. 38: 20-21.

40. Parran, T. MD. (1943, August). Way cleared to undertake vast cooperative program for training of nurse corps." **Hospitals,** 29-30.

41. PHS No. 38:24.

42. PHS No. 38:19.

43. Petry, L. (1943). U. S. cadet nurse corps—Established under the Bolton Act. **AJN 43.** (8) 704-8.

44. PHS No. 38:89

45. Petry.

46. PHS No. 38: 40-45.

47. Ibid.

48. Ibid.

49. Ibid.

50. Ibid.

51. Robinson, T. M. & Perry, P. M. (2001). **Cadet nurse stories—The call for and response of women during World War II,** (pp. 14-15). Indianapolis, IN: Center Nursing Publishing.

52. Ibid. 9-10.

53. Schwitalla, A. (S.J.) (1943, August). An Appeal to the Catholic Hospitals. **Hospital Progress** (24), 1-3.

54. Goostray, S. (1943, October). Problems of cadet nurse school curriculum—glamour not enough—The job is to educate. **Hospitals,** 65-67.

55. PHS No. 38: 47-48.

56. Ibid.

57. Petry, L. & Spalding, E. K. (1943). The production front of nursing. **AJN.** (9), 900-901.

58. PHS No. 38:61-64.

59. Ibid.

60. Leone, L. P. (1987). The U. S. cadet nurse corps—Nursing answer to World War II demands. **NSNA/IMPRINT,** 46-48.

61. Kalisch, B. J. & Kalisch, P. A. (1975). Slaves, servants, or saints: An analysis of the system of nurse training in the United States, 1873-1948. **Nursing Forum,** (3), 252-259.

62. Parran, T. (1943, August). Way cleared to undertake vast cooperative program for training of nurse corps. **Hospitals,** 29-30.

63. "100,000 are expected to enroll in the new U. S. cadet nurse corps. **New York Times.** (1943, July, 14): p.14.

64. List of dignified guests attending the luncheon for the selection of the U. S. Cadet Nurse Corps were as follows: Dr. Parran, Surgeon General of the U.S.P.H.S.; Mrs. Frances P. Bolton, Representative from Ohio; Miss Sophie Nelson, Vice-Chairman of the National Nursing Council for War Service who presided the meeting; Miss Lucile Petry, Director of the U. S. Cadet Nurse Corps; Assistant Surgeon General Charles C. Hillman, representing General Kirk of the U. S. Medical Corps; Mrs. Herbert Lehman, Federal Security Agency; Rear Admiral K.C.Mellhorn, representing Admiral McIntire of the U. S. Navy; Colonel Florence A. Blanchfield, Superintendent of the Army Nurse Corps; and Dr. George Baehr, Chief Medical Officer, Office of Civilian Defense.

65. Acronyms stand for the following: Women's Army Corps (WAC); the Navy's Women Accepted for Voluntary Emergency Service (WAVES); SPARS (derived from Coast Guard's motto, *Semper paratus*, "Always ready" and the U.S. Women Marine Corps, Women's Reserve.

66. Uniforms chosen for cadet nurses. (1943, August, 14). **New York Times,** p.19.

67. Donahue, P. M. (1996). Nursing the Finest Art. (2nd ed.) St. Louis: Mosby: 126

68. Dietz, L. (1963). **History and modern nursing.** (p.172) Philadelphia, PA: F.A. Davis Company.

69. Public Law 74, 78th Congress.,—Congressional Session No.1. (1 July 1943, July, 1).

70. Dietz.: 168-173.

71. New York city hospitals confer merit awards. **AJN, 44** *(12), 1188-1189.

72. The Churchills admire American uniform. (1943. September 5). **New York Times.** p.19.

73. PHS No. 38:30.

74. Henderson, J. (1945). One blueprint for recruitment. **AJN, 45**: (12):, 1002-1005.

75. Office of War Information in Cooperation with U. S. Public Health Service, Federal Security Agency. (1943, September). **Information program for the United States cadet nurse corp**s. (USPHS booklet from the Cadet Nurse File). Bethesda, MD: National Library of Medicine.

76. Ibid.

77. Ibid.

78. Ibid.

79. PHS. No.38: 26-32.

80. The special task force to recruit student nurses was under the direction of Anson Lowitz, a vice president of the J. Walter Thompson Co., New York. Among other groups volunteering private effort in behalf of the Cadet Nurse Corps were: The Writer's War Board, Parent Teachers Association, the Rotary International, the

Daughters of the American Revolution, Kiwanis, Lions, The Auxiliary of the American Legion, the Fraternal Order of the Moose, the Elks, the War Activities Committee of the Motion Picture Industry, and the General Federation of Women's Clubs. Agencies and associations also made outlets available for the distribution of literature.

81. PHS No. 38:26-32.

82. Kalisch, B.J. & Kalisch, P.A. (1973. Cadet nurse: The girl with the future. **Nursing Outlook**. 21, 444-449.

83. Ibid.

84. Ibid.

85. Cadet nurse corps celebration. (1994, Summer). **American Association for the History of Nursing Bulletin,** p.8.

86. PHS No. 38:26-42.

87. Kalisch, B. J. & Kalisch, P. A. (1973). Cadet nurse—the girl with the future. **Nursing Outlook** (7): p. 444-449.

88. Capping ceremonies. (1944). **American Journal of Nursing,** 44 (1) p. 65-66.

89. Ibid.

90. Petry, L. (5 April 1944). Memorandum to Directors, Schools of Nursing, No. 4. **National U. S. cadet nurse corps induction.** [RG 90]. College Park, Maryland. National Archives and Records Administration II.

91. Kalisch, B. J. & Kalisch, P. A. (1973). Cadet nurse—the girl with the future. **Nursing Outlook** (7): p. 444-449.

92. Capping ceremonies. (1944). **American Journal of Nursing,** 44 (1) p. 65-66.

93. Ibid.

94. Petry, L. (5 April 1944). Memorandum to Directors, Schools of Nursing, No. 4. **National U. S. cadet nurse corps induction.** [RG 90]. College Park, Maryland. National Archives and Records Administration II.

95. Henderson, J. Memo for General Release. (17 April 1944). **National induction ceremony,** [RG 90]. NARA II.

96. Henderson J. News release to Washington, D. C. newspapers. (29 April 1944). **U. S. Cadet nurse corps military drill,** [RG 90}. NARA II.

97. National induction as seen by a cadet nurse. (1944). **AJN 44** (6) p. 592-593.

98. A mass induction of the United States Cadet Nurses. (14 May 1944). **The New York Times.** p. 26.

99. Kalisch, P. A. & Kalisch, B. (1974). **From Training to Education: The impact of federal aid on schools of nursing in the United States during the 1940's.** (Vol. 1 of Final Report of NIH Grant NU 00443, p. 358).

100. Corps unity stressed at national induction. (1945) **Cadet Nurse Corps News**. Vol. 1 (2), p.4. (Cadet Nurse File). Bethesda, Md. National Library of Medicine.

101. Petry, L. Memorandum to Directors, Schools of Nursing, No. 12. (3 June 1944).

102. **U. S. Cadet Nurse Corps will Celebrate its first birthday . . . . July 1.** [RG 90] College Park, Maryland: National Archives and Record Administration II.

103. Cadet nurse corps celebrates second birthday. (1945). **AJN, 45** (8): pp. 656-657.

104. Corps birthday July 1 observed in churches. (1945). **Cadet Nurse Corps News.** Vol. 1(3). p. 2.

105. Dear cadet nurses. (1945). **Cadet Nurse Corps News.** Vol. 1 (1) p.1.

106. Cadet parade. (1945). **Cadet Nurse Corps News.** Vol. 1 (4) p. 4.

107. Cadets here and there. (1946). **Cadet Nurse Corps News**. Vol. 1 (6) p. 2.

108. Music is important. (1946.) **Cadet Nurse Corps News.** Vol.1 (7) p. 3.

109. Cadet nurse named jubilee queen. (1947). **Cadet Nurse Corps News.** Vol. 2 (1), p. 3.

110. Triple duty. (1947). **Cadet Nurse Corps News.** Vol. 2 (3) p. 6.

111. Bulges to be blitzed. (1945). **Cadet Nurse Corps News.** Vol. 1 (1) p. 1.

112. Gray and scarlet—Badge of distinguished service. (1945). **Cadet Nurse Corps News.** Vol. 1 (2) p. 1.

113. Cadet police pick 'em up. (1945). **Cadet Nurse Corps News.** Vol. 1 (3) p. 4.

114. Marching along together. (1945). **Cadet Nurse Corps News.** Vol. 1(4) p. 4.

115. Public Law 74-78th Cong., 1st Sess. (1 July 1943). An act to provide for training of nurses for the armed forces, governmental and civilian hospitals, health agencies, and war industries, through grants to institutions providing such training, and for other purposes.

116. Editorial. (1942). Married student nurses. **AJN, 42** (8), 855-7.

117. Editorial. (1942). What about married nurses. **AJN, 42.** (4), 400-1.

118. PHS No. 38: 49-51.

119. U.S. Public Health Service, Division of Nurse Education. (1944, January 18). **Estelle Massey Riddle**. (Memo to Negro Press). College Park, MD. (RG 90).

120. Carnegie, M. E. (1986). **The path we tread: Blacks in nursing 1854-1984.** Philadelphia, PA: J.B. Lippincott, p. 26.

121. U.S. Public Health Service, Division of Nurse Education. News Release. (1944, August 21). **Cadet nurse Annie Banks.** (RG 90.) NARA II

122. Hine, D. C. (1989). **Black women in white.** 1989. Bloomington: Indiana University Press, p.p. 152-3.

123. Kalisch, P. A. & Kalisch, B. (1974). **From training to education: The impact of federal aid on schools of nursing in the United States during the 1940's.** (Vol. I. of Final Report NIH Grant NU 00443, pp. 110-114. (Here after referred to Kalisch & Kalisch.)

124. Thomas Ray Bodine Papers. (no date). From camp to college—The story of the Japanese American student relocation. Pamplet from National Japanese American Student Relocation Council. Hoover Institution of War, Revolution and Peace, Palo Alto: Stanford University. (Bodine was the Field Director for the National Japanese American Student Relocation Council for the West Coast 1942-1945).

125. Editorial. (1943). The problem of student nurses of Japanese ancestry. **AJN,** 43 (10), pp. 895-6.

126. Bodine Papers.

127. Robinson, T. M. (2001, September). **The plight and perseverance of the Japanese American student nurse during World War II.** (Paper presented at the annual conference of the American Association for the History of Nursing, Charlottesville, VA). For more information regarding the Nisei Cadet Nurse please refer to: Robinson, T. (2004). **Nisei cadet nurse of World War II: Patriotism in spite of prejudice.** Boulder, CO: Black Swan Mill Press.

128. Kalisch & Kalisch. 627.

129. Robinson, T. M. & Perry, P. M. (2001). **Cadet nurse stories—The call and response of women during World War II.** Indianapolis, IN: Center Nursing Publishing, pp. 158-9.

130. Craig, L. N. (1940). Opportunities for men nurses. **AJN 40,**(6), p.p. 666-670.

131. Rose, J. (1947). Men nurses in military service. **AJN 47,** (3) p.146.

132. Kalisch & Kalisch. pp. 627-651.

133. Male cadet nurses also. (1944, July 6). **New York Times,** p. 14.

134. Federal Security Agency News Release. (1944, November 14). **Report on the U.S. cadet nurse corps.** Note* Cooperating groups as listed in the news release included the following: Recruitment committees of the National Nursing Council for War Service and their affiliated State and local councils, schools of nursing, the American Hospital Association, State boards of nurse examiners, the Office of War Information, the War Advertising Council, The War Activities Committee, Rotary International, the General Federation of Women's Clubs, Women of the Moose, United Daughters ot the Confederacy and other public-spirited volunteer organizations as well as guidance counselors in high schools, colleges

and universities. (RG 90). College Park, MD: National Archives and Record Administration II.

135. PHS No. 38: 42-45

136. Petry, L. (1944). Making the most of the senior cadet period. **The American Journal of Nursing, 44** (2). (reprint). (RG 90). College Park, MD: National Archives and Record Administration II.

137. Petry, L. (1944, July 14). **(Letter to directors of nursing in schools of nursing participating in the U.S. cadet nurse corps program)**. (RG 90). NARA II.

138. PHS No. 38, p.p. 42-45.

139. Senior cadet period with army gives military background. (1945). **Cadet Nurse Corps News**. Vol. 1(2), pp.1 & 4. (Cadet Nurse File) Bethesda, MD: National Library of Medicine.

140. Sorenson, M. M. (1945). The senior cadet program in an army hospital. **American Journal of Nursing, 45**. (6), 200-203.

141. Kalisch, P. A. & Kalisch, B. (1974). **From training to education: The impact of federal aid on schools of nursing in the United States during the 1940's**. (NIH Grant NU 00443, 842-4).

142. Ibid.

143. Senior cadets experience polio nursing care. (1946). **Cadet Nurse Corps News**. Vol. 1(10), p.3. (Cadet Nurse File). Bethesda, MD: National Library of Medicine

144. Dunn, Mary J. (1945, November). Senior cadets in public health nursing. **Public Health Nursing.** (reprint). (RG 90). (College Park, MD: National Archives and Record Administration II).

145. Parran, T. (1945). The cadet nurse corps. **Journal of American Medicine Association,** Vol. 127 (15), 995.

146. PHS NO. 38, p.p. 61-64

147. Kalisch, P. A. & Kalisch, B. J. (1973). The women's draft: An analysis of the controversy over the nurses selective service bill of 1945. **Nursing Research,** Vol. 22 (5), pp. 405-6.

148. Edey, M. A. Ed. (1967). **Time capsule/1944 A history condensed from the pages of time.** (p. 230). New York: Time-Life Books.

149. Kalisch & Kalisch. Women's Draft. 403.

150. Leone, L. P. (1996, January 21). Interview by author. San Francisco, CA.

151. Maddox, R. J. (1992.) **The United States and World War II.** Boulder, Colorado: Westview Press, 305-312.

152. PHS No. 38:7

153. President announces corps status. (1945). **Cadet Nurse Corps News**, Vol.1, No.4, p.1. (Cadet Nurse File) Bethesda, MD. National Library of Medicine.

154. Petry, L. (1945). **Cadet Nurse Corps News**, Vol. 1. No. 5, p. 2.

155. Ibid.

156. Parran, T. (1946). Surgeon general's message to the Corps. **Cadet Nurse Corps News**, Vol. 1. No. 6, 1 & 2.

157. Ibid.

158. Ibid.

159. Miss Petry to head division of nursing. (1946). **Cadet Nurse Corps News**, Vol. 1. No. 7., p. 1 & 2. (Cadet Nurse File). Bethesda, MD: National Library of Medicine. In 1949 Petry was promoted to the rank of assistant surgeon general. It was the first time a nurse attained the flag officer rank. Not until the 1970s did nurses in the Army, Navy, and Air Force enjoy such recognition.

160. Veterans' medical chief voices plea for senior cadets. (1946). **Cadet Nurse Corps News**, Vol. 1. No 9, p. 2.

161. Kalisch, P. A. & Kalisch, B.J. (1974). **The study of the impact of the U.S. cadet nurse corps on American nursing profession through an historical analysis and synthesis. (**Final Report of NIH Grant NU 00443, 797-804).

162. PHS. No. 38: 43.

163. Health leaders congratulate corps on birthday. (1946). **Cadet Nurse Corps News**, Vol.1, No. 9, p. 1

164. Ibid.

165. Petry, L. (1945). A summing up. **AJN, 45** (12). 1027-8.

166. Christy, Teresa. (1980, August). Clinical practice as a function of nursing education. **Nursing Outlook**, 493-4.

167. Donahue, M.P. (1996). **Nursing The finest art, an illustrated history, 2nd ed.** St. Louis, MO: Mosby, 296.

168. Nutting, M. A. (1926). **A sound economic basis for schools of nursing and other addresses.** New York: G. P. Putman's Sons, 187.

169. National Nursing Council for War Service. (September 1944). **Colleges and universities schools of nursing,** (RG 90). College Park, MD: National Archives and Records Administration II.

170. Dock, L. L. & Stewart I.M. (1938). **A Short History of Nursing, 4th ed.** New York: G.P. Putnam's Sons, 179.

171. Petry, Lucile. (1945). A summing up. **The American Journal of Nursing, 45**(12).1027-8.

172. National Nursing Council for War Service. (see above).

173. Kalisch, P. A. & Kalisch, B.J. (1974). **The study of the impact of the U.S. cadet nurse corps on American nursing profession through an historical analysis and synthesis.** (Vol. 1 of Final Report of NIH Grant NU 00443, pp. 675-7 & 720).

174. Ibid. Vol. 2, 1479-1485.

175. Lynaugh, Joan E. (2008). Nursing the great society: The impact of the nurse training act of 1964. **Nursing History Review,** 16, 13-27.

176. Bullough, V.L. & Sentz, L. Editors. (2000). **American nursing: A biographical dictionary,** Vol. 3, New York: Springer, 37-38. Bonnie and her husband Vern L. Bullough were an exceptional nurse team in the field of research, teaching and historians in nursing. Bonnie died in 1996 of an autoimmune disease. Verne died in 2006.

177. Bullough, B. (1976). The lasting impact of World War II on nursing. **AJN 76** (1), 118-120.

PART 2

Cadet nurses continued to serve through the postwar years. Cadet nurses march through downtown Waco, Texas to honor veterans on Armistice Day, 1946. (Photo Courtesy—Willie Mae Boyd Collection)

11

Excerpts from the Cadet Nurse Corps News

Author's note: In April 1945, Dr. Thomas Parran, Surgeon General of the U. S. Public Health Service announced the inauguration of the Cadet Nurse Corps News. He said, "This is your official organ and it is recognition which you have long deserved as a medium for personal expression and for disseminating information about the Corps. The News should provide an added tie to your common bond of service to our Nation at war."

The first issue of the Cadet Nurse Corps News introduced Lucile Petry, Director of the Corps, to cadet nurses throughout the country. Petry appeared in subsequent issues, Petry's "Memo to You" is reprinted in this chapter along with other excerpts.

Also in this issue congratulations were extended to the 85% cadet nurses polled in 63 schools of nursing who signified their interaction of applying for military service after graduation.

April 1945 (Cadet Nurse Corps News. Vol. 1 (1): 2.)
Editorial

We're sorry we can't bring her around and introduce each of you in person—"Cadet Nurse Mary Brown, meet your Director, Miss Lucile Petry."

We're sorry, because you'd love knowing this diminutive—there's only five feet one inch of her—dynamic "first" Cadet Nurse. Her arresting gray eyes are sympathetic, lively and intelligent. There is a sense of urgency in the air whenever Miss Petry speaks of nursing. Her calm, soft voice would tell you just how important you are as a student nurse. Her pride in her own gray and scarlet uniform would make you doubly proud of yours.

That's the kind of loyalty Miss Petry inspires in everyone. It's one of the reasons why she's a four stripe officer in the commissioned Corps of the United States Public Health Service as Director of the Division of Nurse Education. Another reason is her impressive list of A-1 performances as nurse, instructor, and administrator . . .

She's thrilled over the way you are standing by on your jobs as student nurses, pitching in enthusiastically as Senior Cadets in Federal Hospitals, and signing up on graduation with the Army Nurse Corps or Navy Nurse Corps. It would do you good to hear her praise.

June 1945 (Cadet Nurse Corps News. Vol. 1 (2): 2) Editorial

The wonderful announcement of Germany's unconditional surrender brought to our lips a prayer of Thanksgiving . . . a prayer that resounded throughout the world as the first act of a dreadful drama was brought to conclusion. The first thrilling flash of joy and gratitude was followed by the realization that the sorrow and suffering is not yet over. The situation is still critical and we must attack our work with the renewed determination not to relax our efforts until the day when final, total Victory is proclaimed.

Our President gave us our cue when he addressed the following message to all wartime agencies: "The tasks which lie ahead are no less important, no less urgent, no less vital to the future stability by our free institutions than the tasks which are behind us . . .

"These patriotic citizens who have devoted themselves unstintingly to the Nation's welfare in time of war have earned the lasting gratitude of the American people. They have helped pay that debt which every citizen in the Democracy owes to his Country and its institutions. But that debt is unpaid, at least until we have finished the war and solved those urgent problems which leaves us in its aftermath. I reiterate with all the emphasis at my command that the Nation cannot yet allow any man to leave his post of duty."

President Truman's words apply to you just as directly as they do to all other persons concerned with completing this war. Our fighting men need more than ever to know that you, as student nurses and later as graduate nurses, will continue your enthusiastic support of the war effort. You must give them the assurance that in their final battle they will receive good nursing care—the kind of care that has been saving 97 out of every 100 casualties. They will want to know that while they are being cared for, their families are receiving similar care through your service in civilian hospitals.

Although demobilization of service men began after the collapse of Germany, the Army is remobilizing "only well men." Casualties will continue to receive Army medical care, and the ratio of nurses must continue to be proportionately high. Here is where you can best serve your country.

You can know the satisfaction of helping to speed Victory. Even while in training you can give actual military service by spending your Senior Cadet period in an Army hospital. Upon graduation, you can continue the magnificent contribution which the Corps has made to the war effort, by joining the Army Nurse Corps.

Until the war in the Pacific is over—you will have finished the job you began when you entered a school of nursing and put on the gray and scarlet uniform of the Cadet Nurse Corps.

July 1945 (Cadet Nurse Corps News. Vol. 1(3):2.) Editorial

In a world currently given over to destruction, the nurse stands out—significantly—as a constructive force. While other young men and women build planes and tanks, toss grenades, plant mines, or learn the intricacies of a bomb sight, she carries on the greatest constructive task in the world—saving and rebuilding human bodies and minds.

With healing hands, she has the grave responsibility of giving her service. Her Florence Nightingale pledge—taken at capping—dedicates her nursing skills to an entire world; her Cadet Nurse pledge—made or reaffirmed at Induction—dedicates them to men and women wounded in World War II. And when their combat ends, her recreative job has just begun.

As a nurse, she knows how much longer it takes to build up than to tear down—years of study lie behind her ability to bandage wounds inflicted within the space of seconds. Her training is in itself a patriotic service, she knows she cannot stop until the last gun is fired. She must see to it that every wounded man who needs nursing care has it. Her V-day will not come till the last man who can be healed is sent home, a well man.

Author's note: By the time the third issue was in print, V-E Day had occurred and the Surgeon General of the Army announced the Army Nurse Corps needed only replacements. When the fourth issue was published (September, 1945), the War was over. President Truman announced the Corps status. The 30,000 cadet nurses who had been recruited for the Fall classes would receive Federal aid through to graduation. October 15, 1945 was the final date for new admissions.

November 1945 (Cadet Nurse Corps News. Vol.1 (5), p. 2.) Thanksgiving . . .

Author's note. This issue announced the uniform policy for new cadet nurses. With victory, congress requested all war-created agencies to cut down on expenses immediately. In compliance the Division of Nurse Education canceled the uniform contract. All other regulation benefits would be available to all students alike.

The true Thanksgiving spirit was expressed in the following letter written to Miss Petry and Dr. Parran by 34 brand-new cadet nurses. Their sentiments represented, the spirit of each member of the Corps. This is their letter:

> A little more than an hour ago, we were the recipients of the wonderful news that our August class of the United States Cadet Nurses is to be given the opportunity and privilege of completing our course of study at Broadlawns

Polk County Hospital School of Nursing with the financial assistance of the Government.

We therefore wish to take this opportunity to express to you our enthusiastic and heartfelt thanks for thus permitting us to carry through our ambitions.

We fully realize what this means to us. Each passing day of our careers, we will be conscious of our good fortune, and will strive to fulfill our obligation to our country, our school and to ourselves. Our school is surely one of the finest and we are proud to be a part of it. We sincerely hope that it will one day be proud of us!

The August 1948 Class

Memo To You
By Lucile Petry

YOUR PLEDGE . . . Despite the Japanese surrender, neither the "termination of hostilities" nor the conclusion of the "duration of the war" has yet been officially designated. They may be declared as different dates. Until the "duration of the war" is officially concluded, your pledge continues in effect. As loyal graduate Cadet Nurses, you have an obligation to render nursing service for such duration.

I have had great evidence of your devoted and enthusiastic response to duty. I have confidence that each of you will justify the faith of your Government and its citizens by continuing your vital contribution and serving where you are most needed. Categories of nursing listed as essential by the Procurement and Assignment Nursing Service will continue to guide you in interpreting your pledge. You are needed to help this Nation maintain a solid health front.

January 1946 (Cadet Nurse Corps News. Vol. 1 (6): 3)
Student Government Organization Started at Indiana UTSN

Students in the Indiana University Training School for nurses took the first step in organizing self-government policies in establishing "The Student Union." The objectives included the fostering of cooperation and unity among the students and faculty, the stimulation of individual responsibility and loyalty, and the adherence to the ideals and standards of the school and of the nursing profession. *Author's Note. A definite first in the formation of student government in schools of nursing.*

March 1946 (Cadet Nurse Corps News. Vol.1 (7): 2.)
Memo to You
Lucile Petry

Today, all thinking Americans are following the activities of the United Nations Organization with keen interest—mindful of the plans being made to secure enduring peace—aware that while these long-range plans are being formulated, there are immediate ways in which we, as individuals, can help assuage the terrible aftermath of war in countries less fortunate than ours.

I know that all of you are anxious to help alleviate the suffering in Europe. Some of you have learned from your local postmaster that 11-pound packages may be mailed weekly direct to friends and members of your families in certain European countries. On a broader scale, you have been cooperating with the International Nursing Council, through the American Nurses Association (ANA), in its drive to collect clothing for our sister nurses in other parts of the world . . .

Continue your good work to assist a needy nurse in a foreign country. Form a group in your hospital to handle a project for your school. A collection of the following items will assist a needy nurse in a foreign country. Include uniforms and aprons that you no longer wear, serviceable low-heeled shoes, warm stockings, coats and long sleeved sweaters. A combined shipment will be sent to nurses in war torn lands through ANA.

May 1946 (Cadet Nurse Corps News. Vol.1 (8):2.)
Memo to You
By Lucile Petry

This month I should like to talk particularly to those of you who are completing your Senior Cadet training period, and will soon annex the proud title of "R.N." to you names . . . Each of you has, I know, done your share and more during your country's emergency. A grateful Nation is proud of your past record, and confident that your will continue to meet the critical needs that still prevail when you become full-fledged professional nurses.

The opportunities which lie ahead of you bring their own rewards, together with their own serious responsibilities. You should always remember that in the practice of nursing, the learning process is never finished, but continues through the professional life of the individual. I hope you will not confine your learning merely to technical and professional subjects, important though they are, but that you will study and weigh carefully all of the issues involving your profession, gather all available information, study it, and then take a positive stand . . .

There are many problems that will interest you more than ever now that you are about to leave your student days behind, and enter actively into the practice of your profession . . . do your part to help in the development and improvement of professional nursing standards.

September 1946 (Cadet Nurse Corps News. Vol.1 (10):2&4.)
Director of CNC Addresses Graduates

For the first time in its history, Meharry Medical College, Nashville, Tennessee, invited a nurse to deliver its commencement address. Miss Lucile Petry, Chief of the Division of Nursing and Director of the Cadet Nurse Corps, addressed the graduates of the schools of medicine, dentistry, and nursing on June 24.

Selecting as her theme the words spoken by Prophet Jeremiah, "Make bright the arrows, gather the shields," Miss Petry outlined the changing aspects of the task facing the school graduates. "We, an army of health workers," she said, "find ourselves in a setting when there are more older patients, more chronic diseases, earlier diagnosis, demands for health confirmation and for psychosomatic care, and emphasis on preventive aspects of all care. Are we ready to do battle in a changed warfare?" . . .

Two points of attack were outlined . . . research and education . . . "No longer will the researcher work alone in his laboratory. His team mates will be with him. His knowledge must be used to define human values even to participation in the formulation of the biggest idea conceived by man—world government for peace."

Miss Petry added that education must make the researcher a wise interpreter along with health workers, doctors, dentists, and nurses and it must bring people actively together toward the goal of optimum health.

January 1947 (Cadet Nurse Corps News. Vol. 2, (1): 2&4.)
Memo to You
By Lucile Petry

The beginning of a New Year is the time for stocktaking. Maybe you do it because it's customary—maybe you undertake it seriously . . . . Try this brand of inventory.

What do you read for fun? Write the names of the books you read during 1946—at least all that you can remember now. Before you tuck the paper away for reference on December 31, 1947, study it a bit . . . . Who wrote the books you listed? How much variety does your list show? Novels, biography, poetry, religion, travel, drama, who-done-its, foreign or domestic affairs? Or maybe something special appeals to you—perhaps you collect cook books (and have read them) or you choose books that are suitable for reading aloud. Perhaps you follow the rule of reading a classic between every two best sellers. Perhaps you read in a foreign language or are a good critic of translations, or you like psychological novels for practice in analysis of character and personality—applying what you learned in mental health and psychiatry. Have you tried Shakespeare for this? Do you enjoy the sounds of words, the patterns they make, the pictures they call up, the moods they create . . . .

What will you read for fun in 1947? To what boundaries will your professional reading extend in 1947? Our foundations in nursing biological and physical sciences, medical science, sociology, and psychology—are deep and merit deep soundings. The frontiers of our profession's tomorrow are wide and multidirectional and merit exploration.

July, 1947. (Cadet Corps News. Vol. 2 (3): 1, 3 & 6.) Corps is Lauded

(Note.—An excerpts of an editorial appeared in "Drawsheet," a publication of the Kahler Hospitals School of Nursing in Rochester, MN)

The advent of the Cadet Nurse Corps brought big changes in most schools of nursing. For the first time, we found students enjoying privileges never granted before: the most outstanding of which was the privilege of choosing places to work during the last 6 months, either on favorite floors here, or in affiliating hospitals . . . Without the Cadet Nurse Corps, many of us would not be as far along in training as we are; indeed, many of us may not have deemed it possible to come at all.

Memo to You
By Lucile Petry

Whether our careers in nursing are to be brief or long, most of us—students and graduates alike—chose nursing because we are interested in people. We want to meet their needs. Some of those needs are emotional. Satisfaction comes from seeing a frightened child fall asleep after our comforting, or from the smile on the face of an old man who forgets his loneliness at our good-natured busyness at his bed.

Other needs are physical. Satisfaction comes from leaving the accident victim, now scrubbed of street dust and blood, now stitched, well positioned in his traction, pain relieved. In our mind's eye we can almost see the healing processes begin . . .

Sometimes we understand the physiology and the psychology which guided our right actions. Sometimes we perform these right actions only because someone has shown us the way . . . someone who has searched for good ways to meet these needs of patients, and has explained and demonstrated them to us.

The teacher of student nurses has added new dimensions to her satisfaction. She deals with students as well as patients. Students, too, are people with needs to be met. In meeting these needs to be met the teacher of nursing multiplies her usefulness. Because she teaches others, she cares for hundreds, rather than tens of patients on this day in the hospital. I call upon you to consider teaching as the field of nursing in which you will practice after graduation . . . And if you teach, be the best possible teacher. Patients and student nurses merit the best!

January 1948 (Cadet Nurse Corps News. Vol. 2 (4): 2& 6.) Farewell Messages from Agency Chiefs

A memorable chapter of the Nation's wartime history will close when the final Cadet Nurse class graduates in 1948. Although this nurse training program is ending, the 125,000 nurses educated under its aegis will exert a great influence for a long time to come. As members of the nursing profession, you will carry considerable prestige in your communities. Because of this capacity for service and your position in the community life, you, as a nurse also will have a heavier share of responsibility than the average citizen . . .

Thomas Parran, Surgeon General.

The proud profession of nursing, to which you have dedicated your minds, hearts, and energies, is vital and basic to the health of our people. The Nation's nurses are the largest single group of health workers in the country. Cadet Nurses, as students and graduates, represent nearly half of this significant number . . . I want to express my appreciation for the work you have done, and my confidence in the quality of the service which you will continue to render throughout the years.

Oscar R. Ewing
Federal Security Administration

Memo to You
By Lucile Petry,

As I have watched your development in nursing education, I have tried to pace my memos to match your growth. Soon all cadet nurses will have attained graduate dimensions. I think it is fitting, therefore, in my final memo, to tell you what stature I think you may aspire in your postgraduate world.

Because there are so many of you, you will represent an important segment of the nursing profession. Intelligence, interest, education and application can make you agents for bolstering and elevating health and nursing service standards; apathy can cause you to sit on the sidelines. You will decide the course.

Good bedside nursing is the first requisite, but it is not the whole job. Nursing today is a component part of the total health picture, in which medicine, research, hospital administration, community planning and other factors all figure. That means we need greater social and professional awareness in order to discharge our duties properly. Toward that end, it is essential that we understand existing conditions and seek their betterment . . .

May I share my vantage point with you? I see more patients needing more nurses in hospitals and homes. The demand will be at emergency proportions the years when the smaller postwar classes graduate. Your patients will call for you eagerly.

By answering that call, you can reach the stature demanded by your all-encompassing world of today. My very best wishes for success and happiness to each one of you.

The last class of cadet nurses graduated Fall of 1948. Lucile Petry (Leone) continued to make headlines in nursing history. In 1949 she was appointed Assistant Surgeon General in the U.S. Public Health Service, the first woman to hold the prestigious rank of admiral which entitled her to wear the gold braid. In 1952 Lucile Petry married Dr. Nicholas C. Leone, a Public Health Service researcher. When Lucile Petry first arrived in Washington D.C., her plan was to stay six months but as she said later, "I wound up staying for 25 years." She then moved to Dallas, Texas with her husband where she served as professor and associate dean at Texas Women's University for more than a decade. One of Petry Leone's students said she had enriched her life in the following dimensions: the joy of learning, the joy of teaching, the freedom to think, the freedom to say what you think, the acceptance of new ideas, and the fun of living. A prolific writer and sought-after speaker, Petry Leone advocated for women and for men as well, who were aspiring to become professional nurses.

In 1971, Petry Leone retired again and moved to San Francisco. She became active once more as Coordinator of International Students and Visitors for the University of California San Francisco. This was a notable retirement effort after her earlier teaching and public service careers.

Petry Leone was well versed in many disciplines and held a high regard for nursing history and history in general. She told a friend nurse-historian, "You tell us where we've been, why we went there, and enlighten the choice of goals for our next venture. Knowledge that makes sense of our lives."

Petry Leone touched my life personally. I learned from her and was encouraged to pursue my goal in writing about the U. S. Cadet Nurse Corps and to record cadet nurse stories. She helped me view history (and nursing) through a broader perspective. I thank her for becoming the nurse historian that I am today. I, Thelma Robinson, am extremely fortunate to have been privy to her knowledge, her perspective, and her reflections regarding the Corps and to experience her enthusiasm for living a life of fullness.

12

Letters Home

Margery Shanafelt Bitter

Author's note: Margery said that her fifty-year-old memories were both refreshed and adjusted when she discovered a box of her letters written to her parents among her Mother's things. These letters written home, give us an authentic glimpse into the life of one cadet nurse.

Whether my sister and I would go to college was never in doubt—it was assumed. Where we would go wasn't a question—Iowa State College. The University of Iowa was considered "fast." Good girls went to Iowa State.

How we would go wasn't in question. We would go in made-over clothes, live in co-op dorms, get jobs, and write checks on Dad's zero-balance checking account for what we had to. Mr. Helchet, the banker, would periodically call Dad in to sign an extension on the farm mortgage to cover the overdraft.

Iowa State had no nursing curriculum, but it did have Premed, so I would take that, using the University of Minnesota catalogue as a guide for picking courses and then transfer to the University to complete the five-year program in nursing. It seemed logical enough at the time.

In the summer of 1943, hired men were hard to come by, and I volunteered to go home and work as a hired "man" instead of getting a job following my second year at Iowa State. My folks were excited about the advent of the Cadet Nurse Corps, but I wanted nothing to do with it, considering it an intrusion on my long-held plans. I assumed it would mean entering the service, and I didn't want to hear about it. Only after I arrived in Minnesota in September of '43 did I succumb to the lure of the financial advantage. As I recall, only one girl in my class did not join the Cadet Corps.

September 1943

Dear Folks . . . I went down to see what I could do today, but there isn't anyway I can get into the school of nursing this quarter, so I'll have to pay my own way. I'll write my fee check tomorrow, and I think it will be $77.00. Football season tickets are $7.50 and here is a question—should I or should I not spend $13.50 for a season ticket to the Minneapolis Symphony concerts? I will never have another chance to hear such a string of guest artists and wonderful music for so little (there are 18 concerts), but it looks like quite a bit of money. I got a job waiting tables at a sorority for meals. Board will be $30.00 for the quarter. Other expenses, based on my account book, would be: incidentals $1.50/ week; postage 30 cents/week (for mailing my laundry home); church 10 cents/ week; and transportation home/ $9.00. I'm afraid I can't get it much under that. Thought I should let you know the worst right off. Next quarter I'm in the School of Nursing. I'll get $45.00/ month for room and board, $15.00/ month allowances. Wish I could get in [the Cadet Nurse Corps] now! . . .

Love, Marge

November 11, 1943

Dear Folks . . . If I don't forget to put it in, I'll send the application for the Cadet Nurse Corps home for your signature. Decided I'd better get it in or they'll be having the quota filled and no room for me . . . .

December 12, 1943

Dear Folks . . . I have a little surprise for you! For the second time in my life I know what I want for Christmas, and this time it's not a Santa Claus suit. I need a watch with a second hand on it! Now, quit laughing! I know that there is no such thing on the market, but the fact remains that we *have* to have one when we go into the hospital. It can either be a wrist watch or a lapel watch. It's up to us to beg, borrow, steal, or manufacture one. I thought I'd better tell you so you could start working on it . . . .

January 1944

Dear Folks . . . Got my first little present from the government today in the form of a receipted fee statement for $70.00 and a requisition for $30.00 worth of books . . . .

February 1944

Dear Folks . . . After six months of rooming houses it's pretty good to be back in a dorm. The Nurses' Home (Charles T. Miller Hospital, St. Paul) is lovely. We have one big parlor and several little ones, and a recreation room and a nice dining room. All of us probies [all student nurses began on probation] have single rooms. They weren't kidding about how wonderful the food was here. For lunch we had vegetable soup, crackers, baked hash with tomato sauce, salad, raisin brown bread, sweet pickles, gingerbread with whipped cream, and milk or coffee. Sounds OK, doesn't it? Everything is good, too . . .

We have a tennis court in the nurses' home lawn, and last night there was a baseball game going on in it. The players included a bunch of nurses, two interns, a convalescent patient in a wheelchair (he played outfield) and 6 dirty little boys from the nearby slum districts. Quite a lively game! . . .

March 1944

Dear Folks . . . Well, here I am at last, a probie, the lowest form of life except for grub worms and freshman medics! Spent all last evening trying on uniforms and aprons and sewing on name tapes. We got 8 blue uniforms, 9 white aprons, and 10 sets of white collars and cuffs . . . .

April 1944

Dear Folks . . . We've been on duty for the last 3 mornings . . . so far we don't do much except to give a. m. care (bath, breakfast, temperature, pulse and respiration, etc.) and do odd jobs, but we get to help with most any kind of treatments. Already I have a pet patient—a little old lady. Tonight, the sailors on the farm campus are having an open house for the Miller nurses . . . .

April 14, 1944

Dear Folks . . . You know the pictures of the Cadet Nurses in *uniform* on the posters? Well, I'm coming up in the world! Now I can say that my shoes have been worn with a uniform. They pulled out a couple of uniforms for two of the girls to have their pictures taken for the newspaper the other day and one of them borrowed my shoes! It makes me so hopping mad to have them come out with one of the uniforms every time there's any sort of public event or pictures to be taken and then they snatch them back. They really are beautiful, but it seems that they should include a blouse . . . .

April 1944

Dear Folks . . . We rotate again this week. I go to 6A. That's a new top floor in more ways than one. They (patients) pay $12.00 a day, demand service, and get it. Don't know how I'm going to like it. Something tells me I'll wish I was back on 2B, but time will tell. I can pass medications now, and gave my first hypo(dermic)

Wednesday. Dad, you are interested in penicillin—we have 4 patients on 2B who are getting it. One has a venaclysis (running into his veins continuously day and night) . . . .

[Author's note: At that time, aqueous penicillin was mixed in the Central Supply Room, and every three hours someone went from each floor to get syringes filled in the CSR for each patient. I remember being scared I'd drop that precious tray in the elevator. It was so expensive.]

. . . Some of the [cadet nurse] uniforms, or rather parts of them, came this week, but we don't expect ours 'til June. There is to be an induction ceremony May 13 for which they had hoped to have us in uniforms, but there's small chance of that—at least for us probies. Incidentally, I think either the President or Eleanor, the First Lady, is going to deliver a radio address for the occasion. You should listen in if you happen to be around . . . .

May 13, 1944

Dear Folks . . . Gee, this is another beautiful day! Yesterday was the first one we'd had and it certainly was a honey. I could hardly believe it. Things like that just don't happen! It rains on days when you especially want it to be nice. Somebody slipped up. I certainly wish you could have been here. All the schools in the twin cities met at Northrup Auditorium on the University campus and 1,400 of us cadets were there. The other 1,000 couldn't get off duty. About a third had their outdoor uniforms and the rest of us were in hospital uniforms with white caps. The hospital uniforms are all variations of blue and white, so it was quite impressive. We almost filled the main floor of the auditorium with the gray uniforms in the center and the white caps on both sides. We had all sorts of governors and mayors and the Army and the Navy big shots on hand, too . . . .

June 5, 1944

Dear Folks . . . We've given up hope of having our uniforms before vacation. It's so disgusting. They've been ordered over two months. They just can't get 'em out of Washington cause they're all tied up in red tape. We're about the only school in the country that hasn't had them for ages. After being associated with the Corps for almost 6 months, I think it's almost time I was at least seeing a uniform somewhere besides a poster. We just laugh and laugh every time we see a big sign that says, "Wear the Uniform of a Cadet Nurse!" I'd like to know just how you go about it! . . .

Margaret and I dug up some uniforms and were going to the show last night, but the line was so long and it was so late that we gave up and went to the USO instead. We always have such a good time there. I'll certainly be glad when we get all of our uniforms without borrowing. We sang around the piano for a long time and then played ping pong and danced . . . .

July 1944

Dear Folks . . . The diet kitchen goes on and on about the same way. Every day triple splits; every meal serve trays, carry trays, scrape dishes, strip trays, set up trays for the next meal. Only yesterday I broke the monotony as only I can! I was in a hurry to get a late tray out and was tearing along close to the wall toward a corner. Equally in a hurry and tearing along from the other way was none other than the sophisticated and notoriously immaculate Dr. Hensen. There was a sickening thud, and then a deadly silence while I stood horrified and watched the milk run off his perfectly immaculate pinstriped lapel, onto his vest, then drip from the vest onto the pants where it spread out in great dark splotches. Then I began getting violently red and stammering some sort of tongue twister about, "I shouldn't have been coming so fast a little . . ." and he was muttering about he would just have to take a trip to the dry cleaners and it couldn't be helped and he guessed I wasn't expecting to see him. I was setting the dripping tray on the desk and mopping madly at his suit with the napkin . . . .

August 1944

Dear Folks ... Did I tell you about my prize patient, Mr. Wagoner? He weighs just a little over 300 pounds, is paralyzed on one side, and incontinent. I have him assigned to me every single time I'm on. They give me him and Marcia, who is 15 years old and weighs 90 pounds. Guess they think I like variety. I made a post operative bed and helped give an intravenous this morning. You know when I was little how I used to reel off a whole string of things I wanted to be when I grew up? I sure enough picked the closest thing to a combination of all of them. So far this week we've learned how to shave a male patient, give bed shampoos, and baptize people in case of an emergency. What a life! ... Love, Marge ....

November 1944

[Finally the cadets were all in uniform and in demand to perform.] Dear Folks ... Our glee club is getting to be almost too much for us. We are strictly amateurish and haven't even been organized very long, and suddenly we find ourselves not only giving a program at the Central Presbyterian Church, but also singing at a banquet at the Radison Hotel in honor of our Dr. Ward, who is president of the American Medical Association. Of course no one much will be there—just all the most important people in the medical world from all over the U.S. I simply cringe at the thought, but we're going to do it. One of the songs we will sing is a round to the tune of "Are You Sleeping." It goes like this:

Polio Myelitis, Polio Myelitis
Varicose veins, varicose veins,
Jaundice, Impetigo; Jaundice, Impetigo,
Labor Pains, Labor Pains.

We figure if we can't be good we might as well be appropriate ....

December 1944

Dear Folks . . . We went shopping this morning and found it discouraging business. I got some Jell-O for you, but not lemon or lime. The only pajama material we could find in cottons was some terribly cheap stuff, so I'm still looking. However, I did get some rayon. I'll send it home with my laundry. We saw a whole rack full of flashlight batteries and thought we really had something so we said "We'll take 4 apiece." The clerk said she didn't have any and we said "What's that, then?" She lifted 'em up and showed us that they were just a fake for display purposes. Were we disgusted! No Deft [laundry soap] yet, either . . . I am at the leg make-up stage now—except at work where I wear stockings with as many as 3 full length sewed up runs. Soon as I get back to working in the hospital and have an occasional chance to go down town and stand in line I'll be able to get some. They sold 60,000 pairs at Dayton's this week, but I think there were 100,000 people there to get them . . . .

February 1945

Dear Folks . . . "This is my "long day" [day off]. That's something to shout about—having Saturday for a long day. It theoretically happens every 6 weeks, but seldom does. Furthermore, I was off from Friday at 1:00 p.m. 'til Sunday at 2:30 p.m.! Pretty slick! I'll doubtless pay for it. In fact, I start paying Sunday when I go on 2:30 to 11 p.m. The 7 to 11 p.m. is "relief," the biggest rat race of the day . . . Only three nurses are on to pass medications, do treatments, take care of the lights which start coming on big time, and settle the whole floor for sleep. No one ever gets off before 12 midnight. It's the time when everything that's going to happen, happens. The most people die, and the most emergencies occur, and the most nurses go crazy. That's life! That's the way it goes . . . .

March 1945

Dear Folks . . . It's a beautiful spring morning; much too nice to stay in and write a case study, but that's what I have to do. We have a mess of hours in our room this week. Margo's on nights 11 p.m. to 7 a.m. and sleeps in the morning. I work relief all week—3:30 to 11:00 p.m. so mornings are the only time I have left to get anything done, and Helen works varying day hours between 7 a.m. and 7 p.m. Margo makes herself a little tent by hanging blankets over the upper bunk. She says she sleeps fine, and we can have it light in the room without bothering her. She puts my old clock in the closet because it ticks so loud. Helen's out in the lounge typing her case study. Guess I'll join her . . . .

May 1945

Dear Folks . . . Now we are assigned to "Contagion" at Minneapolis General Hospital. Yesterday we had a class at the campus and it was so nice that we walked there and back. It's about a 40-minute walk. Barb and I had an Alpha Tau Delta meeting on campus in the evening and we walked back from that too. We got in our walking for the day. We came up Washington Avenue and past the railroad yards and a lot of factories. When we got home we found that we were completely covered with black soot from head to toe. It was just as if we were made up for a minstrel show. That part was funny, but our clothes were *not*. My green coat will have to go to the cleaners . . . .

May 1945

Dear Folks . . . Barb and I are pretty well settled in our "little mud hut" [Minneapolis General Nurse's Quarters]. We have red, yellow and blue crepe paper window curtains of our own creation to brighten things up. The work is very dull in one way and interesting in another. There are so many nurses on Contagion that we are always looking for something to do. The hours are wonderful. We never have split shifts. Sometimes you only have one patient, and sometimes two nurses are assigned to one patient. Barb and I keep ourselves occupied trying to clean things up, but it's kind of useless. Most of the patients on station L are children, so it's exactly like station 33 where we both spent five weeks of pediatrics. We do have some very interesting patients, though. This is the first experience I've had where the charts had a place where it specifies whether or not the patient is being held for the police or workhouse . . . Questions? Why were we overstaffed? Was a polio epidemic expected? . . .

August 1945 [After V-J Day]

Dear Folks . . . The big St. Paul Victory Carnival Parade is supposed to come right down Summit Ave. at 2:00 this p.m. From what I hear it is supposed to be a parade to end all parades. If it is on time I'll get to see part of it before going on duty. They predict it'll take about four hours to pass. It's 1:30 and the people are already lining the curb all along Summit Avenue. I had no idea it was such a big affair. Guess they are broadcasting it all over the U.S. Maybe you will hear it. Must go get ready for duty now so I can watch as much as possible . . . .

September 1945

Dear Folks . . . We are coming up in the operating room world! This morning I first scrubbed for Dr. Zimmerman! Boy, was I scared. Even with Miss Furguson standing behind me giving moral support. It went pretty well, though. He only glared at me a couple of times, which is a good average for two operations. Whee! I'm a big girl now!

Tomorrow I scrub for another Caesarean. They are lots of fun, even though they are a little messy. This will be my last major scrub as I have all my required in. I hate to leave the O.R. We're even getting acquainted with the RNs a little bit. Tomasoni asked us down to her room the other night. She is a lot of fun, even if she is a head nurse . . . .

October 5, 1945

Dear Folks . . . Just got home from capping ceremonies for the new probies. It was very nice. We served coffee and doughnuts afterwards. We still feel gypped that we never had a capping. Our new probie class seems to be a very nice one. We've been having lots of fun with our "little sisters" . . . .

October 1945

Dear Folks . . . Last Night was an Alpha Tau Delta meeting and we pledges were supposed to entertain the actives. The girl who was supposed to arrange the main entertainment went home for the weekend and didn't get the person to fill in as she was supposed to. She didn't tell us. Imagine what a spot that left us in! We didn't find out 'til people were arriving. We had the whole album of records of the Nutcracker Suite and a phonograph, so Barb told the story and we played the records. That filled in fairly well, and fortunately Barb and I had worked up a mock ballet, and that really saved the day. She wore blue shorts and a shirt, a white uniform apron, red sock-slippers and a nurse's cap. It went fine and we even came out with the music (waltz of the flowers) . . . .

November 1945

Dear Folks . . . [Now assigned to public health field work.] Oh, to not have to tramp the streets today! Saturday is always a hard day, as there are only two or three nurses on, and today it is 16 below. At least no snow is predicted. Don't know about the wind. I am all ready to go out in my knee-length snuggles, sweater dickey under my [public health] uniform, anklets over my socks, [with black shoes] red sweater, scarf, gloves, mittens, overshoes, coat and hat. But what is to become of my poor ears? . . .

Later: Today I had to put in one more day in T. B. [tuberculosis] public health work. Went out with a PH nurse. It was a beautiful day—and we were out in the country. Everything was beautiful and we enjoyed the ride . . . .

January 1946

Dear Folks . . . Most of my work [Senior cadet field work] here in Washington County, Iowa, is with Amish families who have their babies at home with the help of the Public Health Physician. I will never forget my first home delivery, which was observed silently by a very tall and stern looking grandmother. I fumbled nervously as I bathed the baby on the wooden plank table under her watchful and I thought, disapproving eye. To calm myself I talked to the baby. After a bit Grandmother asked, "Do you speak German?" Of course I had to say no. She said, still unsmiling, "Then how do you expect the baby to understand you?" I relaxed after a good laugh, and I will never forget her humor and kindness . . . .

May 1946

Dear Folks . . . This is my long night in the nursery and it is always confusing. I was going to stay up today and sleep tonight, but I was so tired when I got off duty this morning that I went to bed for a short nap and when I woke up it was five minutes till three and Helen was calling me to get up for my 3 o'clock class. Now I don't feel like sleeping and if I sleep tonight I won't sleep tomorrow and then I will be all tired out to go on duty tomorrow night. Such troubles! I love nursery, but I've never worked quite so hard. We have 48 babies now, and we do not sit down or slacken our pace once from 11 p.m. 'til 7 a.m. It's just a mad race every minute. Last night when we were taking the babies out to breast, I had to wait just a minute for a mother to get ready, and I sat down on the arm of the chair in her room. I don't believe I ever appreciated waiting on anyone so much in all of my life. The cribs are just high enough so that you have to stoop at a backbreaking angle to work with the babies, and you get so you can't even straighten up when you go from one crib to the next. We think we made some sort of record by "pantsying'" all 48 babies in 15 minutes last night. Our poor little baby with erythroblastosis (RH negative factor) is still alive, but he isn't improving much. He is a grayish gold color now instead of bright yellow, but it is the worst jaundice I have ever seen. He is such a sweet little thing, too! . . . Love, Marge

[Note: What I remember most about the nursery is how stiff those wartime diapers were, how thick and dull the metal safety pins were, and how our scalps would get sore from rubbing the pins in our hair to help them go through the material better.]

May 1946

Dear Folks . . . I have certainly fallen down on my letter writing since I've been on nights. I have hardly been in my room this week even to sleep. We've been shopping and running around and trying to get ready for finals, until everyone's in quite a spin! Tomorrow night is my last night in the nursery, but I go back on days in the nursery for another week, for which I am eternally grateful. Most kids [fellow students] only get three weeks in the nursery. That means one week less on the OB [obstetrics] floor for me. Happy day! Tonight I am in charge, and the RN has her night off. Hope we have a nice smooth easy night of it. Last night we had our usual baby, half an hour before we were supposed to be off duty and had to clean up on overtime. I've been doing the book work for the last couple of nights . . . .

June 1946

Dear Folks . . . We had a rugged time Friday night when I was in charge. In the first place we had one baby who had to be watched continually and be given oxygen and CO_2 about every 10 minutes to keep him from getting blue, and one who was in critical condition—she died the next afternoon. We had four new babies, two of them within 10 minutes of each other just at the time when we were taking the babies out to breast. We were proud of ourselves, though, cause we got off *almost* on time and Miss Olefson couldn't find *one thing* wrong with the book work—not that she didn't try . . . . Love Marge

Margery Shanafelt Bitter entered the University of Minnesota as a nursing degree student in September 1943 and joined the Cadet Nurse Corps in January 1944. Degree cadets received federal funding through their first 3 years of parallel training with the diploma cadets. As a degree candidate, she took the state board examination after finishing the last 3 quarters, and then worked in the delivery room at the Charles T. Miller Hospital for the remainder of her senior year. She graduated with a bachelor of science degree in public health nursing, in May 1947. Bitter remembers the illustrious Dean Katharine Densford. Bitter practiced public health nursing in the San Juoquin Valley, California for 2 and 1/2 years. After a 16 year hiatus during the raising of her four children, Bitter became a school nurse just in time to take part in the developing role of school nurse partitioner. She was one of the first group of experienced school nurses trained at the San Diego State University. She developed the concept of school nurse practitioner in the context of the Follow-Through program for first through third grade disadvantaged students. She became proficient and involved in performing neuro-developmental assessments and planning for children with special needs. Her specialty became recognized beyond the minority community.

Retiring after 20 years with the school district, Bitter continued to conduct training seminars for school nurses in California, before becoming preoccupied with her 11 grandchildren. After 17 years, Bitter continues to assist in teaching T'ai Chi 3 times each week. Looking back through the years, Bitter concludes, "I have always found that I have been well prepared to take on any challenges life presented, and there have been many. We carried lots of responsibility as student nurses during those war years, and the practical experience gave me a degree of confidence that probably exceeded the benefit of our technical training."

13

A Lifetime Education **FREE**

Hilda Morrison Harned

*Author's Note: Growing up in the Great Depression, the Cadet Nurse Corps proved to be a boon to many young women. Still recovering financially in the 1940s, parents often did not have the means to assist their daughters in gaining an education beyond high school. Hilda Morrison Harned was one of thousands of teenage girls who benefited from receiving a "Lifetime Education **FREE**."*

I am from a rural family with five children all within a nine year span. I was the fourth child, born July 28, 1924, in rural Lake Country, Kentucky in the midst of wheat harvest. We were tenant farmers with very little money to spend, but we always ate well and were protected from the elements. Everyone was assigned chores—mine were to gather the eggs, carry in wood, clean the lamp chimneys, and dry the dishes.

We walked three miles across farm fields to attend a one-room school house. Discipline wasn't a problem because our parents would have taken care of an issue once we got home. There were two "restrooms," one in sassafras bushes to the right and a similar one to the left. Our school uniforms were similar—dresses made out of feed sacks, overalls, and bare feet. We presented school plays for our parents for Halloween and Christmas. After graduating from 8th grade I attended high school in town, again walking several miles.

We always attended church as a family. Travel was by Model T, later by Model A [Fords]. We were all 4-H members. Mother was a homemaker and Dad served on the County Fair Board. Then came Pearl Harbor. Like everyone else, my family supported the war effort. No problem with rationing. We gathered up scrap iron and raised hemp. We prayed a lot and cried when one brother was lost in the Battle of the Bulge.

When I graduated from high school, I went to the city of Louisville to live with an aunt and to attend business college. I had to get used to street cars, tokens, taverns, and bright lights, and in class to be addressed by Miss Morrison rather than my given name. To support myself I started working at a newly constructed army hospital as a file clerk and a "runner." This one-story, multiple building had miles of corridors, and people needed a guide to get where they were going. I became interested in nursing and noticed signs in front of the post office with an attractive cadet nurse in a neat uniform with caption that read, "A Lifetime Education **FREE** if you can Qualify."

While working as a "runner" I met a nurse, a wife of a GI from North Dakota who was stationed at Fort Knox. She got a job working at Nichols General Hospital and rented a room from my aunt. We became close friends and she told me stories about living in a nurses home, scrubbing for surgery, demanding supervisors, night duty, etc. I was backward and timid and did not make friends easily. We talked about the Cadet Nurse Corps. We talked about how I was going to overcome my shyness. She was a graduate of Trinity Hospital School of Nursing in Minot, North Dakota.

I had never traveled out of Kentucky, but my nurse friend and I decided that I should make application to her school of nursing. If I was accepted I would be on my own for three years and hopefully I would learn to overcome my shyness. (To have given up and to fail never entered my mind.) My aunt was very protective of me and did not approve of our plan. To this day I believe that she tore up my acceptance letter and it took a phone call to find out if I had been accepted.

I was entering a midyear class of 16 students. It was December 1943—World War II was raging. My brother had left for the Army. Rationing was in effect, and I had some difficulty in getting a stamp to purchase my nurse's white oxfords. My parents had always encouraged us to get more education after high school, but they felt that they were giving up a daughter to the war effort and knew that they would not see me very often. (I would come home only once a year for the next three years.) Telephones were used only for emergencies.

I boarded a train in Louisville and arrived at Union Station in Chicago—somehow I managed to find the Great Northern line and climbed aboard the "The Empire Builder." My journey to Minot, North Dakota would take two days. The train was crowded with all types of service men. What an opportunity I missed by being shy.

I arrived after midnight and was met by a very stern housemother who was undoubtedly disgruntled at having to meet me. The snowdrifts were up to the eve of houses and the temperature was subzero. She took me to a large house on the campus of Minot State Teachers College. She opened a door and said, "This is your bunk—goodnight." There was a lump on the other bunk, but it did not stir. Soon it would be Christmas and here I was—WHERE?

When I awoke my bunk was surrounded by a sea of curious faces . . . my classmates could not understand why someone from the South had come to North Dakota for nurse's training. The ice was broken, their curiosity and friendliness broke the spell of my shyness and those friendships which began that morning have endured for more than 50 years.

The school was breaking up for the holidays. A senior student heard that I would not be able to go home so she came and took me home with her . . . family, food, and midnight church. I will be forever grateful.

Memories—the demerits, the restrictions, the giggles, the waking up from working nights and seeing your Sunday coat going out the door, the having your towel disappear while you were in the shower, the scrubbing of your teeth after helping eat a berry pie that just happened to be missing from the diet kitchen.

I loved wearing my cadet nurse uniform and felt just like the woman on the poster. We cadets wore our uniforms and sat together when we attended the funeral of a V-12 Navy student who had attended our college. I wore the summer uniform when I was home on vacation, and on V-E and V-J day we cadets wore our uniforms to church.

I liked having the support and respect of the upper class women and being part of a team. I liked the nights when I was in charge of a floor knowing that there was a supervisor somewhere in the building. I liked being junior nurse on call on night duty and helping my classmates on the wards. I enjoyed the emergency room activity and as a senior nurse on call, I assisted the surgeons in the operating room. I remember setting patient's flowers out in the hall so they would not use up the oxygen.

My hardest assignment was during the polio epidemic, and I spent 71 days applying hot Kenny packs . . . and at night we would all think that we had the symptoms of coming down with the disease. I learned to pick up the limbs of a polio patient carefully so there would be no pain. I climbed inside an iron lung to experience how it would feel . . . it was frightening. Some experiences were very sad like the little boy of an older couple who died when a peanut become lodged in his bronchi and the hydrocephalic baby with the beautiful face.

Rules were strict signing in and out when we left the nurses home; boys in the parlor only during certain hours. It was part of our training to stand when a doctor or upper class man came to the desk. I never resented it and surely did like it when my time came; however, the rumble of change was in the making.

For fun, we walked a mile or more in very cold weather to the train station so we could wave to the GI's on the troop trains. We also visited the USO (United Servicemen Organization). We exchanged V-mail letters with friends in military service. My weekly letter from home always included a silver dime—we saw all of the Van Johnson and June Allyson movies. We saved money from our stipends so we could occasionally eat downtown as we needed a change from the routine staple of macaroni and cheese.

Our student hospital uniform was white, short sleeves with a cadet Maltese Cross on the pocket. On the last day, our student uniforms were torn to shreds by underclass women and we left the wards for the last time wearing a hospital gown—with the split in the back. For graduation I wore a long sleeved white uniform with cuff links and the hospital pin, and I could now sign my name followed with RN.

The next day I flew back to my home in Kentucky. The following day I had an interview and the next day I began a job that lasted 25 years. In those days a country doctor cared for the whole family and I became part of the team . . . injuries, sickness, babies, broken hearts, deaths . . . we cared for three generations in our rural community. I attended over 1,000 births, many in the homes and others in our birthing center which was in the basement of our clinic.

When the doctors retired I went to the local nursing home to help out for a few days and began another career, first as staff nurse, then as Director of Nurses and Administrator. I had gone from delivering babies to encouraging people to live every day no matter where they were and, then to help them die in dignity. My best memories are being of service to so many different people—good, bad, sad, or happy times—all have made me what I am.

Harned concluded her story with these words, "And for us, cadet nurses of World War II, hasn't it been great? Gray hair, extra pounds, artificial this and that, but what does it matter when we think back on the history that we have been privileged to be a part of?"

*Hilda Morrison Harned describes her training days as a cadet nurse with fondness and affection gratefulness to her cadet nurse classmates who gave her courage and confidence in overcoming her shyness as a teenager After receiving a "life-time education **FREE**, Harned gave 46 years of nursing service to her surrounding community of Hodgenville, Kentucky, receiving many awards including the American Nursing Association Nursing Home for the Year, the Rotary Club Service Award, Chamber of Commerce Business Professional Person Award, and Key to the City. She also served as Chairman of her church board. A great nurse who gave back generously to her community.*

14

Weird Night on Duty

Dorothy Geiger Kibbe

Author's Note: One of the challenges of being a student nurse in the past was the "night duty assignment" and trying to stay awake in class the next day. Problems occurred and strange things often happened, and like Dorothy, a student at Yale University School of Nursing, alone to find a solution.

Back in 1944 through 1947, New Haven Hospital faced a critical shortage of professional personnel. This was a problem in hospitals throughout the United States. It was caused, of course, by the shifting military demands for doctors and nurses during World War II. Hence, the Cadet Nurse Corps was created in an attempt to relieve the crisis.

As a consequence cadet nurses were literally the basic staff for hospitals. There were only enough professional nurses available to maintain a skeletal management by head nurses, supervisors, and instructors. Students were needed to provide the bulk of patient care. We faced many dilemmas in the course of our nursing education and practical experience while we were still students.

One night I was a student who was assigned to Tompkins East I, a men's urological ward. The desk and charting area ran across the ward B, the entrance from the corridor. Eight cubicles on each side filled the body of the ward. The unit carried a full census of 16 men, all attached to catheters, drip bottles, and drainage bottles.

At the end of the long ward was the utility area, medication room, hopper room, and tub room.

I took report at 11 p.m. with no unusual problem facing me. Dutifully, I made rounds of the patients. Medications, irrigations, and position changes all were done on schedule. My fears of getting everything done and done right eased as the night shift rolled on. About 3 a.m. I sat down at the desk to do some charting. "Piece of cake!" I soothed my nerves. The ward was quiet like a tomb.

The moments of peace were brief. The silence was broken with a rhythmic "Slap! Slap! Slap!" coming from the middle of the darkened ward. I hopped up to peer into the dim shadows. I fully expected to see a male patient plopping his bare feet on the linoleum floor. I expected to see tubes and catheters dragging along the floor after him.

Nothing came into view. I saw no human walking around. I checked all the beds. Sixteen men were in their beds. Puzzled I went back to the desk to get a flashlight. I searched every nook and cranny carefully. Again, nothing! I worked my way back down the ward, cubicle by cubicle. Then I heard the "slap! slap!" sound again, and out from under the bed walked a full grown DUCK who waddled into the circle of light coming from my flashlight. A DUCK! A real live quack, quack duck!

Returning to the desk, I placed a page call for the night supervisor . . . I somehow felt a solution was beyond my wisdom and experience. After a lengthy time gap, the supervisor responded to my call. In level tones, I tried to describe the situation. She gave it some silent thought. Then I heard her voice, crisp and clear. "If you are kidding me, I shall have to report you for wasting my time on frivolous matters. If you are not kidding, you are on your own to figure out what to do with a duck. I have much more serious problems to handle. I can not come to Tomkins East I."

Well, that was that! Instructors kept telling us we had to learn to be resourceful and responsible. I walked down the center aisle of the ward. Vigorously I flapped the skirt of my uniform, nudging the reluctant duck toward the tub room. Once we were both inside I slammed the door shut. The creature did not respond well to captivity in such a small room. Feathers flew; wings flapped. The bill snapped open and shut repeatedly in obvious threats. Amid all the chaos I managed to get the faucets turned on with a flood of water filling the tub. No, I did not check the temperature of the water with the wooden thermometer hanging on the wall. But yes, I did swish my hands in the water to make sure I would not be boiling the duck.

With a final flurry of effort I scooped him up and literally threw him into the tub. As I hastily slammed the door shut, I took a last look at him. He was merrily swimming in ovals around the tub. And I swear his orange bill widened into a bit of a smile.

I went back to finish my charting in peace. When the head nurse came on duty at 7 a.m., I merely reported the census as 17—sixteen men and one duck!

Naturally I was curious to find out how the duck got so far into the interior of a large hospital set smack in the middle of the city of New Haven, Connecticut. The research labs were adjacent to the Urological Ward. Only a double swinging door separated the lab from the hospital corridor. The duck had escaped from a cage and had set out to explore. It gave me a weird night on duty but I suspect the duck rather much enjoyed the frolic.

The ability to express a situation in comical terms proved to be a great survival technique for many cadet nurses like Dorothy. Through childhood and adolescence, Dorothy Geiger Kibbe had the desire to be a doctor. She went to Gettysburg College for four years and completed the premedical program. The premed male students had no problem in being accepted at medical schools with expenses paid. Not so for women during this time. Her father and she sat up one entire night with facts and figures trying to see a way for her to finance medical school. She had been accepted at the Albany Medical School. There was no source of that kind of money within the family. Banks and private individuals were reluctant to make such large donations to a young girl for medical schools.

Kibbe talked to her advisor at Gettysburg, and he came up with the idea of the Cadet Nurse Corps. She applied at Yale University School of

*Nursing. She attended Yale for 32 months and enjoyed every minute. She did not regret being a nurse instead of a doctor and spent 41 years of active nursing. She also raised a family of three children. At age 5, her son asked her a serious question: "Mom, if I get sick, will you take care of me or will a real **nurse** take care of me?"*

Even in retirement, Kibbe remained a "real nurse." She moved to Nippenose Valley, a rural area of Pennsylvania, and became intimately involved in the lives of Amish families. They were wonderful neighbors and she saw their needs. One problem was severe farm accidents. She went to the American Red Cross for manuals and set up training sessions in the one-room schoolhouse. She taught the Amish people how to deal with emergencies and equipped them with first aid skills. She also taught illiterate adults how to read and found them eager and good students. Kibbe repaid her cadet nurse training many times over by giving more than 50 years of nursing service.

15

I Never Wanted to Be a Nurse

Shirley Morrison Francisco

Authors note: Despite her initial ambivalence and reluctance, Shirley's decision to enter the Cadet Nurse Corps proved to be beneficial. She said that the Corps was the beginning preparation for almost 50 years of participation in an interesting, exhausting, exacting, frustrating, but always a rewarding profession.

I grew up in a rural area (Warren County, Pennsylvania) and attended a one-room school and later rode five miles on the school bus to a small town high school. We didn't know about television, but there was always something to do. We enjoyed records, radio, and reading. Music was an important part of our family life. My father, mother, and brother played the violin, piano, and guitar. We received three daily newspapers and almost a dozen magazines a month.

The Pearl Harbor attack by Japan changed the life in our community, as it did all over the country. Many young men left quickly for the military service, and only three boys remained to attend our high school graduation. They too left soon after we graduated. My father was in the oil business; he and my older brother worked long hours producing this much needed-war commodity. Everyone bought war bonds, observed the rationing regulations, wrote V-mail letters to service men and sent cookies, and listened anxiously to the war news every evening on the radio.

I never wanted to be a nurse. After graduating from high school in the spring of 1944, a girlfriend and I worked in a small, experimental manufacturing plant, making radio tubes for the U.S. Navy. We thought we were contributing to the war effort in this way. After a few months, we decided there might be a less monotonous way to contribute. She wanted to enter nursing school and I reluctantly agreed to accompany her, at least to the entrance exams.

My family was not sure that I would want or be able to accomplish what was required of a nurse, but they were supportive. My sister-in-law was a registered nurse, so they knew a little about the requirements. We were aware of the Cadet Nurse Corps because a member of our high school graduating class had already joined. She left for nursing school before graduation but returned for the ceremony, looking very stylish in her uniform. There were also many advertisements for the Corps picturing attractive young ladies in uniform. We hoped we would look like them when we became cadet nurses.

The Meadville City Hospital School of Nursing [in Meadville, Pennsylvania] to which my friend and I applied, was about forty miles from our homes. We knew two girls who already attended there. The school had a good reputation.

Admission requirements for the school included a long day of testing on site. We nervously worked our way through the written tests, interviews, and physical exams. We saw student nurses hurrying by on their way to class and duty and admired their crisp uniforms and caps. Our acceptance letters were to be mailed, and after we received them my friend, much to my disappointment, decided to attend a school of nursing in another state. So, there I was—go back to the factory or on to the school of nursing. Nursing school was the inevitable.

Leaving home seemed like a big step at the time. I had been living away from my home while working, but committing to nursing school for three years was much more daunting. The big question of what clothes to pack was partially answered by a lengthy list of items to bring which was included in the acceptance letter.

Our class started in May, 1945 and would be the last class of cadet nurses to be accepted into the Corps. We attended the summer session of a highly rated private, liberal arts college to study the required basic sciences. My classmates and I trudged about a mile uphill each morning from the nurses home next to the hospital for classes in chemistry, anatomy and physiology, microbiology, sociology, and psychology. The early morning fog made our hair stringy, but we enjoyed returning to the hospital in the afternoon and studying while sunbathing on the roof. Who knew then that sunburn was dangerous to your health?

Dormitory life proved to be enjoyable. The oldest buildings at the hospital had been made into dormitories for the students, and most were double rooms. Roommates for the most part were compatible and there were frequent get-togethers for griping, sharing of experiences, success, sympathy, and advice. It seemed to us that there were too many strict rules. Lights out at 10:00 p.m.; morning chapel at 6:45 a.m. for which one arrived, well groomed, awake, and ready for the day. There were regular room inspections, one late night until midnight per week.

The news on V-E day in June was cause for elation. A group of us, who were free, immediately walked down the street to a nearby church to give thanks and to pray for final victory. V-J Day in August was a time of jubilation. One could hardly dare hope that the war was finally over and our soldiers would be coming home. Nearly every family had a loved one serving in the War. One of my brothers was a combat engineer and after attending Stanford University survived the Battle of the Bulge. My other brother was on the front lines in Italy and Austria.

We received our cadet nurse outdoor uniforms in the Fall, but with the end of the war the uniform became less important. While the upperclassmen continued to wear the grey and scarlet, our class began the transition back to "civilian" attire. A talented classmate helped us transform our summer cotton into midriffs, a popular style then.

We were now "probies" [student nurses on probation] and was there ever a lower form of life? We stepped aside to allow doctors,

RNs, upperclass students, visitors, and everyone in the world to go through the doorway before we did. We were not allowed to enter the front door of the hospital. If seated and a doctor appeared, we jumped to our feet. Clinical instructors inspected our bed-making and assessed each room to make sure that each item was placed in the prescribed space. The open ends of pillow cases never, never faced the door. The bed linen corners were mitered, or redone until approval was granted. We could be called back on duty to rectify the slightest error, and often were. We decided the school was a combination of the military and a nunnery.

The end of the probationary period was marked by the capping ceremony, complete with lighting of candles, reciting the Nightingale Pledge, and finally receiving the coveted white cap atop our proud heads (pure pleasure). Our student uniforms consisted of a blue short-sleeved dress with an attached white apron and bib. Our caps were one piece, heavily starched by the laundry, and we wore white stockings and shoes. An insignia on the left sleeve indicated that we were cadet nurses. We received three clean uniforms each week, and uniform inspection included clean shoe strings and the absence of jewelry. A medication error resulted in losing one's cap for a week.

Ancillary help was scarce and students, especially the probies, scoured everything in sight. Linen closets, medicine cabinets, sinks, furniture, bedpans, and urinals were scrubbed, sometimes several times a day. Rubber rectal tubes were cleaned and boiled. The aroma of burning rubber sometimes permeated the halls as some hapless student, busy with chores, forgot to monitor the boiling process closely. Sitting with a patient, just to talk, was forbidden. We soon discovered that the best way to keep out of trouble was to keep busy with cleaning. We carried a little booklet in our uniform pocket which contained a list of "must learn" procedures, and each time one of these was successfully demonstrated to an instructor, it was happily checked off.

As we rotated through the various clinical assignments, we began to develop a bit more confidence in our own knowledge and abilities. The educational approach in general, however, was not designed to enhance a student's self-esteem. Registered nurses were not readily available as most were in the military. Many classes were taught by physicians with a focus on medical aspects instead of nursing care. We provided service to the hospital and worked all of the different shifts. Often we worked a split shift from 7:00 a.m. to 11:00 a.m., then back on duty at 7:00 p.m. Our off hours were spent attending class and studying. When on night duty from 11:00 p.m. to 7:00 a.m. we tried our best to stay awake in class.

My favorite rotation during this period was the obstetrical or maternity department. New mothers were kept in bed for several days and the babies out of sight in the nursery with the exception of feeding time. Our fingers bled from trying to push dull safety pins that had been autoclaved through the thick material of the large breast and abdominal finders that all new mothers had to wear. One disconcerting aspect of deliveries at that time was the administration of ether to mothers during delivery. Fathers were not allowed in the delivery room, and visiting regulations were vigorously enforced to discourage the introduction of stray germs.

Moving on to the dietary kitchen was a challenge. There were vast amounts of Jell-O and custard that had to be prepared each day. Diabetic patients were visited and complaints acknowledged with attempts to better please with future meals. An advantage to this rotation was that fresh fruit somehow found its way back to the dorm to be shared. Raw potatoes were transported from the diet kitchen where they were sliced, fried in grease, and devoured with ketchup.

It was in the medical/surgical wards and private rooms that many of the "must learn" procedures were checked off. Narcotics were in pill form and prepared for injection. This was done by dissolving the prescribed pill in sterile water heated, placed in a bent spoon and suspended over an alcohol lamp. The solution was drawn up in the syringe and the syringe shaken until the solution was clear. Syringes and needles were scrubbed and kept in an alcohol solution. Needles were sharpened and reused. During this rotation we experienced our first responsibility of caring for the patient after death. Postmortem care was an awesome moment for the new student. Through lectures and example, our instructors impressed upon us the necessity for approaching this responsibility with compassion and dignity.

My least favorite rotation was the three months spent in the operating rooms (OR). There was no air conditioning and no disposable items. The surgical masks were hot, itchy and irritated my face. Students scrubbed for minor surgical procedures and assisted the RN scrub nurse with major surgeries and circulated—sometimes for two rooms at once. The duties of the circulating nurse were to retrieve items needed for the procedure and to take sponge count. One day I was circulating for a major surgery and found the sponge count one short. I reported this to the OR supervisor who was not known for her fondness for students. Somehow she made me feel that this was my fault. After rechecking my count she informed the surgeon and he groped around inside the incision, pulled out the missing sponge and remarked casually, "This is why we have sponge count."

After three months, I was glad to be back on the medical-surgical ward where patients could talk to me and my hands were not red and rough from constant scrubbing with brushes and harsh soap. My reprieve was short-lived as I was called back to the OR for another month. It was summer and T and A [tonsil and adenoid] season. There was a shortage for scrub nurses as every child in the county and neighboring counties were doomed to have their tonsils and adenoids removed that summer.

In surgery, instruments were scrubbed, counted, wrapped, and autoclaved. Rubber gloves were scrubbed, rinsed, hung on racks to dry, turned inside out, dried again, then powdered, wrapped, and autoclaved. The operating rooms were scrubbed and "set up" for any emergency. All of this was considered a learning experience for the student nurse. Two blessings: we didn't have to do the laundry; and the sterile technique would forever be engraved in our brains and behavior forever.

The three-month rotation at a state mental hospital was a highlight in my nurse's training. I tried desperately to get those patients exhibiting catatonic posturing to relax and talk to me, but it never happened. We became familiar with paraldehyde used for calming patients. Often it would be spit back on to our uniforms. Hydrotherapy, induced insulin coma, and cold wet sheet packs were remarkably effective for reducing agitated behavior. Electroshock treatments were a weekly routine inducing the patient into a grand mal seizure, with student nurses valiantly hanging onto each limb trying to be unconcerned about the procedure.

An unforgettable experience for me had to do with "hoarding." We had discussed this sinful concept and knew that patients were not allowed to keep little bits and pieces of things which they treasured in their assigned cubicles. One day when the patients were in the day room, a new aide and I were assigned to clean out the locked storage area. Unlocking the door to the small room, we proceeded to put everything the patients had collected into a bag to be thrown out. Suddenly, a large, very agitated patient (who had a reputation for violence) appeared in the doorway, obviously disturbed that we were throwing out her collection. She came toward us with fist upraised. The aide ran out of the room and slammed the door behind her. A cardinal rule was that one never let a patient come between you and the doorway. I was sure that I would not survive to receive the scolding due me.

I looked at the patient and quavered, "I'm sorry." The patient stared at me, lowered her arms, sat on the floor, and began to cry. I would have joined her had it not been for the head nurse and nurse aide coming to my rescue. I did not like carrying keys around my waist and constantly unlocking and locking doors. On my final evaluation, I was asked to come back to work after graduation. I was fascinated by the patients, but not the treatments at that time, and knew I was not ready.

Not long after the war, some miraculous new medications made their appearance. Penicillin and sulfa became widely used. Polio was a devastating mystery and we learned about iron lungs. We burned our hands on hot woolen packs applied to affected legs. Large oxygen tanks on a dolly were wheeled to patients' rooms. Brains and brawn were necessary to give patient care. "Specializing" patients returned from OR and not yet recovered from anesthesia was part of the daily activities. There was no recovery room, no intensive care, no "beepers" to warn us that intravenous solutions were not dripping correctly.

There seemed to be no restraint that a determined patient could not wriggle out of and no side rails that could not be climbed over or slithered through, with a fall to the floor as a result. This meant that the supervisor and the doctor had to be notified and an incident report written in triplicate. Bones must have been stronger in those days as there were rarely any fractures from these mishaps.

Occasionally the ladies of the Hospital Auxiliary gave a tea for the students. A few tickets to local cultural events, such as visiting bands or an orchestra, were available to students. If we happened to be free on such occasions, we welcomed the change of pace. After the war, gas rationing ceased, but students rarely had a car. Getting around was accomplished by walking, bus, or train. Transportation was not a problem.

The camaraderie shared throughout the triumphs and terrors of nursing school provided support and fun for the students. Our monthly cadet nurse stipend did not allow for grand shopping sprees but we were avid window shoppers. Card games, walks, movies, phone calls, mail, food packages from home, gripe sessions and trips to a nearby lake were enjoyed. Dates were admitted to the "living room" by the ubiquitous house mother and their arrival announced to the lucky students. No men were allowed past the living room/waiting room. Each year there was a graduation dinner and dance which all students attended.

Except for colds and a severe sunburn, I was healthy during the three years of my training days. One exception occurred during my last year when I developed a high fever with aching and severe chills. There was no student health service then, but my concerned roommate reported my illness to the evening supervisor and she brought a staff doctor to my room. I was shivering under a pile of blankets donated by helpful classmates, and after a cursory examination, he ordered that I be admitted to the hospital and given sulfa. By morning, I was feeling a bit better but my skin was red hot. An almost retired doctor diagnosed scarlet fever. My first time in the hospital and I was in isolation. After a week of this, sustained by surreptitious visits by classmates, a young doctor (with better eyesight) wrote a diagnosis of erythema roseolus and discharged me to the dorm, with an awareness that I was allergic to sulfa.

As students, we appreciated the doctors who were kind and enjoyed teaching as well as respecting our observations. A few of the older doctors were arrogant and could make our lives miserable, but we learned how to deal with all kinds.

The war was over and a new director of nurses came on board during our last year. She informed our senior class that we would not spend our last six months of training outside of our home hospital. Many in the previous classes had the option of choosing to serve as senior cadets at a veterans hospital or in public health service, but we would not have that choice. On the plus side, six more months and we would be graduating and we could ask for a specific assignment. I enjoyed working nights and requested a large medical-surgical unit consisting of two separate hallways with private and semiprivate rooms. No one else was foolish enough to voluntarily do all of that walking (sometimes running) and my request was granted.

The hospital served us a late supper at 10:30 p.m., and then on duty at 11:00. We made rounds every hour checking vital signs, giving medications, monitoring the oxygen, charting intake and outputs for the day, and always the cleaning chores. There was the nursing desk to wash and wax, ordering supplies, checking charts for needed pages, and flowers to be tended. It was believed that flowers removed oxygen from the air and [it was] healthier for the patients to have the flowers outside their rooms. How we dreaded gladiola season! These tall blooms had a penchant for tipping over at the slightest breeze through the hallway. The night supervisor was the only RN on duty with the students staffing all of the floors. She had to be very brave and trusting.

All was not well with the new director of nursing and the last class of cadet nurses. She had decreed that our nursing caps would be secured to our heads with pearl hat pins. This we tried but were dismayed when our caps fell off or hung askew over one ear. We resorted to the tried and true white bobby pins concealed under the folds of the cap to anchor the caps to our heads in order to preserve our dignity. But the director could spot a bobby-pin-held cap at an amazing distance and those with infractions were labeled impudent.

One day I discovered that my name was on the "campused" list for disobeying the rules. My bed was not made when a daytime inspection of the dorm rooms took place. I strongly protested that the reason my bed was not made was because I was sleeping in it after working nights. That made no difference and I had no privileges (could not leave the hospital grounds for a week). I called home collect asking my parents to send money for transportation out of there, but my mother convinced me that I should not let petty tyranny prevail with such a short time remaining in the program.

During our senior year, one member of our class was secretly married when her fiancé returned from the military. This was forbidden and our friend was devastated with the thought that she would have to leave. Three of us "impudent" students were on night duty and we decided that something had to be done. After working all night we met outside the superintendent's office and when he appeared, we ambushed him. We spent the better part of the next hour explaining to him why this antiquated rule of not allowing student nurses to marry needed to be changed. Probably to get rid of us, he finally agreed to take our plea to the Board of Directors. The superintendent was as good as his word and the rule was changed. Our school of nursing became a forerunner of other schools to allow student nurses to marry. All of us "impudent" students managed to graduate.

Although my experience as a cadet nurse ended with graduation from a hospital school of nursing, and my "training" was in large part service to the hospital, I consider myself fortunate to have had the opportunity to work with so many different people in so many different settings throughout a long and satisfying career in the profession of nursing. For someone who never wanted to be a nurse, I have had a long and satisfying journey.

Shirley Morrison Francisco received the highest grade in her class. Over a span of twenty-some years, she was either a part- or full-time student, earning a bachelor of science degree with a major in nursing, a master's degree in psychiatric-mental health nursing, and a doctor of philosophy in psychiatric—mental health nursing. Francisco practiced nursing for almost 50 years and demonstrated that there is always something new to learn and one is never too old to learn it. While teaching nursing her emphasis was on humor related to family functioning. She had plenty of examples to share with her students as she along with her husband raised a family of five children. She gives credit to the support of her loving husband, for without him she would not have been able to attain both successful parenting, her educational goals and long career in nursing.

16

You Are In the Army Now

Grace Obata Amemiya

Author's Note: "How gracious and compassionate they were," Grace, an American Japanese said, "to accept us without animosity." As a senior cadet nurse serving in an Army hospital, she cared for wounded soldiers who had returned from the war fronts and from Japanese war prisons.

The sign on the gate read, "Schick General Hospital—All traffic will stop at gate—Speed limit 15 miles per hour—Cameras Prohibited—by order of the C.O. [Commanding Officer]." Along the fence was another sign, "Climbing over fence will not be tolerated—by order of the C. O."

These were the signs that greeted us cadet nurses. I was a student nurse from the St. Mary's School of Nursing at Rochester, Minnesota and a member of the U. S. Cadet Nurse Corps in the fall of 1945. While at St. Mary's, I had enlisted in this program and had chosen to serve at an Army hospital for the last six months of my formal training. I was assigned to Schick General Army Hospital in Clinton, Iowa.

This was a new and different experience and environment. At this sprawling hospital we would be caring for the soldiers who had returned injured or ill from the war fronts, some former prisoners of war, and others transferred closer to home from other military hospitals. Their needs were varied. Some were healing from wounds and broken bones, and there were others whose broken spirits or broken minds needed mending. Many had left home as teenagers and had seen war at its worst. We were privileged to work with a wonderful group of Army nurses and medical staff, and our goal in caring for these men was to return them to their home as soon as possible.

As officer candidates, we were treated as officers, eating and sleeping in officer quarters, but always mindful that the Army nurse officer was in charge of us cadet nurses. As students we regularly attended classes and numerous lectures taught by the medical and nursing staff. We were exposed to related materials that we might not have had the opportunity to study about in a civilian setting. We marched and drilled on the parade grounds with the other Army nurses and Red Cross personnel. This was a friendly group. There were times, however, that we cadets were corrected for our conduct and reminded that, "YOU ARE IN THE ARMY NOW."

One day we were told that the Italian prisoners of war who worked in the dining room as bus boys had gone on strike. We learned that the cause for their strike was that they were not provided with Italian olive oil with which to cook their meals. They were denied their case, as prisoners of war would receive no special privileges regarding their ethnic food of choice.

Our soldier patients were always playing pranks on each other, and it was amazing what they would come up with. When the ambulatory patients were able to get off-ground passes, many evenings they would return to their bed ready to fall in, only to find that their beds had been short-sheeted, or "water-balooned." Condoms filled with water had to be carefully removed. Loud grumbling words were heard as they corrected the situation before falling into bed. Those who had committed the deeds would quietly chuckle under their covers and then spend the next day acting very innocently about the previous evening's happenings.

The therapy rooms were always busy. For some the healing limbs needed physical therapy. For others the need was occupational therapy where the patients created beautiful things for their family and friends. One day I received a lovely scarf which had been made with parachute silk and stenciled.

When we were off duty, we would go shopping in town, bowling, visiting the library, and scouting out places for dinner. We did a lot of walking, often ending up at the park. At the time, Iowa was a dry state, which meant no liquor sold. To accommodate the thirst of some of our patients for booze, some of us would take a taxi over the bridge to Fulton, Illinois to make the needed purchases. On these trips we went in civilian clothes and felt very daring.

As officer candidates we were cautioned that we were not to fraternize with enlisted men. A dear friend, and former classmate at the University of California in Berkley, was now a sergeant in the Military Intelligence Service and was planning to stop by at Clinton to visit me. He was en route to his overseas assignment in the Pacific. I had to have permission to meet him so I dutifully talked to the Captain in charge of us. She said I could go off hospital grounds and meet him, but I was instructed not to wear my cadet nurse uniform. With permission granted I had a wonderful visit with my friend off-base in civilian clothes.

Some patents called me "Irish." My maiden name was Obata. Upon hearing this, I was kidded about my Irish name. They were sure I spelled it O'Bata and that my father was Irish. I would play along with this banter, telling a tale that I was from Hawaii, my father was an Irish fisherman, my mother was from Japan, and they had met in Hawaii. Of course I would follow up with the truth that I was born in California to parents who had immigrated from Japan in the early 1900s. Irish? Not so. Just an American citizen of Japanese ancestry. I later married my soldier friend who had visited me—whose birthday falls on March 17th. Irish? Nope, Japanese like me.

The question often arose as to what a Californian was doing in the Midwest. This provided me an opportunity to tell of the incarceration of American citizens of Japanese ancestry during the war. More than 110,000 of us were placed in one of ten American concentration camps, surrounded with barbed wire and sentry towers and machine guns pointed in our direction. Our crime? We were of Japanese descent. Only after a year and FBI clearance were we allowed to leave camp and relocate outside of the restricted areas. Many had not heard of the concentration camps and were surprised and fascinated with our story.

There were three senior cadet nurses of Japanese descent from St. Mary's Hospital School of Nursing at Schick Army Hospital. An occasion arose when our Captain in charge called us into her office. She told us that our hospital would be receiving a few soldiers who had been prisoners of war and had been subjected to the Bataan Death March. She wanted us to be aware that there could be some angry or dangerous reactions by these patients upon seeing an Asian face caring for them. She wanted to avoid any unpleasant incident which might occur and possibly endanger our safety. We were advised to have an escort with us when we were going to and from duty and especially when returning to our quarters.

When several of our patients heard of our situation, they offered to serve as our escorts. Fortunately, we did not encounter any adverse incidences. In fact, our patients who had been prisoners of war were curious about us, and they freely visited and conversed with us. They shared their observations regarding the treatment and living conditions of the women and children in Japan in order to survive during the war years. They told us how fortunate we were to be American citizens living in America. Their discussions occurred occasionally of heartbreaking memories of brutality, but humorous incidences were also related.

With the war ending, the government planned to close down the hospital. This was a disappointing time for the city of Clinton and surrounding areas. Local citizens had worked at the hospital, and volunteers had brought cheer and comfort to the soldier patients with gratitude for their war time service. The Army hospital had given an economic boost to the local community that would soon be gone. Ward by ward the hospital was emptied. Equipment and furniture were sent on to other places or discarded. It was an end of an era for Clinton and for all of us who were stationed there.

We cadets will forever be grateful for the experience of having served at an Army hospital. We matured as individuals. The experience made us more caring and better nurses. We were brought closer to those who had served in the war. We had a deeper understanding of how war had affected the soldiers' lives as well as the lives of their families and loved ones.

In the Fall of 1941, Grace Obata Amemiya had completed two years of pre-nursing studies. Fulfilling her dream to become a nurse, she enrolled at the University of California School of Nursing San Francisco. A few months later Pearl Harbor abruptly changed her course. With her family, she was interned at the Turlock Assembly Center in California and later moved to the Gila River Relocation Center in the desert of Arizona on the Gila River Indian Reservation.

Anemiya worked as a nurse aide serving her incarcerated people in the camp hospital for more than a year and began searching for a school of nursing that would admit "her kind." She was excited to learn that she was finally accepted into the St. Mary's Hospital School of Nursing in Rochester, Minnesota, making her eligible to join the U.S. Cadet Nurse Corps. She was one of more than seven thousand senior cadet nurses who served in a military hospitals.

After graduation she married her soldier friend when he returned from military service. Anemiya worked as a nurse helping her husband through graduate school to become an agronomist. His profession took the family to Colorado and Texas, finally settling in Ames, Iowa where she resides today. She had two sons, the eldest mentally disadvantaged. The second son and his wife live in San Francisco. Her husband and first son are deceased.

Today, Amemiya is a sought after speaker at schools, churches, and service organizations. While there is a sense of light heartedness, her mission is to educate people by sharing her story. She is living history in regard to a "dark side" in American history. She says, "When our generation—the generation who experienced internment—goes, it's something that the next generation will need to know about."

Sometimes she is asked if she feels bitter toward her government for the incarceration of her people, to which she replies, "I am not about to let something I had no control over make me bitter. You learn to do what you can do the best you can with whatever circumstances are thrown at you."

Thanks to the Cadet Nurse Corps, Grace Obata Amemiya earned a diploma in nursing, however, through the years she never forgot her dream of receiving a degree from the University of California (UC). In 1942 Amemiya and about 700 Japanese American University of California students were forced by the U. S. government to abandon their studies and sent to inland internment camps.

On July 17, 2009, Amemiya in testimony told the UC Regents Committee on Education Policy that the forced internment was hard to accept. She said that it was a shocking experience and added, "Yes, you can start your life over again with just two suitcases."

Referring to herself and other Nisei students, Amemiya continued, "We, with patriotism in spite of prejudice, did our best."

Sixty-seven years later, the University of California Regents formally acknowledged the historic injustice and voted to grant special honorary degrees to the hundreds of former students like Amemiya who never finished their UC Education because of the World War II Japanese American internment. For Amemiya, at the age of 88, her dream of a degree in nursing will come true. (Jill Tucker, "UC to grant Japanese W.W.II Internees degrees," San Francisco Chronicle, 17 July 2009.)

17

Life as an Army Nurse

Shirley Wales

Author's Note: In February of 1945, Dr. Thomas Parran, Surgeon General reported that 40 per cent of the nurses who had graduated from the U. S. Cadet Nurse Corps had been accepted by the military service. This record was made during the time when the public believed the war was about to end. Shirley Wales was one of these cadets who served with the Occupational Forces in France.

Soon after graduation from Butterworh Hospital School of Nursing, in Grand Rapids, Michigan, I joined the Army and went to "Boot Camp" at Camp McCoy, Wisconsin (June 1945). A sergeant drilled us in marching and to do push-ups. I can still hear his voice calling loudly, "Lieutenant!" While there we cared for Japanese prisoners of war who had been burned by flame throwers and were having skin grafts. Some of our patients were Korean soldiers who avoided the Japanese, and many had tuberculosis. During the polio epidemic, we were sent to Milwaukee on temporary duty. There were so many little ones in iron lungs, and we used the Sister Kenny's hot woolen packs to ease their painful spasms. It seemed there was little we could do.

We were then sent to Camp Grant, and from there on to the "staging area" in Georgia where we were joined by many nurses from all over the United States. We were sorted alphabetically and marched onto the waiting troop trains. A long ride took us to Camp Miles Standish, then on to Boston where we boarded a huge ship, the "General A. E. Anderson."

We sailed on December 14, 1945 and experienced a stormy crossing. Many of us were sea sick. One could look down at the top of the wave, then way up from the bottom. The best memory on our "cruise" was listening to the young soldiers singing carols on Christmas Eve. We dreamed of all the good things we would like to eat (oranges, apples, bananas) which were not available.

When we landed in Le Havre in northern France on the English Channel, we found a city in the midst of rubble. We waded through the mud and rain in the clothes we had worn for days and were sent one place after another being greeted with consternation. "What! 400 Nurses??" Finally at midnight, on the top of a hill, a warm welcome and a FEAST—turkey and trimmings and bottles of red wine on the table.

Our first home was a tent with eight cots and a wood stove. We took turns sleeping and stoking the fire during the night, setting our clocks at different times. It seemed that the latrine was at least a quarter of a mile away, but on our first night, we gratefully showered, shampooed, and washed our underwear. Our tent was always smokey and the air filled with soot.

Our duty wards were large Quonset huts with 40 beds. We worked 12-hour shifts but were never too tired when off duty to go to the Officer's Club, where we danced to the music of a band made up of prisoners of war. Our chaplain introduced us to a nice French family, and we shared dinner and fellowship with them every Sunday night.

There was anti-American sentiment in the area as the Germans had been very good to the French people, making sure the port was guarded. We could see where the "Buzz Bombs" had been aimed at England. There was a strict curfew as there was danger for our G.I.s and danger for those who did not obey.

Spring came and we shed our "fatigues" and wore our seersucker uniforms. One patient, badly burned, puckered up his lips and whistled. Later there were trips to Paris, and I was glad that I had been a good student in French. The beautiful cathedrals had been spared in the bombing raids.

There was one lieutenant who kept coming back and wanted a date, but I thought him much too fresh. My captain head nurse intervened and said, "He's a nice boy. If he wants to go out with you GO. Now that's an order." One thing led to another and we became engaged in Geneva, Switzerland. This place seemed like the Garden of Eden compared to the rest of bombed-out Europe. The people were warm and friendly and treated us like family. One early morning we watched cattle with jingly bells being driven through the village on the way to the mountains where they would spend the summer. The herdsman dressed in lederhosen yodeled as they strode along with their herds.

My short career as Army nurse ended in October, 1946, and was an experience I will never forget.

Wales was married in December and once again found herself living in a Quonset hut in G.I. student housing, still shoveling coal while her husband attended the university. Her husband was an engineer, and the family moved frequently. After her three children were born, she became a full-time mom with all the trappings of motherhood, Sunday School teacher, Cub Scout Den Mother, Brownies and then through the years, a Senior Girl Scout leader.

During the periods when Wales was inactive as a nurse, she remained on call. During a terrible hurricane she was with a Red Cross unit for four days. She tenderly cared for her husband when he had a heart attack, then a stroke, and she brought him back to health. As the saying goes, for Wales it was true: "Once a nurse, always a nurse."

18

The War is Over!

Janet Veenboer Banta

Author's Note: Anyone who is of the last generation can tell you what they were doing on August, 15, 1945. After a leave of absence to marry her college sweetheart before he left for overseas duty, Janet Veenboer Banta had returned as a graduate nursing student to the Frances Payne Bolton School of Nursing. A few days after V-J Day Janet wrote what she had experienced on that historic day.

August, 1945, on the campus of Western Reserve University in Cleveland, Ohio, the heat was oppressive. Sitting in the large and poorly ventilated amphitheater, we found it difficult to listen with a semblance of interest to the never-ending, monotonous reports on "The Social Component of Medicine." The faces around me were warm, tired, and shiny, shoulders were drooped, and almost as a body we had given up taking notes because it was far too energy consuming. My friend Ginny sat behind me with her knees sprawled, trying in spite of her warm uniform and heavy white stockings to find a cooling breeze somehow or somewhere. I had given up completely and was resigned to the half nauseated, half drugged feeling brought on by the combination of a lagging class and the mid-afternoon heat of August. (There was no air conditioning back in 1945.)

I couldn't blame my lethargy entirely on those factors, however. Early that morning, 5:45 a.m. to be exact, I had been awakened after four cherished hours of sleep to feel my roommate, Lennie, shake my bare shoulders and to hear her jubilantly shout, "Wake up Janet, wake up! The war is over, it's real this time, it's really over!" It was one of the few times in my life when I awoke easily and jumped up to turn on my radio to hear more of this wonderful news. Could it really be true? A previous false alarm had aroused within us a sense of caution, a hesitancy that would not have otherwise been felt. Through the static of my worn-out radio, we found out the real truth. No, the news had not been confirmed. No, the President had had no word. No, no, no! There was only the possibility that the long coded message sent to Switzerland by the Japanese government contained the long-awaited, much hoped for acceptance of surrender.

Nursing classes droned on. Still, here we were sitting in class. We had to go on learning about biliary obstruction, thyroidectomies, paralytic ileus; we had to answer questions and write a quiz. Each one of us would shift from one hip to the other, cross and uncross our legs, intermittently try to fan the air around us into circulation, and try to keep drooping eyelids from closing. Yet around us all was an air of expectancy. Dormant in our prosaic class lay an embryo of hope, the possibility of something greater than we had dared dream—PEACE!

Mrs. Morris, our instructor, had more cause than any to nervously await such heartwarming, soul-reaching news; her husband had been gone for three long and painful years. Dottie, sitting next to me, was absorbed in thoughts of her Abbie and the wedding that might happen sooner now than she had dared hope. Constant in my mind, coloring my thoughts, and filling my daydreams was the knowledge that my Jim would be back—maybe not soon, but at least HE WOULD BE BACK! That is, IF it were true that Japan would unconditionally surrender. IF there were no long negotiations to keep from halting the fighting. IF only we were not dreaming.

At noon we had almost despaired of learning definite news, especially of the sort we wanted. In the late afternoon I was back on duty in my medical-surgical unit. As I went about the ward, sticking a variety of derriere with penicillin and changing foul-smelling dressings, my mind was still wandering to thoughts of peace. I resolved to put it aside, to focus on my patients, and to ignore any further rumors. Only the official presidential statement could possibly convince me that we would have peace at last.

It was a waiting game and the day had been exhausting. Besides the sticky, depressing heat, the wind had blown enough pollen about to start my hay fever in royal style. Giving one sneeze after another and constantly blowing my sore, red nose had furnished a good portion of my day's activities. After a meager wartime dinner of usually avoided and much disliked liver and onions, I pulled my weary being as far as Lennie's room, where I collapsed, uniform and all. "Tonight," I began to plan aloud, "I shall clean my room, write Jim a letter, and go to bed. Oh, yes, and wash my hair." This was to be my evening, although I still had distant hopes it might take another form.

I lay back, stuffing my pillows between my head and the radiator, my legs dangling uncomfortably over the edge of the bed. Although I switched on the radio I have little recollection of what was said. Lennie sat, reading her latest book, **The Fountainhead**. Neither of us took note of the program beyond a chance observation that Lowell Thomas had a very pleasant speaking voice. So pleasant, in fact, that it was no trouble at all for me to doze again. Through a semiconscious haze I heard Lowell say, "Goodbye until tomorrow, or until we hear from the President."

In a matter of seconds a special newscast came through. "The President has admitted newsmen to a conference," the announcer said. "We will contact Washington any minute for what we expect to be a momentous announcement." When Washington was reached there was no hysterical, jubilant announcement of "Peace at last!" Quietly and in a matter-of-fact voice, the newscaster told us that President Truman had received Japan's full acceptance of the Pottsdam Ultimatum. Japan had unconditionally surrendered. The war was over.

Lennie and I sat stiff, staring at each other, trying to realize that these calm words meant the cessation of the nightmarish way of living that had been inflicted upon us. Nightmarish not because we had been deprived of necessities as well as luxuries—neither was true. But our friends, brothers, husbands, the boys who sat next to us in chemistry, who teased us in those tender adolescent years, who made our lives rich and meaningful—they had faced the fire of the Germans and Japanese and had to steel themselves to be equally hard and destructive to their ruthless foes.

Ahead was the task of bringing the boys back, their finding civilian jobs, building the homes of which we had dreamed. A world of peace; happy couples together hand in hand, families reunited, fear and worry lifted from our hearts. Now we could begin to believe in the reality of the future. The war was over! At last, the war was over!

The news had come quietly. Did we acknowledge it? We were frozen into silence for all of thirty seconds. Then as the reality of peace settled upon us, we became jubilant, almost hysterical. With tears in her eyes, our friend Margie came running down to the room where Lennie and I were sitting to screech the news and to smother each of us in a hug of victory. We felt sorry for the people going by on the streetcar. They could not know, not yet. Margie and I had had a standing date to go down to Trinity Cathedral, our favorite Cleveland church, if and when victory should arrive. We got dressed and then took time to stop in the rooms of our classmates, repeating over and over, "Japan has surrendered!"

We stood in the hall saying to each other, "The war is over. The WAR is over. The war is OVER. THE WAR IS OVER." The words rolled off our tongues, extricating the deep significance, the joyful meaning of each syllable and inflection.

When at last we left for church our group had grown: Yorkey, Penny, Mary, Ruth, Mim, Margie, Lennie, and myself. We went downstairs to watch the panorama of Euclid Avenue. In the lounge I saw our classmate Margaret standing at the desk. Near her was a soldier with battle ribbons and a face etched by wind and sun and war. As Margaret and I jubilantly greeted each other, I was wondering what the boy in uniform was thinking. What were his memories as people were shouting, "The war is over."

Mrs. Payne, at the switchboard, looked at me and said, in her usual dry and tired voice, "You aren't happy are you, Mrs. Banta?" Knowing her own joy at having her son safe at last, I laughed and said inanely, "Oh no, Mrs. Payne, we don't want 'em back—." I was sure the light in my eyes and laugh on my lips would belie my words. In the lounge, Lennie and I waited for our classmates to join us. We knelt on the low window seats so as to better watch the activity outside. Cars rushed by, horns tooting, people shouting. An ancient automobile passed, covered with vibrant humanity and crowned with one triumphant high school boy perched on the roof shouting his jubilation to the world.

Our group had assembled and we waited in the safety zone, an area by the street car tracks where passengers waited for the next car. Car loads of people passed us on both sides. Everyone was waving and jubilant in this great moment. A club coupe with two soldiers stopped and offered a ride for three of us. Laughing and a bit hesitant, we shoved three of the undergraduate nursing students into the car and wished them luck. I later wondered what sort of an evening they had, and whether they got home before their curfew.

We at last saw a streetcar which, to our amazement, had ample standing room. Before long, Lennie and I were bemoaning the fact that we had worn high heels—the street car ride was tedious; it took us twenty minutes to progress the four blocks to 105th Street. Four girls in the back seat raucously yelled and waved to each sailor they passed, and they teased the motorman in the streetcar behind us.

Looking around the car, I was surprised at the number of people sitting, mute and solemn, as though nothing was happening. As though there were no happy people filling the streets. As though there were no streamers and confetti and paper floating from windows onto the street. Surrounding us there was a flurry of exultation. Was it because these people were alone, lacking the companionship with which to share joy? Was it because their own hearts were too heavily laden with sorrow or worry to celebrate?

As we neared the city, crowds had gathered and our car inched its way down the tracks. Someone started singing the Air Corps song, and soon our mixed and discordant voices were accompanied by the rhythmic tooting of car horns. The Marine Hymn, Anchors Aweigh, and the Caissons Song followed in succession. An excited group of schoolboys started teasing the girls in the rear of the car, and before we knew it, five of them tumbled into a heap on the crowded floor, some grappling and scuffling about our feet. In the heat of the shoving people and stuffy air we decided to get off and walk the remaining blocks to Trinity Cathedral.

We discovered that the walk in our high heels was longer than we had anticipated. Dodging raindrops and picking our way across the busy streets, we finally arrived at the sedate steps of the church just as the rector was locking the doors. Obligingly he let us in, explaining that we had just missed the V-J service. The church was dimly lighted, and we felt warm and welcome as we stood before the shining altar. Empty but for a few people, the majestic pillars and beams of the church echoed to the clicking of our high heels. As we knelt in the pews, the heat of the damp evening caught up with us. At first it was difficult to find the peace we were seeking as perspiration dampened our brows and our cheeks were still burning from the outside heat. It took a few moments to still our minds and our hearts. Kneeling there we thanked God for at last bringing peace to our world, and we prayed that our leaders together would build a world of love and brotherhood instead of hate and war. As I left the Cathedral I felt gratitude and joy instead of the hysteria and wild rejoicing that had been my first reaction.

With hot and complaining feet we worked our way downtown, marveling at the sight of the crowds, their amazing happiness, the penetrating noise, the demonstration of uncontrolled emotions, the melee. In a rash moment I threatened to kiss the first Marine I saw, and as I was engrossed in watching another couple embrace under the light of a marquee, my friends shouted, "A marine, a marine; Janet, there goes a Marine." Ducking ahead I managed to get away before they harnessed me and held me to my threat. "At least," I maintained, "I didn't see him—you did." I had decided that

Jim might not appreciate my efforts to acknowledge his connection with "the best outfit in the world."

We lost part of our group as they sped down Prospect to put Penny on her bus for duty at the City Hospital. We had tried to keep up, but our blistered feet would not cooperate. We turned back to watch a group of grimy street urchins in tattered clothes organize an impromptu band with drums and makeshift horns that they used to lead a susceptible group of people in a parade.

Longing for something to quench our thirst we headed for the Statler Hotel. Trudging through the lobby we were met with "Closed, V-J Day" signs as we hunted in vain for a drinking fountain. We moved on to a theater and paid for the price of admission mainly to get a drink and rest our tired aching feet. We enjoyed the movie, "Thrill of a Romance" with Van Johnson and Esther Williams. The scenes could not compare to our own hope for the romantic scenes looming bright in our own life and future.

We left the theater at 11:30 p.m. and dodged across the still busy Euclid Avenue to jump onto our streetcar just as it was about to leave for the nearest stop. The trip home was quieter, and I leaned my head against the steel window bars. Half asleep I watched the scenes pass by. I fought with the "Canadian Soldiers" (Flying beetles, so called because they were thought to have come across Lake Ontario from Canada) which settled on my skirt, sleeves, and hair. As we reached our stop we struggled to our weary feet and stumbled off the car into a drizzling rain. The three of us had slipped out of our shoes much to the amusement of the streetcar passengers. Three dirty, bedraggled, barefoot girls limped into the dorm.

It was late, nearly two in the morning, when Margie paused in my room to say goodnight. A new world had opened up as we reminisced, planned, and dreamed. The evening's memories lay behind us, never to be forgotten and to be shared with generations to come.

In 1945, Janet Veenboer Banta was a graduate student in the Frances Payne Bolton School of Nursing at Western Reserve University in Cleveland, Ohio. Her school was named for Congresswoman Frances Payne Bolton, who instituted the Cadet Nurse Corps. At the war's end, Banta was midway through the masters program, having entered in August 1943. She had taken leave of absence in October 1944 to marry her college sweetheart who had just completed the United States Marines Officers Candidate School at Camp LeJeune, North Carolina. After Lieutenant James S. Banta boarded ship for the far east, Janet returned to her home in Michigan and waited to reenter her nursing program with the next class beginning February, 1945.

Cadet nurses at this school lived in a quadrangle of dormitories. Banta's dorm, Mather, faced Cleveland's main thoroughfare, Euclid Avenue. Streetcars mentioned in this chapter, clattered past the bedroom windows. With many of the graduate nurses in the Armed Services, the cadets were the major staffing personnel of the large University Hospitals and they were pressed into action, which challenged their abilities providing valuable experience.

Janet Veenboer Banta graduated from Western Reserve University with a master's degree in nursing in 1946. She and her husband raised five children, then she obtained a second master's in education and taught nursing at the Kirkhof School of Nursing, Grand Valley State College in Allendale, Michigan. She retired as Associate Professor, Emeritus in 1988. She spent more than twenty years in nursing, primarily in teaching. The Bantas' grown children are spread around the country and they have eleven grandchildren.

19

Cadet Nurses, Stand By

Gail Churchill Sorensen

Author's note: Reflecting back on those cadet nurse days, Gail Churchill Sorensen said that the camaraderie with her classmates was always number one. She celebrated fifty years of becoming a graduate nurse by writing her memoirs which she has shared with family, friends, and this project. In 2006 she invited her classmates to her home in Homer, Alaska for a 60th class reunion.

Fear made us run, our chests heaving, our sides aching.

WHAP-WHAP-WHAP-WHAP! Our shoes slapped the sidewalk as we flew past the spooky dark alleys, past the Happy Hour Dance Hall and the Nicollet Avenue Bar where hollow-eyed drunks leaned against the doorjambs. But it was not dark alleys or drunks we feared; it was Miss Abigail Whippet, the Director of Nurses of Abbott Hospital School of Nursing in Minneapolis, Minnesota.

Words from her thin unsmiling lips followed us, proclaiming, "must be in by 10:00 p.m . . . tardiness will not be tolerated . . ."

WHAP-WHAP-WHAP-WHAP! Must be in by ten . . . must be in by ten. The words raced through our brains in cadence with our feet.

"Faster," Ruth gasped. "I think we'll make it . . . there's the sign."

The sign read, "**Abbot Hospital and Janney Children's Hospital.**" Another block and we'd be safe at 1905 First Ave. South, our home for the next three years . . . if the door wasn't locked.

Ruth's hand darted to the hidden button that unlocked the door. Nothing! Giving me a look of agony, she rang the door bell. We waited as if for the executioner.

Tiny Abigail Whippet had said it clearly. "Our rules are strict. If you don't abide by them, you'll be dismissed." She spoke with the authority of a general, her stern eyes slowly scanning each of us, drilling her words into our brains. Her five-foot-two-inch body seemed to grow, and her gaze withered us to a size that would fit under her thumb. We called her "Mighty Mouse" behind her back, and we feared every ounce of her ninety-five pounds.

The brown door before us slowly opened, and there stood housemother Helen Hodgkins who seemed as big an obstacle as the door.

"Miss Ruth Peterson. Miss Gail Churchill." She adjusted her gold-rimmed glasses and frowned at her watch. "Six minutes past ten."

"We got lost," I gasped. "We ran and ran, but . . ."

"We went downtown and . . . we don't know Minneapolis very well." Ruth panted. Ruth's soft brown eyes overflowed and tears mingled with the sweat of her hot, crimson face.

For an eternity we stood in judgment as her gray head contemplated our fate. "Being late is serious." Our heads hung lower, convinced that we were doomed. I felt a small sob escape my chest as I thought about the shame—kicked out the first week.

She spoke slowly. "I don't believe you intentionally broke the rules."

She paused. Were we still doomed? "I will record this incident as an unavoidable tardiness . . ." Kindness flickered across her face, then sternness returned as she added, "never let it happen again."

"Oh, it won't," Ruth beamed. "It won't."

"Thank you," I murmured.

Carefully, quietly, as if sneaking away from a great peril, we hurried to our floor apartment. As the door clicked behind us, we collapsed against it. Home! Safe!

We loved the infant Cadet Nurse Corps, our country, and this school. Abbott Hospital seemed elegant as we entered through the big glass doors that opened into a living-room-like lobby with comfortable chairs and tasteful paintings. We felt proud as we turned left into the long hall that led to the classrooms. Midway down the hall was Miss Whippet's' office, its open door, a gapping hole of potential disaster which made us hurry silently, trying to be invisible. Clustered at the hall's end was the heart of the school that gobbled up our days: the classrooms, laboratories, and instructors' offices. Microbiology, anatomy, psychology, chemistry, dietetics, nursing arts I, hygiene. Study, study, study. Tests, tests, tests. Keep up an 80% average or out you go!

The school's student nurse uniforms arrived, and we were informed that from now on we would wear them to class all the time. The Abbott uniform was not a simple piece of clothing; there were six parts to assemble. First was a white dress that buttoned down the front with clip-on buttons. Then a board-stiff collar and cuffs were pinned to the dress, and next a bib was pinned to a wrap-around skirt, making a smooth-belted apron that buttoned in the back. Assembly took twelve clip-on buttons, eleven safety pins, and a pair of mother-of-pearly cuff links.

Monday morning, like white flowers that bloom overnight, we had blossomed into nurses, proud and starched with black lettered mother-of-pearl name pins. Crescent-shaped "probie" caps sat atop our heads and, by afternoon, chaffed bright-red bands circled our necks, painted there by the stiff sharp collars. We looked and felt as if we belonged. Then we read on the bulletin board that we would start floor duty the following week. The day came. With excitement, anticipation, nervousness, we waited for the elevator to take us above to the great unknown.

Congestive Heart Failure, read the diagnosis on my patient's chart. "Ye Gads, heart failure! I think mine will fail too," I thought as I anxiously entered the room expecting to see a near-corpse.

"Good morning," a robust-looking man with a cheerful voice greeted me.

"Good morning, Mr. Christensen," I replied, still convinced, in spite of his appearance, that one false move on my part would send him straight to the great beyond. And then it happened. I tripped on a caster at the foot of his bed and jolted him severely. I thought everything would be over—his life, my career.

"Oh, I'm sorry. Are you all right?" I wailed.

He seemed more amused than damaged. "I'm just fine. How are you?"

How was I? I couldn't tell him I was flustered, scared, and nearing panic. "Clumsy," I grinned weakly as I continued his bath. Then I wished I could go out and start over again. I was making a terrible mistake—washing the wrong arm first!

When the bath was over, he thanked me for a pleasant morning, gave me a piece of chocolate candy, and didn't seem amazed that we both had survived.

More classes were added. We saw by the new schedule that we would have ethics with Miss Whippet! As the first ethics lecture began, we sat, quiet and tense. Not even those who sat at the back of the long narrow room would dare doze off today.

"It has come to my attention," she began, "that many of you have been franking your mail."

We had. Like others in the service of our country, we wrote "Free" where the stamp would go and "Cadet" in the return address. It seemed a logical thing to do.

"As Cadet Nurses, you may not frank your mail. Franking is reserved for the Military services. The Cadet Corps is under the Public Health Service. Franking is not only unethical, it is illegal."

An uncomfortable silence filled the room. We were guilty. We'd repent and sin no more. "As nurses you are expected to be ethical beyond reproach," she avowed.

"You will often have information about your patients which is very private, and it is essential that this information be kept strictly confidential. There must be no hospital conversation when you are walking down Nicollet Avenue, no discussion of patients while you are having a sundae at Bridgeman's or riding the street car." She paused briefly, silence reinforcing her words, then added, "Violation of this trust will be subject to immediate dismissal."

"All patients must be respected and called by their proper names: Mr. Smith, Miss Andrews, Mrs. Williams (never by their first names) and you must never use such terms as Grandma, Pops, or Dearie."

These points being welded into our souls, she continued, "When sick, a person's faith is of great comfort to him. To aid in his spiritual care you must be aware that what you believe may be different from your patient's beliefs. For example, Catholics do not eat meat on Fridays. If you are Protestant you probably think that is unimportant, even foolish."

"If you are Baptist, you probably think baptism should be done only when a person is old enough to decide for himself. If you are Catholic, you probably believe Heaven is denied to anyone, no matter how young, if he isn't baptized. It is not the duty of the nurse to decide the right or wrong of these profound issues, but it is her duty to give emotional and spiritual care by being aware of these beliefs and respecting them. For example, if there is danger that a newborn baby of Catholic parents will die, it is important that the priest be notified and if death is imminent before the priest arrives it is vital that you baptize the baby by sprinkling water on his forehead and saying, 'I baptize you in the name of the Father, the Son, and the Holy Spirit. Amen.' Even if you are not Catholic the church recognizes the baptism as valid because you are a nurse."

Nurses can baptize! The responsibility seemed awesome—nurses' actions could actually affect who entered the gates of Heaven?

She continued, "If the infant's parents are Baptist, of course, you would not baptize the baby. Also remember that those of the Jewish faith do not eat pork . . . Jehovah Witnesses will not accept blood transfusions . . ."

Silence remained as she concluded, "Nurses are to care for people, not judge them." Her thin lips closed and she left the room. Though gone, her presence seemed to remain, and we quietly left our seats, whispering to each other, "She's a good teacher."

Training's fast pace was beginning to invade everything we did. We walked fast, ate fast, brushed our teeth fast, played fast, packed as much fun as we could into every free minute. Besides the many classes, we often worked on the floor both morning and evening, and like a train ahead of schedule, we were reaching the pinnacle on our journey: capping—the end of our probationary period.

The ceremony took place at Westminster Presbyterian Church, a huge gray stone building that oozed a dignity which was contagious. As the processional called us to our destiny, our immaculate white shoes carried us, starched and bareheaded, past our beaming families and friends to the front of the sanctuary.

There was the invocation, and then the choir members (made up of student nurses) stood and sang like St. Peter's angels. With somber dignity the satin-robed minister stepped to the podium, let his gaze wander over us approvingly for a moment, and began his address. "Congratulations, you have reached a great milestone. You have worked and studied hard to earn your nursing cap, a symbol of the most noble of professions . . ."

The moment had arrived. Miss Monkmand and Mrs. Stafford marched to the front of the sanctuary and stood behind a linen-covered, candlelit table with forty-three hemstitched caps waiting for us. They sat perkily in rows, the most beautiful caps in the world, gleaming jewels brighter than the candles which glowed from their crystal holders.

"Miss Dorothy Ames," Mrs. Stafford announced in a tone that said, "This is someone important." Ames floated as if in a dream-come-true to the marvelous table and stopped in front of

Miss Monkman, who placed the precious cap on her head and secured it with two white pins. With a smile Mrs. Stafford handed Ames a lighted candle, then announced, "Miss Marjorie Anderson." As Andy approached with poise and dignity, Ames stepped up on the raised dais behind the table, turned to face the audience, and waited to be joined by her classmates.

"Miss Shirley Wharton." Hers was the last cap, the last candle, and as she took her place with the others, the sanctuary lights dimmed. Flickering candles lit our faces, and our reverent voices joined together as we recited the Florence Nightingale Pledge.

The magical ceremony, the magical caps had transformed us. We were no longer "probies." We had earned the Abbott cap.

Seven a.m. found us on floors scurrying about taking temperatures, giving medicine, serving breakfast, giving baths. Our assignments changed from one patient to two, then three, four, five, and more. Hurry. Hurry. Hurry. Get the charting done. Report off. Get to class on time.

Mrs. Chase came into our lives, the life-sized mannequin with opening for the urinary meatus, vagina, and anus. Each week, with the help of Mrs. Chase and Mrs. Stafford, we mastered new procedures, and each week we added to our "Red Book," the record of procedures done for real patients.

Another class entered training. Schools of nursing were doing all they could to solve the nursing shortage. Most graduates joined the military, leaving civilian hospitals stripped bare and dependent upon students to provide care. We were no longer the youngest or the greenest, and we were proud to be "big sisters" to the newcomers, to help teach them the ropes.

In spite of the war effort, Abbott Hospital School of Nursing was eager to produce proper young ladies as well as nurses. Teas were common. I would have failed "tea-going" if we were given grades. I often forgot that enema results and fuzz in the belly buttons wasn't proper "tea conversation."

We were "circulating" for minor surgery. Coming on duty one morning, I looked at the schedule with dismay. Dr. Ward—local tonsillectomy. Circulating nurse—G. Churchill. Scrub nurse—M. Doll.

Our luck had run out. We had been warned that he was terrible in surgery, and we knew he did ornery things. We'd seen the "moon faces" he had drawn on charts to criticize the nurses. "Patient says her hot packs were cold," he'd write, and draw a sad face with tears dripping from its eyes.

"I won't cry, no matter what," I vowed. Neither of us said any more about our dread of Dr. Ward as we rushed about preparing for the case. When he entered the room, his patient, sedated and calm, was positioned in a chair, a barber-shop-type drape around her shoulders. Dr. Ward's head light and instruments were laid out as he wished. Lots of big tonsil sponges—the kind he liked—were ready on sponge sticks. We felt everything was perfect.

He looked around with a scowl, sat on the stool we had positioned in front of the patient, picked up the mouth retractor, and said to the patient, "I need to hold your mouth open with this." He held out his hand; Doll handed him a filled syringe. "What's this?" he snapped.

"Ten ccs. of 1% Novocain," Doll answered. He grunted, plopped the syringe back on the table, and held out his hand again. Doll guessed that he wanted a scalpel. Wrong.

He glared at her, "What do you want me to do with that? Cut her tongue out?" He picked up the metal tongue depressor, and his glare switched to me.

"Fix that light. I can't operate in the dark. And then come hold this."

I adjusted the light so the beam would bounce off his head light and shine into the patient's throat. "Hurry up. Now sit on that stool and hold her tongue out of the way. Hold it just like I've got it."

I grasped the handle of the tongue depressor and looked to see where it was positioned. "You going to do this operation? Get your head out of the way," he growled. Then, whap, he slapped my hand. "Can't you hold that like I told you? Now do it right."

He grumped through the surgery and when Doll's gaze and mine would meet, we'd roll our eyes at Dr. Ward. No way would he make us cry. When the surgery was over he scrutinized us as he ripped off his gloves. No, we weren't crying—not even close. "Humph!" was his final insult as he threw his gloves on the floor. Thankfully, most surgeons weren't like Dr. Ward. Most of the physicians enjoyed teaching and helping us learn.

A new marvel entered our lives: the cadet nurse uniform. Wearing it, we could ride at reduced fares and enter the serviceman's gate at the bus depot, thereby being assured a spot on an overcrowded bus. The summer uniform was made of gray and white striped cotton material. Its red-epaulet jacket and straight skirt looked good on the girls who looked good in anything, but for some of us, it fit like a sack. We weren't eager to wear it. Then the gray wool winter uniform arrived. Handsome. Beautiful.

The uniform opened other doors. We were striding down the street in our cadet uniforms one evening when we saw the sign. USO. "That's the United Service Organization, and it's for those in uniform," we mused. "Let's go," we all said at once.

A band was playing, and servicemen were dancing with the hostesses. Ruth's foot started to tap to the boogie beat, and a soldier swooped her off to the dance floor. Soon we were all dancing or playing cards or ping pong or checkers. A table in the corner held food and drink, and instantly we knew this was a place Madame Astra, the fortune teller whom we had encountered earlier, would expect us to visit often—a place, as she predicted, with young men and happiness.

Obstetrics . . . a favorite service for many of us. There was a thrill in watching a new life begin. We felt privileged to share it with a patient as we faithfully timed her contractions, listened to the baby's heartbeat, rubbed the soon-to-be mother's back, encouraged her to breathe deeply, and waited. We joined the gambling games of guessing the sex, and when the baby was born, the weight. It was exciting and the happiest place imaginable . . . when everything went well.

But everything was not always perfect. One baby was born with six fingers which saddened the mother, initially, and then seemed insignificant when her roommate had a baby with a "Rh" blood type (a beautiful eight-pounder who became jaundiced and grew weaker every day).

Medical science had discovered the cause of the condition through experiments on rhesus monkeys. The most severe cases were doomed to death as the cure was decades away. Sometimes bad blood replaced with good blood could save a few infants born with the Rh factor. The baby was given a complete blood exchange, but the infant grew more jaundiced and weaker.

The doctor talked to the parents. "I don't have much hope . . ."

They pleaded, "Please try again." We set up the procedure, but the baby died during the blood exchange transfusion.

The sadness of the Rh baby's death had not left the nursery, when Miss Howe hurried in and said, "Help me get the incubator set up. A 'preemie,' eight weeks early, is about to be born."

My first glimpse of the tiny naked infant triggered apprehension. Almost transparent bluish skin covered his fragile, listless skeleton, but he was breathing, alive. Gradually, the tiny three-pounder became pink as the warm, humid, oxygenated air of the incubator surrounded him. Only the fragile hands and feet at the end of his bony limbs remained blue. The tiny heart pulsed, fast and visible in his chest, a chest that heaved irregularly as he tried to fill his immature lungs. He was feeble and so small, but we were determined. We'd save this one. Although more vigorous babies wailed, demanding attention, I dared not leave the side of the newborn infant.

Check his breathing . . . 40, irregular.

Check his heartbeat . . . 110.

Check his color . . . extremities cyanotic.

Suction mucus.

Check the incubator . . . proper temperature, proper humidity, proper oxygen.

Watch.

Worry.

The intern who had assisted at the birth came into the nursery. He looked hopefully into the incubator, then turned away. The infant was blue and listless. We were grateful for the young doctor's presence and even more so as he started helping us change the diapers of the demanding crying babies in the nursery.

Then it happened. The chest was still. "Dr. Wells, he's gone bad," I said trying to keep panic from my voice as I grabbed the resuscitator and gently squeezed air into the delicate infant's lungs. The baby gasped and again the wee chest moved, struggling for life. Dr. Wells gave him a stimulant.

More watching. More worrying. More and more I helped him try to breath. *Precious baby, breathe again. Precious baby, breathe again.* I silently wailed each time I squeezed air into his lungs. Then the feeble lungs could work no more. I looked pleadingly at Dr. Wells. Sorrowfully, he shook his head. There was no more we could do. The heartbeat, barely visible between the frail ribs, became a mere whisper of movement. With mist in my eyes, I watched life vanish.

Be professional. Control your emotions. Function through sadness. Nursing is often hard, we'd been taught. I checked the time. It was important to record the moment of death. Eleven p.m . . . the end of the shift . . . the end of a life . . . the end of a mother's dream.

"Mental illness is just becoming recognized as a disease with causes and cures instead of being a mystical, unfathomable, insane condition," Mrs. Ballard, our psychiatric instructor, said. We cadets were now experiencing our psychiatric affiliation at the Rochester State Mental Hospital. "With more help, more research, we believe many of these people might get well. However, at the present, the state budget is thirty-seven cents per day for each patient's care. That includes everything—housing, clothing, laundry, medicine, nursing care, food . . ."

But poor as the hospital was, the patients received excellent care thanks to the donated services of the famous Rochester Mayo

Clinic staff and to the few dedicated nurses, psychiatric technicians, and trusted patients who lived and worked there.

The Rochester State Mental Hospital with many buildings, a mattress shop, a barn, and other farm buildings was a community all of its own. For days and weeks, our lives were satisfying without leaving the grounds with well-kept lawns and old majestic trees. We played tennis, attended the weekly movie, used the library, picnicked by the outdoor fireplace, wove on the loom in the occupational therapy room, and played ping pong and shuffleboard in the nurses' home basement.

In the outside world, the war still raged. We felt its sting occasionally: when a classmate was killed in action, when a brother was sent overseas, and when our loved ones were somewhere in the thick of fighting. Our lives went on learning about our patients with mental illnesses and about how we could best care for them.

One day we watched with interest as a car stopped outside and a tall, well-built lady stepped out. She stood straight as a general, adjusted the flowered hat she had on her head, looked at the two white-clad attendants who stood by her side, pulled herself even straighter, whipped her hand to her forehead in a salute, and commanded, "Forward march." Her name was Gladys Brady, and she was wearing an attractive navy blue suit adorned with many brooches and three different colored sashes that flipped from side to side as she marched with high-kneed steps into out lives.

Stopping just inside the door which locked behind her, she scrutinized us. What should we expect from this loud, colorful woman? She looked at the cadet nurse patches on the sleeves of our uniforms. "CADET NURSES," she shouted, "CADET NURSES, STAND BY!"

"Would you come into the office, please?" Miss Johnson asked.

She sang loudly, "Come, come, come to the office." Although the male attendants remained in case they were needed to control her, Mrs. Brady cooperated with the admitting procedures and flamboyantly entered her bare room, dressed only in a bathrobe. She sang. She stood her mattress up against the wall and recited poems to it. She laughed, and we couldn't help but laugh too as we peeked through the tiny hole in her door. At last the sedative we'd given put her to sleep. "We'll schedule her for electric shock therapy as soon as possible," Dr. Webb said. "She's been here before and responds well."

The next morning breakfast was served on a tray in her room. She pounded a cadence with her spoon, then waved the spoon as if conducting a band, and finally picked up a piece of toast and started to eat. Assuming she was eating, we went about other duties. Then we heard her loud commanding voice shouting, "CADET NURSES, STAND BY."

What a sight we saw as we peeked into her room! Her robe was tied in knots and flung in a corner. She stood bare naked in the center of the room. Her metal oatmeal bowl was upside down on her head like a helmet, the contents dripping down her back and face. "CADET NURSES, STAND BY," she shouted again as she brought her hand to her forehead in a salute, then stood at attention, motionless.

The next day Mrs. Brady was scheduled for electric shock therapy. We escorted her to the therapy room and positioned her on the padded table. We rubbed electrode paste onto her temples. "Rub it in well for good electrical conduction," Dr. Webb instructed.

He turned to a black metal machine with a multitude of electrical wires sprouting from it. He adjusted the amount of current, the duration of the shock, and then attached an electrode firmly to each temple. "Stand back. Don't touch the patient," he cautioned.

We stood in awe as he pressed a button and Mrs. Brady's body stiffened, and then started to jerk violently with a full blown grand mal seizure. It was not a pretty sight. At last the jerking slowed, her body relaxed and she gurgled and gasped for air. "Turn her on her side. Quickly. Suction her airway," Dr. Webb ordered.

She lay limp and unconscious as we moved her to a recovery room. What a strange treatment this seemed to be. What would she be like when she awoke? We watched her closely, and at last she stirred and groggily responded. Then she slept and slept.

The next day Mrs. Brady was a different person. She was aware, understood that she'd had a treatment, couldn't remember well what she had done before she came to the hospital, but seemed to know that she had been ill and was better now. She was friendly, cooperative, and helpful to other patients. She was given another treatment the next week, and in a few days she went home.

Not everyone who had electric shock treatments responded well (some didn't seem to be helped at all), but after caring for the hundreds of patients who had been in the hospital for months and years, we rejoiced. There was hope. At least for some.

For three years, I'd been looking forward to the end of training, and now that it was almost here, a great sadness came over me when I thought that we'd probably never all be together again. Where had the three years gone? I felt an urge to have them back, but then I mused about the changes that had taken place. We were now at peace. Penicillin cured . . . and with only two shots a day instead of eight. Patients with infections, especially children, seldom died. Better, longer-acting insulin had been developed. Orthopedic surgery was using new metals, even making artificial hip joints. And there was a blessing for our busy feet; nurses now wore low-heeled, comfortable shoes. Yes, it was better to move ahead.

I was returning to Abbott Hospital School of Nursing after spending my senior cadet nurse experience in the Mayo Orthopedic Hospital in Rochester, Minnesota and excited to see my friends. We would soon be out of here.

Laughter greeted me before I opened the door. Mike, Nickel, Joyce, Edblom, Haar, Tess, and Ost were circling Ruth like a pack of wolves ready to rip her apart. "Churchie, you're just in time," Ost said as she gleefully grabbed Ruth's apron and gave it a yank. Pop, went the apron. Rip went the bib. One quick pull and her dress was slit to the hem. Rip, rip, rip and there she stood in her underwear.

Tradition demanded we do that. Ruth's training days were over. The old white cotton uniform was gone, but hanging on the closet door was another white dress made of satin and lace. She would wear it tomorrow as she started her new life as Mrs. Robideau.

We collapsed with laughter and the joy of the the moment. "You should have seen Mike when we ripped her uniform last night," Nickel snickered.

"Did it at the hospital and left her standing in the hall in her slip," Edblom chuckled.

"They didn't tell you the worst part," Mike sputtered. "The rascals wouldn't help me get my clothes to come home in, and I had to come home with a sheet wrapped around me, and then . . . I opened the nurses' home door and there SHE was . . . my heart sank."

"Then I realized that she no longer power over me, and I said, 'Good evening, Miss Whippet' and when she was out of sight, I laughed and skipped all the way to my room."

One by one the faded student uniforms were ripped, some completely gone, some still hanging like the shells of newly-hatched chicks. And as each of us shed the old protective shell, as our time came to leave the comfortable, familiar nest, we paused only briefly. We were ready to scatter, eager to soar. But the three years together had created a bond, an unbreakable thread of camaraderie and friendship, bonding us always over distance and time.

Had the war continued Gail Churchill Sorensen would have joined one of the military nurse corps. Instead she says that her biggest contribution to nursing was being willing to always go back to nursing when the need presented itself. Forty years of nursing were spent in a variety of positions that included the following: general duty in a small town 17-bed hospital, receiving nurse at a state mental hospital, 4-H camp nurse, emergency room nurse in a big city hospital, instructor for a school of nursing, nursing supervisor for a nursing home, nurses' aide trainer, director of nurses for a 10-bed hospital in Alaska where besides nursing, the nurses were responsible for cooking, cleaning, and laundry. One of her most rewarding positions was an instructor of emergency care throughout much of Alaska. She felt greatly honored when the all-male fire department of Homer, Alaska, asked her to join them.

Over the years she has received numerous plaques and certificates of various kinds as well as proclamations from two small cities in Alaska.

Sorensen said that those recognition's were nice but most meaningful of all was the look on a patients' faces and the words, "I don't know what I'd have done with out you."

Sorensen had a happy marriage of more than fifty years and enjoys her three sons and their families. With her husband she fished commercially for crab, shrimp and halibut in Katchemak Bay and was a 4-H leader. Today she is an avid gardener, a cross country skier and she plays the drums in a city band. She said that having a work skill that was in great demand was always a blessing.

20

North to Alaska

Charlotte Allen Rogers

Author's note: Alaska was in Charlotte Allen Roger's blood. After graduating from her school of nursing, she spent the summer with her uncle, Jesse Allen, one of the first White men to explorer the Brooks Range. After that experience, she decided to begin her nursing career in Alaska. Several years later, as a single mom, she returned to California to raise her two children. She then returned to Barrow, Alaska where she served in the Alaska Native hospital until her retirement.

I grew up in the back hills of West Virginia and our family had the first radio in my town of Richwood. My father was a butcher for a logging company. Sometimes he would let my sisters and I watch him cut up cows and pigs at the slaughter house. We sat absorbed in anatomy. He was a surveyor before he and my mother married. My dad had gone through eighth grade, which was good for that time in our area. If you had gone through eighth grade you could teach school.

My mother was a high school graduate, a great reader, and a very religious Catholic woman. She was interested in world events, literature, and classical music. We belonged to a lending library by mail. I remember receiving *Jason and the Golden Fleece* through the mail library.

My sister, Gin, and I remember hanging onto our mother's dress tail standing at the front door when she told a visiting nurse she would not allow her to vaccinate us for small pox. There was a small pox epidemic 25 miles away. I got my first small pox vaccination when I entered nurse's training.

My mother was tubercular and had a pulmonary hemorrhage when I was six months old. She was sent to a tuberculosis sanitarium at Tarra Haute, West Virginia, and I was sent to live with the neighbors. I didn't see my mother again until I was three years old. There was no chemotherapy at that time, and for the rest of her life, my mother was a latent or active tubercular patient.

When I was five years old, our family sent us kids to a Catholic boarding school in Huntington to get us away from our mother, who was sick again with tuberculosis. To get there, we rode the caboose on a logging train until it got to the junction where we met the passenger train. I always got sick on the passenger train due to breathing the coal exhaust. We were at the boarding school for three years.

Then the Depression came, the banks failed, and we came home and started attending a three-room school. The family all helped in caring for our mother, and we learned about contagion. We boiled dishes, burned contaminated sputum bundles, etc. I remember my mother coughing and coughing until she would hemorrhage.

We kids were jealous of the cats because Mother would pet the cats but keep her distance from us kids. Of course we were all contaminated anyway. I took care of my mother from the time I was 12 years of age. That was the year she was pregnant with my brother, Bob. I stayed out of school a full year to take care of the baby and my mother so my sister could finish high school.

A railroad ran down the middle of town in the logging community where we lived. About 40 families lived in a 10-mile area. They were either loggers, railroaders, or company store people. The three-room school included grades up to and including the eighth grade. Two or three-grades were in one room, and you could learn so much if you were inclined. I was always interested in history and listened with fascination to the upper grades discuss the Revolutionary War. Folding doors opened up to make an auditorium where we had Christmas programs and pie and box dinner socials. My dad auctioneered for the box socials. We also watched black and white movies.

The school had outside pit toilets and a pot-belly stove. When the stove was fired up the kids sitting close would be roasting and the kids further back would be freezing. When it got too cold for the teacher, we could go home. That was great; then we would go sledding. We improvised a sled by using a raft that we turned over, clumped on snow, and then poured on water which froze and made great runners. Then we hiked up an old mining trail where we climbed onto our makeshift sled. Someone would give us a push, and off we would go, flying down the hill.

In March we went skinny-dipping just so we could brag that we were the first kids in town to jump in the river. In the summer we swam everyday or we would go sailing on our home-built rafts and play pirates. We fished with a willow pole and a fishing line of string in the Big Hole below the bridge for chubs and suckers which we didn't eat. Sometimes we fished Lick Branch for trout even if there was a "NO FISHING" sign posted. We wandered through the woods and were on the look out for rattlesnakes and copperheads. We played stick ball or scrub or work-up with a ball made out of twine. We also shot marbles with stealers and played for dibbs. I was a great marble shooter. I feel sorry for kids today; everything they do is organized, and they are always watched.

At the end of the 1930s there was a great deal of discussion regarding the pros and cons of the United States getting into the war on the side of Great Britain. The war was on everyone's mind, and I told my dad that I was going to volunteer as a nurse if we got into the war. I had been the primary caregiver for my mother since I was 12 and it was the natural thing to do. Then came the bombing of Pearl Harbor.

I had enough credits to graduate from high school, so I enrolled at the St. Mary's School of Nursing in Huntington, West Virginia, in February 1942. My two sisters at home would care for my mother and little brother. I was awarded a $50 scholarship which paid for my books. The school furnished my uniforms and board and room, and that was all I needed. I came home from nursing school in May and graduated with my high school class.

The Cadet Nurse Corps became available about a year later and was a financial lifesaver for me. The stipend was helpful as I didn't have any money. We had to buy our own hose, and I remember getting holes in the heels and would turn the hose under so the holes wouldn't show. The hose would get shorter and shorter until we couldn't fasten them with our garter belt. Fortunately our uniforms were 10 inches from the floor so hose weren't seen much. We always wore the outdoor cadet nurse uniform when we traveled home.

There was segregation at St. Mary's Hospital. The Blacks were in the old wing where the cockroaches were, but there were also poor Whites there as well. One time a doctor came by and asked me for a patient's chart using her first name. She was a Black woman by the name of Annie Johnson. I said, "Yes Doctor, here is Mrs. Johnson's chart." He said, "I want Annie's chart."

I replied, "Yes, Doctor, right here it is." It was going through my minds that he must know her well enough to call her by her first name but I didn't. My mother had taught us to be respectful to older people.

The doctor then said emphatically, "I want Annie's chart and we don't call them Mrs."

I was shocked and automatically said, "Well I do! She has as much right to be called Mrs. as anybody."

One woman was upset because a Black woman was on the obstetric floor and her baby was in the nursery. We cadets laughed at her. The Black woman was a college professor and had demanded her rights.

One of my patients had tetanus, and he took a lot of care. I always left him facing the door so he could see people coming into the room. The slightest noise or touch startled him and he would go into a spasm. He had been frolicking with the hired girl when his wife caught him and jabbed him in the rear with a pitchfork. That's how he got tetanus, but he recovered.

Isolation impressed me and I remember the children who had diphtheria. We intubated them by placing a tube into the larynx so they could breathe. It was hard nursing to care for those children with diphtheria, but we saved the kids. One time we had a patient with small pox. Children with pertusis (whooping cough) would cough and cough until they would vomit. If parents today who choose not to vaccinate their children had any notion how terrible those diseases were, they would not object to immunization.

One newborn had gonorrhea of the eyes. We had no treatment at all except to wash the kid's eyes out with boric acid solution every five minutes, 24 hours a day for days. I'm proud to say that we saved that baby's eyes.

My mother and sister died while I was in nursing school, and I lost time which I had to make up. I planned to join the service and went to White Sulphur Springs Army Hospital for my physical, and they kept taking X-rays. Six weeks later I received a notice saying that I had chest pathology and was not eligible to join the service. Today, my lungs show apical scars due to my exposure to tuberculosis.

I think one of our fine accomplishments for that time was that the students ran the hospital because all of the graduate nurses had gone into the military. I was charge nurse on a medical floor when I was a junior cadet. After graduation in 1945, the Director of Nurses wanted me to go to Georgetown University to get a degree in nursing, but I had decided that I was going to Alaska. Early summer, I hiked and camped with my Uncle Jesse in the Brooks Range in Alaska. From the Kobuk River, we followed the Iko Blarney Creek up to the head waters, and I was hooked. Alaska would be the place I would begin my nursing career.

Back in West Virginia for the few remaining months of summer, I spent time with my nephew who contracted polio. I took him to a hospital which was set up for polio patients. I was asked to stay for a month as they did not have a graduate nurse on nights. There were 20 patients in various stages of polio, including a young girl in an iron lung (a tank in which the entire body except for the head is enclosed). Pressure is regularly increased and decreased to provide artificial respiration. Fortunately the girl was able to breath on her own and no longer needed the clumsy respirator before I left.

In September, I landed in Anchorage and stayed with a minister of the Seventh Day Advents the first evening. The next morning I was driven to Palmer. I hadn't been smoking, as Advents don't approve, and when I got out of the car I will never forget the wonderful smell of Sitka spruce.

I first worked at a small hospital that was built to be a bungalow. The doctors lived a good distance from the hospital and babies don't wait. I delivered a lot of babies, and one woman named her baby after me. Then I moved on to Fairbanks and later in my career to the bush community of Barrow, the most northerly town in the United States with one of the largest Eskimo population.

Obstetrical nursing was always interesting and rewarding. The native mothers from the small villages would come into a regional hospital before they were to deliver. Once I was asked to go out in a helicopter to help bring in a mother who was about to have a baby. She lived in the village of Nuiqsut, which was a 40-minute flight from Barrow. The reason they picked me was that there was no doctor available and I had delivered more babies than anyone else. There was no ambulance in the village so we dressed her in her parka and warm boots and moved her in the back of a truck. You never know when a plane might need to make an unscheduled landing, and I wanted to keep the mother's feet warm and dry.

It was cold, about 40 degrees below, and I told the pilot, that if the baby was born we would tuck him in on the inside of his coat. The helicopter had little heat. I started an intravenous and tucked the tubing under the mother's shoulder to keep it warm so it wouldn't freeze. Fortunately we got the mother back to Barrow in time for her delivery.

We always tried to get the mothers into the native hospital in Anchorage if we expected them to deliver premature as it was best that the baby travel in his primary incubator, the mother. Our makeshift incubator consisted of a metal box with hot water bottles. We had less infection than most hospitals because of our smaller number of patients.

Della Keats, a native healer, would come to the hospital to treat her people. We had great respect for her. Some of the women didn't want to come to Barrow and spend six weeks away from their families and would deliver in their village with a native midwife.

Outside of nursing my love was floating rivers. On my first trip I floated the Yukon River from the head waters in Whitehorse, Canada, to Marshall, Alaska, a total of 1700 miles. We started the last of June and got off the river in October when the ice was beginning to form. When we stopped at a village, we would send out messages on the bush line, Tundra Topics, which is the bush message service out of Fairbanks.

As I had worked in Fairbanks, I knew a lot of the Alaska natives who lived in the villages along the river. The people were always happy to see us as we were someone to talk to. We carried a letter for 1,000 miles to mail and also delivered a haunch of bear downstream. My nurse friends and I were among the first women to float the Yukon. I floated the Yukon three times as well as the Noatak. I love rivers and would do it again anytime.

Charlotte Allen Rogers spends summers in her log cabin with a view of three glaciers, on Katchemak Bay in Homer, Alaska. She is an avid gardener and nature lover and, until recently, spent a week camping each year in a remote area of Denali National Park. The lure of the old days growing up in hills of West Virginia gave Rogers the love of nature and inspiration for the challenge of living and bush nursing in Alaska.

A Summing Up

During World War II, more than 185,000 young women answered the call, "Become a Nurse: Your Country Needs you." Under the Labor-Federal Security Act of 1942 participating schools of nursing increased their enrollment to 6,558 students. This small number did not alleviate the nurse shortage. The Bolton Act (1943-1948), which created the U. S. Cadet Nurse Corps, added the staggering number of 179,294 cadet nurses. From the Corps' inception to termination, 124,065 cadet nurses saw their training through to graduation.

As the result of the Corps program changes and improvements in nursing education were implemented in the participating 1,125 schools. Due to the shortage of nurse teaching staff, many schools discovered that they could purchase better instruction in the sciences from neighboring junior colleges and universities. Other improvements were implemented. Although the Corps program was established primarily to expand the quantity of nursing service personnel, nursing leaders took advantage of this opportunity to improve nursing education.

The U. S. Cadet Nurse Corps offered those who joined, a lifetime education-FREE. I asked each participant in the *Cadet Nurse Story Telling Project* if this promise had been fulfilled. Overwhelmingly the answer from the former cadets, who had been children of the Great Depression years, said "Yes." More than 75% of the participants in this nationwide project reported that without the Corps they would not have had a career in nursing.

As a cadet nurse, my diploma provided me, Thelma Robinson, the basis for a nurse education with a realization that I needed more, not only as a nurse but as an individual. I wanted to learn more about nursing in the community as well as the hospital and to have a better understanding of people and the world in general. The Corps gave me an eagerness to move forward in my learning and to gain new skills and insights so that I could broaden my horizon and provide a better nursing service.

The heritage of nursing is a rich one and it has been a privilege to be a part of its pioneering efforts. We learn from the past in order to understand the present so that we can better plan for the future.

Index

Appendix

LIST OF SCHOOLS PARTICIPATING IN THE U. S. CADET NURSE CORPS
WITH NUMBER OF CADETS ADMITTED FROM
FY 1944 to FY 1946

School & City	Fiscal Years			Total
	1943-1944	1944-1945	1945-1946	
ALABAMA				
Garner Mem., Anniston	30	13	10	53
✻ Baptist, Birmingham	156	47	40	243
Hillman, Birmingham	128	-	-	128
Jefferson, Birmingham	38	-	-	38
Hillman-Jefferson, Birmingham	64	52	-	116
Norwood, Birmingham	64	36	23	123
St. Vincent's, Birmingham	76	37	38	151
S. Highlands, Birmingham	86	59	7	152
Moody, Dothan	17	-	-	17
Holy Name of Jesus, Gadsden	49	35	-	84
City Hosp., Mobile	64	34	24	122
Mobile Inf., Mobile	65	23	-	88
Providence, Mobile	58	22	25	105
St. Margaret's, Montgomery	-	15	44	59
Drummond Frazier, Sylacauga	20	26	-	46
Citizen's, Talladoga	14	8	-	22
Druid City, Tuscaloosa	-	19	-	19
Tuskegee, Tuskegee	94	21	22	137
State Total	1,023	447	233	1,703
ARIZONA				
Sage Mem., Ganado	6	20	13	39
✻ Good Samaritan, Phoenix	106	57	25	188
St. Joseph, Phoenix	81	58	42	181
St. Monica's, Phoenix	-	51	47	98
St. Mary's, Tucson	107	92	27	226
State Total	300	278	154	732
ARKANSAS				
Warner Brown, El Dorado	26	11	19	56
St. Edwards Mercy, Ft. Smith	80	5	29	114
Sparks Mem., Ft. Smith	51	32	29	112
Leo N. Levi, Hot Springs	47	21	6	74
St. Joseph's, Hot Springs	31	19	15	65
St. Bernard's, Jonesboro	31	20	4	55
Baptist St., Little Rock	202	90	-	292
St. Vincent's, Little Rock	152	63	3	218
St. Mary's, Russellville	21	-	-	21
State Total	641	261	105	1,007

233

| | Fiscal Years | | | |
School & City	1943- 1944	1944- 1945	1945- 1946	Total
· CALIFORNIA				
San Joaquin Gen., French Camp	67	59	19	145
Gen. Hosp. of Fresno Co., Fresno	91	35	29	155
Good Samaritan, Los Angeles	143	70	27	240
L. A. Co. Gen., Los Angeles	629	272	105	1,006
Queen of Angels, Los Angeles	81	60	6	147
California Hosp., Los Angeles	74	36	22	132
St. Vincent's, Los Angeles	87	47	35	169
Methodist, Los Angeles	-	71	37	108
Hollywood Presbyterian, Los Angeles	-	59	22	81
Highland Alameda, Oakland	249	81	41	371
Providence, Oakland	195	80	30	305
Samuel Merritt, Oakland	173	74	39	286
St. Joseph, Orange	62	48	-	110
Mercy, Sacramento	100	55	23	178
San Diego Co. Gen., San Diego	87	49	22	158
Sacramento Co., Sacramento	-	41	12	53
San Bernadino Jr. College,				
San Bernadino	56	17	9	82
Mercy, San Diego	98	78	45	221
Children's, San Francisco	101	71	31	203
Franklin, San Francisco	86	39	22	147
French, San Francisco	75	35	35	145
Mary's Help, San Francisco	147	75	24	246
Mt. Zion, San Francisco	107	44	28	179
St. Francis, San Francisco	110	72	32	214
St. Joseph, San Francisco	117	48	24	189
St. Luke's, San Francisco	111	49	25	185
St. Mary's, San Francisco	79	50	36	165
Stanford U., San Francisco	132	69	37	238
U. of Calif., San Francisco	279	111	28	418
O'Connor San., San Jose	61	32	8	101
San Jose, San Jose	26	47	16	89
Santa Clara Co., San Jose	87	45	27	159
Knapp College, Santa Barbara	72	29	18	119
Sonoma Co., Santa Rosa	46	31	19	96
Hunt Memorial, Pasadena	-	34	11	45
Huntington, Mem., Pasadena	135	-	-	135
State Total	3,963	2,113	944	7,020
COLORADO				
Beth-El Gen., Colorado Springs	-	47	25	72
Seton, Colorado Springs	201	29	33	263
Children's, Denver	71	48	29	148
Denver Gen., Denver	167	94	58	319
Mercy, Denver	191	34	30	255
Presbyterian, Denver	128	99	-	227
St. Anthony's, Denver	84	59	33	176

School & City	Fiscal Years			Total
	1943-1944	1944-1945	1945-1946	
St. Joseph's, Denver	157	90	53	300
St. Luke's, Denver	156	55	68	279
U. of Colo., Boulder	93	46	-	139
Minnequa, Pueblo	73	52	18	143
Parkview, Pueblo	33	17	11	61
State Total	1,354	670	358	2,382
CONNECTICUT				
Bridgeport, Bridgeport	176	71	56	303
St. Vincent's, Bridgeport	110	81	42	233
Danbury, Danbury	50	29	31	110
Greenwich, Greenwich	40	44	-	84
Hartford, Hartford	4	104	59	167
St. Francis, Hartford	112	126	120	358
Meriden, Meriden	40	61	1	102
Middlesex, Middletown	49	30	29	108
New Britain Gen., New Britain	47	32	43	122
Grace, New Haven	27	31	38	96
St. Raphael's, New Haven	108	50	55	213
Yale U., New Haven	194	106	51	351
Lawrence Mem., New London	106	105	-	211
Norwalk Gen., Norwalk	78	36	23	137
Wm. W. Backus, Norwich	46	21	20	87
Stamford, Stamford	51	51	22	124
U. of Conn., Storrs	2	7	19	28
St. Mary's, Waterbury	78	50	38	166
Waterbury, Waterbury	71	61	43	175
State Total	1,389	1,096	690	3,175
DELAWARE				
Delaware St., Farnhurst	24	11	9	44
Beebe, Lewes	21	13	7	41
Milford Mem., Milford	31	10	10	51
Delaware, Wilmington	126	74	51	251
Memorial, Wilmington	38	43	30	111
Wilmington Gen., Wilmington	19	36	20	75
State Total	259	187	127	573
DISTRICT OF COLUMBIA				
American Univ.	45	128	43	216
Freedman's	93	52	-	145
Garfield Mem.	138	100	45	283
Georgetown Univ.	65	63	75	203
Sibley Mem.	83	6	-	89
Catholic U. Providence	152	92	20	264
St. Elizabeth's	130	20	35	185
Emergency	-	59	26	85
State Total	706	520	244	1,470

| School & City | Fiscal Years | | | Total |
	1943-1944	1944-1945	1945-1946	
FLORIDA				
Brewster, Jacksonville	19	40	26	85
St. Luke's, Jacksonville	50	36	17	103
St. Vincent's, Jacksonville	112	51	46	209
Jas. M. Jackson, Miami	187	71	25	283
Orange Gen., Orlando	21	92	27	140
Pensacola, Pensacola	155	64	46	265
Mound Park, St. Petersburg	93	42	20	155
Tampa Municipal, Tampa	64	65	28	157
Good Samaritan, West Palm Beach	52	58	26	136
Alachua County Hosp., Gainsville	-	-	17	17
State Total	753	519	278	1,550
GEORGIA				
Crawford W. Long Mem., Atlanta	201	170	45	416
Warren A. Candler, Savannah	-	52	30	82
Georgia Baptist, Atlanta	192	123	70	385
Grady Mem., Atlanta	183	69	14	266
Grady Municipal, Atlanta	169	14	63	246
Piedmont, Atlanta	104	59	28	191
St. Joseph's, Atlanta	112	40	19	171
Univ. Lamar, Augusta	61	45	-	106
Univ. Hosp.- Barrett, Augusta	112	103	-	215
Columbus City, Columbus	95	39	22	156
Emory U., Emory	207	119	49	375
Macon, Macon	126	59	34	219
Milledgeville, Milledgeville	15	19	1	35
St. Joseph's, Savannah	81	43	24	148
Warren A. Candler, Savannah	45	-	-	45
State Total	1,703	954	399	3,056
IDAHO				
St. Alphonsus, Boise	71	50	11	132
St. Luke's, Boise	64	50	15	129
Idaho Falls L.D.S., Idaho Falls	62	21	33	116
St. Joseph's, Lewiston	75	40	5	120
Mercy, Nampa	35	59	7	101
Pocatello Gen., Pocatello	54	15	-	69
St. Anthony's Mercy, Pocatello	51	24	5	80
State Total	412	259	76	747
ILLINOIS				
St. Joseph's, Alton	48	57	17	122
Memorial, Alton	42	23	17	82
Copley, Aurora	84	10	11	105
St. Chas, Aurora	30	35	13	78
St. Joseph Mercy, Aurora	68	36	21	125
Lake View, Danville	62	41	23	126

School & City	Fiscal Years			Total
	1943-1944	1944-1945	1945-1946	
Bloomington Mem., Bloomington	33	25	16	74
St. Joseph's, Bloomington	48	52	33	133
Burnham City, Champaign	87	45	32	164
American, Chicago	57	51	11	119
Augustana, Chicago	154	95	46	295
Columbus, Chicago	45	38	22	105
Cook Co., Chicago	280	135	23	438
Englewood, Chicago	82	43	21	146
Evangelical, Chicago	81	51	22	154
Franklin Blvd., Chicago	42	5	-	47
Garfield Park, Chicago	30	28	14	72
Grant, Chicago	78	66	33	177
Henrotin, Chicago	62	28	19	109
Illinois Masonic, Chicago	51	83	39	173
Jackson Park, Chicago	92	42	18	152
Lutheran Deaconess, Chicago	99	51	31	181
St. Francix Xavier-Mercy, Chicago	141	64	33	238
Michael Reese, Chicago	407	147	74	628
Mother Cabrini Mem., Chicago	53	30	15	98
Mt. Sinai, Chicago	97	72	21	190
Norwegian Am., Chicago	91	42	24	157
Presbyterian, Chicago	223	124	64	411
Provident, Chicago	46	54	14	114
Roseland Com., Chicago	76	29	13	118
St. Anne's, Chicago	151	73	53	277
St. Anthony de Padus, Chicago	56	50	10	116
St. Bernard's-Loyola, Chicago	122	58	48	228
St. Elizabeth, Chicago	72	73	47	192
St. Joseph, Chicago	102	81	39	222
St. Luke's, Chicago	252	165	62	479
St. Mary of Nazareth, Chicago	104	64	42	210
South Chicago Com., Chicago	44	35	9	88
South Shore, Chicago	37	25	19	81
Swedish Covenant, Chicago	73	41	24	138
Univ., Chicago	14	26	9	49
Women & Children's, Chicago	85	73	7	165
Wesley Memorial, Chicago	262	153	57	472
St. Elizabeth, Danville	69	35	21	125
Dixon Public, Dixon	29	25	8	62
Christian Welfare, East St. Louis	43	13	12	68
St. Mary's, E. St. Louis	84	55	21	160
St. Joseph's, Elgin	65	49	20	134
Sherman, Elgin	81	36	27	144
Evanston, Evanston	114	66	38	218
St. Francis, Evanston	95	55	60	210
Decatur & Macon Co., Decatur	89	56	21	166
Little Co., of Mary, Evergreen Park	93	78	50	221

School & City	Fiscal Years			
	1943-1944	1944-1945	1945-1946	Total
Deaconess, Freeport	50	21	8	79
St. Francis, Freeport	56	14	11	81
Galesburg Cottage, Galesburg	70	35	29	134
St. Elizabeth, Granite City	19	18	9	46
Our Savior's, Jacksonville	25	20	5	50
Passavant Mem., Jacksonville	20	12	9	41
Silver Cross, Joliet	86	32	35	153
St. Joseph's, Joliet	79	48	25	152
St. Mary's, Kankakee	59	45	25	129
St. Francis, Kewanee	18	11	3	32
St. Mary's, La Salle	35	17	11	63
St. Francis, Macomb	20	17	7	44
Lutheran, Moline	74	54	28	156
Moline Public, Moline	83	54	23	160
Brokaw, Normal	23	29	15	67
Oak Park, Oak Park	105	43	41	189
West Suburban, Oak Park	153	90	50	293
Ryburn Mem., Ottawa	13	15	12	40
Huber Mem., Pana	12	14	8	34
John C. Proctor, Peoria	21	22	10	53
Methodist, Peoria	107	41	28	176
St. Francis, Peoria	211	90	62	363
Blessing, Quincy	89	18	19	126
St. Mary's, Quincy	101	52	-	153
Rockford, Rockford	58	27	16	101
St. Anthony's, Rockford	80	65	79	224
Swedish Am., Rockford	43	39	34	116
St. Anthony's, Rock Island	51	24	9	84
St. John's, Springfield	137	103	59	299
Memorial, Springfield	104	72	27	203
Public, Sterling	10	12	8	30
Mercy, Urbana	26	21	10	57
St. Therese, Waukegan	63	48	25	136
Victory Mem., Waukegan	48	25	21	94
State Total	7,074	4,235	2,205	13,514
INDIANA				
St. John's, Anderson	42	30	24	96
St. Catherine's, E. Chicago	81	45	21	147
Prot. Deaconess, Evansville	82	85	37	204
St. Mary's, Evansville	75	69	20	164
Welborn-Walker, Evansville	26	27	12	65
Lutheran, Ft. Wayne	60	38	29	127
Methodist, Fort Wayne	37	31	17	85
St. Joseph, Ft. Wayne	123	48	37	208
Methodist Episcopal, Gary	79	62	26	167
St. Mary Mercy, Gary	99	58	33	190

School & City	Fiscal Years			Total
	1943-1944	1944-1945	1945-1946	
St. Margaret's, Hammond	86	76	45	207
Indiana Univ., Indianapolis	208	115	64	387
Indianapolis City, Indianapolis	137	88	30	255
Methodist, Indianapolis	-	149	89	238
St. Vincent's, Indianapolis	57	72	79	208
St. Joseph, Kokomo	32	26	17	75
St. Elizabeth, Lafayette	41	62	32	135
St. Joseph, Mishawaka	69	24	17	110
Ball Mem., Muncie	111	66	44	221
Reid Mem., Richmond	-	40	15	55
Epworth, South Bend	91	37	43	171
St. Joseph's, South Bend	108	47	28	183
St. Anthony, Terre Haute	107	46	29	182
Union, Terre Haute	50	45	30	125
State Total	1,801	1,386	818	4,005
IOWA				
Mercy, Burlington	55	28	23	106
Mercy, Cedar Rapids	103	50	33	186
St. Luke's M.E., Cedar Rapids	109	54	33	196
Jane Lamb Mem., Clinton	47	28	13	88
St. Joseph Mercy, Clinton	45	29	3	77
Jennie Edmundson Mem., Council Bluffs	99	49	21	169
Mercy, Council Bluffs	105	31	11	147
St. Luke's, Davenport	58	26	25	109
Broadlawns, Des Moines	137	57	36	230
Iowa Lutheran, Des Moines	114	55	26	195
Iowa Methodist, Des Moines	123	90	48	261
Mercy, Des Moines	134	51	24	209
Finley, Dubuque	64	36	18	118
St. Joseph Mercy, Dubuque	-	37	45	82
Mercy, Iowa City	29	37	30	96
State Univ., Iowa City	374	214	2	590
St. Joseph, Keokuk	30	14	-	44
Ev. Deaconess, Marshalltown	94	42	22	158
St. Thomas Mercy, Marshalltown	41	15	12	68
St. Joseph's, Ottumwa	80	16	31	127
Lutheran, Sioux City	77	22	19	118
Methodist, Sioux City	54	28	23	105
St. Joseph Mercy, Sioux City	-	79	33	112
St. Vincent's, Sioux City	74	41	13	128
Allen Memorial, Sioux City	43	17	24	84
	2,089	1,146	568	3,803

1513

School & City	Fiscal Years 1943- 1944	1944- 1945	1945- 1946	Total
KANSAS				
St. Joseph, Concordia	13	17	13	43
St. Anthony, Dodge City	33	18	10	61
Ellsworth, Ellsworth	13	-	-	13
✴ Newman Mem., Emporia	63	36	12	111
Mercy, Fort Scott	40	17	3	60
St. Catherine's, Garden City	16	4	1	21
St. Rose, Great Bend	41	15	7	63
Halstead, Halstead	87	53	14	154
Grace, Hutchinson	54	33	19	106
St. Eliz. Mercy, Hutchinson	49	19	2	70
Mercy, Independence	26	10	11	47
✴ Bethany, Kansas City	86	36	12	134
Providence, Kansas City	51	33	22	106
St. Margaret's, Kansas City	81	41	2	124
✴ U. of Kans., Kansas City	99	68	27	194
Cushing Mem., Leavenworth	21	8	6	35
St. John's, Leavenworth	16	19	6	41
St. Mary's, Manhattan	24	23	8	55
Axtell Christian, Newton	18	22	-	40
Mt. Carmel, Pittsburg	40	-	-	40
St. Anthony's, Sabetha	18	15	10	43
Asbury Protestant, Salina	53	25	1	79
St. John's Hosp., Salina	-	10	4	14
Mercy, Parsons	8	30	3	41
✴ Christ's, Topeka	66	33	37	136
Jane C. Stormont, Topeka	70	29	24	123
St. Francis, Topeka	32	26	17	75
✴ St. Francis, Wichita	140	80	35	255
✴ Wesley, Wichita	176	69	39	284
Wichita, Wichita	100	81	13	194
St. Mary's, Winfield	27	23	7	57
✴ Newton Mem., Winfield	32	28	6	66
State Total	1,593	921	371	2,885
KENTUCKY				
Berea, Berea	32	21	13	66
St. Elizabeth, Covington	120	54	25	199
Speers Mem., Dayton	33	32	7	72
Good Samaritan, Lexington	115	65	22	202
Nazareth St. Joseph, Lexington	72	67	13	152
Jewish, Louisville	37	27	6	70
Norton Mem., Louisville	93	50	31	174
Kentucky Baptist, Louisville	82	30	22	134
Louisville Gen., Louisville	145	72	20	237
Methodist Episcopal, Louisville	35	20	-	55
Nazareth St. Joseph, Louisville	145	20	48	213

1514

School & City	Fiscal Years			Total
	1943-1944	1944-1945	1945-1946	
St. Mary & Elizabeth, Louisville	43	38	22	103
St. Anthony, Louisville	56	44	25	125
Owensboro-Daviess Co., Owenboro	31	19	11	61
State Total	1,039	559	265	1,863
LOUISIANA				
Baptist, Alexandria	89	30	29	148
Baton Rouge Gen., Baton Rouge	31	28	10	69
Our Lady of the Lake, Baton Rouge	56	28	17	101
St. Francis, Monroe	40	35	22	97
Charity, New Orleans	502	230	126	858
Dillard U., New Orleans	18	12	14	44
Hotel Dieu, New Orleans	142	99	59	300
Mercy, New Orleans	72	31	19	122
Touro Inf., New Orleans	161	103	44	308
Highland, Shreveport	33	55	22	110
N. Louisiana San., Shreveport	59	43	23	125
Shreveport Charity, Shreveport	176	58	44	278
T. E. Schumpert Mem., Shreveport	43	38	25	106
Tri State, Shreveport	81	52	20	153
State Total	1,503	842	474	2,819
MAINE				
Augusta Gen., Augusta	47	14	9	70
E. Maine Gen., Bangor	134	55	34	223
Bath Mem., Bath	-	16	-	16
Webber, Biddeford	3	18	5	26
Central Maine Gen., Lewiston	48	55	26	129
St. Mary's Gen., Lewiston	42	42	26	110
Maine Gen., Portland	139	113	55	307
Maine Eye & Ear Inf., Portland	-	46	18	64
Mercy, Portland	74	55	43	172
State Street, Portland	22	-	-	22
Sisters Hosp., Waterville	74	49	27	150
State Total	583	463	243	1,289
MARYLAND				
Church Home & Inf., Baltimore	65	45	23	133
Franklin Sq., Baltimore	30	31	16	77
Johns Hopkins, Baltimore	491	120	40	651
Hosp. for Women of Md., Baltimore	69	36	18	123
St. Agnes, Baltimore	116	36	44	196
St. Joseph's, Baltimore	85	49	27	161
Sinai, Baltimore	98	73	13	184
S. Baltimore Gen., Baltimore	56	35	25	116
Mercy, Baltimore	174	70	31	275
Union Mem., Baltimore	175	90	40	305

School & City	Fiscal Years			Total
	1943-1944	1944-1945	1945-1946	
W. Baltimore Gen., Baltimore	95	59	32	186
Alleghany, Cumberland	61	64	-	125
Memorial, Cumberland	31	61	13	105
Frederick City, Frederick	20	21	13	54
Washington Co., Hagerstown	90	18	38	146
Peninsula Gen., Salisbury	-	22	13	35
State Total	1,656	830	386	2,872
MASSACHUSETTS				
Symmes Arlington, Arlington	49	27	17	93
Beverly, Beverly	72	46	28	146
Beth Israel, Boston	68	61	26	155
Boston City, Boston	227	134	25	386
Carney, Boston	107	88	47	242
Children's, Boston	83	44	34	161
Faulkner, Boston	92	46	23	161
Mass. Gen., Boston	389	182	120	691
Mass. Mem., Boston	142	82	44	268
St. Margaret's, Boston	60	61	26	147
New England Baptist, Boston	83	45	39	167
New England Deaconess, Boston	7	84	48	139
New Eng. Hosp. for Women & Child., Boston	42	41	19	102
Peter Bent Brigham, Boston	81	61	25	167
✳e Simmons College, Boston	48	32	-	80
St. Elizabeth's, Brighton	95	77	37	209
Brockton, Brockton	18	24	18	60
Cambridge, Cambridge	218	67	44	329
Cambridge City, Cambridge	118	52	35	205
Chelsea Mem., Chelsea	17	33	18	68
Clinton, Clinton	-	-	31	31
Shidden Mem., Everett	46	28	17	91
St. Anne's, Fall River	36	27	19	82
Truesdale, Fall River	75	42	23	140
Union, Fall River	64	29	22	115
✳c Burbank, Fitchburg	114	61	40	215
Framingham U., Framingham	52	35	20	107
Henry Heywood Mem., Gardner	61	41	24	126
Addison Gilbert, Gloucester	4	17	11	32
Holyoke, Holyoke	62	32	23	117
Providence, Holyoke	19	36	35	90
Lawrence Gen., Lawrence	65	39	26	130
Leominster, Leominster	45	25	13	83
Lowell Gen., Lowell	68	46	24	138
St. John's, Lowell	160	76	43	279
St. Joseph's, Lowell	79	39	20	138
Lynn, Lynn	75	39	20	134
Malden, Malden	52	40	23	115

1516

School & City	Fiscal Years			Total
	1943-1944	1944-1945	1945-1946	
Lawrence Mem., Medford	69	13	21	103
Melrose, Melrose	8	38	16	62
St. Luke's, New Bedford	112	47	44	203
Newton, Newton Lower Falls	149	70	39	258
Cooley Dickinson, Northampton	66	41	30	137
House of Mercy, Pittsfield	64	37	24	125
St. Luke's, Pittsfield	19	40	33	92
Quincy City, Quincy	130	62	36	228
Salem, Salem	126	62	45	233
Somerville, Somerville	108	53	25	186
Mercy, Springfield	28	58	46	132
Springfield, Springfield	90	55	23	168
Morton, Taunton	34	29	8	71
Waltham, Waltham	74	36	26	136
McLean, Waverly	53	30	14	97
Choate Mem., Woburn	24	25	13	62
Memorial, Worcester	36	31	18	85
St. Vincent, Worcester	14	56	43	113
Worcester City, Worcester	141	70	41	252
Worcester Hannemann, Worcester	58	42	12	112
State Total	4,496	2,834	1,664	8,994
MICHIGAN				
U. of Mich., Ann Arbor	297	194	119	610
Community, Battle Creek	81	44	22	147
Mercy, Benton Harbor	27	30	18	75
Ev. Deaconess, Detroit	87	48	26	161
Grace, Detroit	291	156	69	516
Harper, Detroit	181	94	54	329
Henry Ford, Detroit	279	141	66	486
Mercy College, Detroit	-	153	159	312
Providence, Detroit	293	100	3	396
St. Mary's, Detroit	86	79	38	203
Hurley, Flint	234	72	40	346
Butterworth, Grand Rapids	214	93	28	335
Mercy Central, Grand Rapids	346	147	101	594
Blodgett Mem., Grand Rapids	61	52	43	156
St. Francis, Hamtramck	34	25	15	74
St. Joseph's, Hancock	37	25	9	71
Highland Pk. Gen., Highland Park	69	63	14	146
W. A. Fotte Mem., Jackson	-	48	22	70
Bronson Methodist, Kalamazoo	73	27	30	130
Kalamazoo State, Kalamazoo	14	6	-	20
Borgess, Kalamazoo	113	86	24	223
Edward W. Sparrow, Lansing	34	38	35	107
St. Lawrence, Lansing	57	47	55	159
St. Luke's, Marquette	59	25	-	84
St. Joseph's, Mt. Clemens	92	52	27	171

1517

School & City	Fiscal Years			Total
	1943-1944	1944-1945	1945-1946	
Saginaw Gen., Saginaw	67	55	48	170
St. Mary's, Saginaw	120	79	12	211
Traverse City State, Traverse City	75	12	2	89
State Total	3,321	1,991	1,079	6,391
MINNESOTA				
St. Francis, Breckenridge	15	16	15	46
St. Luke's, Duluth	150	80	45	275
St. Mary's, Duluth	143	85	-	228
Hibbing Gen., Hibbing	60	36	-	96
St. Gabriel's, Little Falls	28	18	16	62
Abbott, Minneapolis	161	67	51	279
Hamline-Asbury, Minneapolis	144	76	50	270
Eitel, Minneapolis	99	41	21	161
Fairview, Minneapolis	164	82	36	282
Lutheran Deaconess, Minneapolis	85	32	20	137
Northwestern, Minneapolis	188	98	33	319
St. Andrew's, Minneapolis	58	27	8	93
St. Barnabas, Minneapolis	119	63	31	213
St. Mary's Coll. of St. Catherine, Minneapolis	84	-	-	84
Swedish, Minneapolis	189	60	53	302
Univ. of Minn., Minneapolis	857	606	177	1,640
St. John's, Red Wing	26	27	19	72
Kahler, Rochester	423	181	66	670
St. Mary's, Rochester	362	187	64	613
St. Cloud, St. Cloud	92	59	37	188
Ancker, St. Paul	105	44	18	167
Bethesda, St. Paul	154	74	27	255
Mounds Pk. Midway, St. Paul	113	33	36	182
St. Joseph Coll. of St. Catherine, St. Paul	108	-	-	108
College of St. Catherine, St. Paul	237	218	123	578
State Total	4,164	2,210	946	7,320
MISSISSIPPI				
New Biloxi, Biloxi	36	31	13	80
Miss. Baptist, Jackson	118	79	11	208
Vicksburg Hosp. & Clinic, Vicksburg	23	37	2	62
State Total	177	147	26	350
MISSOURI				
St. Joseph, Boonville	18	17	14	49
U. of Mo., Columbia	18	8	10	36
Ind. San., Independence	73	45	37	155
St. John's, Joplin	12	21	3	36
K. C. Gen., Kansas City	163	86	11	260

1518

School & City	Fiscal Years			Total
	1943-1944	1944-1945	1945-1946	
K. C. Gen. #2, Kansas City	68	38	26	132
Research, Kansas City	72	48	28	148
St. Joseph, Kansas City	94	62	35	191
St. Luke's, Kansas City	145	76	33	254
St. Mary's, Kansas City	89	44	25	158
Trinity Lutheran, Kansas City	100	29	18	147
Mo. Methodist, St. Joseph	80	36	14	130
St. Joseph's, St. Joseph	59	36	13	108
De Paul, St. Louis	132	54	46	232
Homer G. Phillips, St. Louis	138	63	20	221
Jewish, St. Louis	135	67	44	246
Lutheran, St. Louis	-	46	23	69
Missouri Baptist, St. Louis	96	92	59	247
St. John's, St. Louis	29	44	30	103
St. Louis City, St. Louis	267	120	59	446
St. Louis U., St. Louis	61	28	17	106
St. Luke's, St. Louis	75	67	39	181
St. Mary's, St. Louis	20	47	38	105
Washington U., St. Louis	232	149	64	445
Burge, Springfield	19	33	9	61
St. John's, Springfield	36	39	24	99
Springfield Baptist, Springfield	48	27	12	87
State Total	2,279	1,422	751	4,452
MONTANA				
Columbus, Great Falls	161	54	16	231
Deaconess, Bozeman	488	216	2	706
Sacred Heart, Havre	73	46	9	128
St. Joseph, Lewiston	45	15	6	66
St. Patrick's, Missoula	119	44	13	176
Charity Central, Billings	297	124	40	461
State Total	1,183	499	86	1,768
NEBRASKA				
St. Joseph's, Alliance	44	27	13	84
St. Francis, Grand Island	72	42	18	132
Mary Lanning, Hastings	94	35	-	129
Bryan Mem., Lincoln	34	44	19	97
Lincoln Gen., Lincoln	99	39	44	182
St. Elizabeth, Lincoln	95	47	30	172
Clarkson Mem., Omaha	54	22	48	124
Creighton Mem., Omaha	167	23	50	240
Immanuel, Omaha	59	44	29	132
Nebr. Methodist, Omaha	152	61	34	247
St. Catherine's, Omaha	136	17	33	186
U. of Nebraska, Omaha	136	74	51	261
State Total	1,142	475	369	1,986

School & City	Fiscal Years			Total
	1943-1944	1944-1945	1945-1946	
NEW HAMPSHIRE				
Nashua Mem., Nashua	64	21	12	97
St. Joseph's, Nashua	52	33	23	108
St. Louis, Berlin	19	26	10	55
Margaret Pillsbury Gen., Concord	28	21	10	59
N. H. Memorial, Concord	30	22	10	62
Hillsborough C., Grasmere	41	18	-	59
Mary Hitchcock, Hanover	99	47	24	170
Elliott Community, Keene	21	31	11	63
Laconia, Laconia	10	23	12	45
Elliott, Manchester	60	39	16	115
Notre Dame de Lourdes, Manchester	56	31	26	113
Sacred Heart, Manchester	52	35	35	122
State Total	532	347	189	1,068
NEW JERSEY				
Atlantic City, Atlantic City	96	69	36	201
Bayonne, Bayonne	79	55	29	163
Cooper, Camden	49	51	33	133
West Jersey, Camden	47	43	25	115
E. Orange Gen., East Orange	43	21	14	78
Elizabeth Gen., Elizabeth	62	37	22	121
St. Elizabeth, Elizabeth	41	26	13	80
Englewood, Englewood	94	55	30	179
Hackensack, Hackensack	129	95	55	279
St. Mary's, Hoboken	76	64	26	166
Christ, Jersey City	128	70	23	221
✳e Jersey City Med. Cen., Jersey City	453	239	74	766
St. Francis, Jersey City	70	47	25	142
Monmouth Mem., Long Branch	95	57	35	187
Mountainside, Montclair	65	48	25	138
All Souls, Morristown	54	23	15	92
Fitkin Morgan, Neptune	20	44	22	86
St. Barnabas, Newark	115	49	27	191
Newark Beth Israel, Newark	54	36	18	108
Newark City, Newark	119	47	26	192
Newark Memorial, Newark	33	16	10	59
Presbyterian, Newark	157	46	40	243
St. James, Newark	47	19	14	80
St. Michael's, Newark	129	77	37	243
Middlesex Gen., New Brunswick	53	32	15	100
St. Peter's Gen., New Brunswick	132	74	42	248
Orange Mem., Orange	121	59	45	225
St. Mary's, Orange	25	21	7	53
Passaic Gen., Passaic	6	20	10	36
St. Mary's, Passaic	56	36	27	119
Barnert Mem., Paterson	36	25	6	67

School & City	Fiscal Years			Total
	1943-1944	1944-1945	1945-1946	
Paterson Gen., Paterson	66	57	22	145
St. Joseph's, Paterson	61	82	57	200
Perth Amboy, Perth Amboy	22	30	19	71
Muhlenberg, Plainfield	75	60	41	176
Somerset, Somerville	49	34	21	104
Overlook, Summit	24	29	18	71
Holy Name, Teaneck	110	38	48	196
Mercer, Trenton	102	53	34	189
St. Francis, Trenton	137	65	55	257
Wm. McKinley Mem., Trenton	33	21	13	67
State Total	3,363	2,070	1,154	6,587
NEW MEXICO				
Regina St. Joseph, Albuquerque	95	55	23	173
State Total	95	55	23	173
NEW YORK				
College of St. Rose, Albany	13	37	27	77
Memorial, Albany	24	21	17	62
Alfred U., Alfred	46	54	25	125
Amsterdam City, Amsterdam	82	33	20	135
St. Mary's, Amsterdam	49	34	16	99
Auburn City, Auburn	104	29	36	169
St. Jerome's, Batavia	12	15	21	48
Binghamton City, Binghamton	93	56	53	202
Binghamton State, Binghamton	21	16	7	44
Brooklyn, Brooklyn	79	77	51	207
Brooklyn State, Brooklyn	53	40	14	107
Pilgrim State, Brentwood	9	12	6	27
Cumberland, Brooklyn	54	30	7	91
Bushwick, Brooklyn	31	22	17	70
Israel Zion, Brooklyn	29	22	15	66
Jewish, Brooklyn	199	92	36	327
Kings Co., Brooklyn	361	229	74	664
Long Island College, Brooklyn	94	82	40	216
Methodist, Brooklyn	121	82	47	250
Norwegian Lutheran, Brooklyn	45	34	20	99
Prospect Heights, Brooklyn	48	47	16	111
St. Catherine's, Brooklyn	44	63	32	139
Buffalo General, Buffalo	130	54	35	219
Children's, Buffalo	23	27	25	75
Deaconess, Buffalo	29	88	61	178
Edward J. Meyer, Buffalo	437	144	61	642
Mercy, Buffalo	-	28	42	70
Sisters of Charity, Buffalo	56	30	42	128
Central Islip State, Central Islip	55	27	11	93
Arnot-Ogden Mem., Elmira	76	34	29	139
St. Joseph's, Elmira	116	32	30	178

| School & City | Fiscal Years | | | |
	1943-1944	1944-1945	1945-1946	Total
Flushing, Flushing	89	61	20	170
Adelphi, Garden City	321	246	166	733
Nathan Littauer, Gloversville	34	11	15	60
Gowanda State Home, Helmuth	6	-	-	6
St. James Mercy, Hornell	42	17	15	74
Hudson City, Hudson	40	33	12	85
Mary Immaculate, Jamaica	63	31	53	149
Chas. S. Wilson, Johnson City	114	51	51	216
Keuka College, Keuka Park	79	95	1	175
Kings Park State, Kings Park	11	-	-	11
Kingston, Kingston	53	23	16	92
Benedictine, Kingston	42	24	20	86
Our Lady of Victory, Lackawana	23	24	32	79
St. John's L. I. City, L. I.	74	53	32	159
Middletown State, Middletown	17	11	-	28
Mt. Vernon, Mt. Vernon	41	31	19	91
St. Luke's, Newburgh	-	17	12	29
New Rochelle, New Rochelle	46	45	24	115
Bellevue, . Y. City	476	262	77	815
Beth Israel, N. Y.	120	45	19	184
College of Mt. St. Vincent, N. Y.	6	37	-	43
Fordham, New York	92	59	19	170
Flower Fifth Ave., N. Y.	164	71	50	285
Harlem, N. Y.	85	59	24	168
Lenox Hill, N. Y.	139	79	57	275
Lincoln, N. Y.	46	33	24	103
Manhattan State, N. Y.	18	14	5	37
Manhattanville, N. Y.	74	71	50	195
Metropolitan, N. Y.	221	73	31	325
Misericordia, N. Y.	68	49	34	151
Mt. Sinai, N. Y.	96	111	59	266
Cornell U. N. Y. Hosp., N. Y.	209	125	49	383
Columbia, U., N. Y.	32	-	-	32
Pres. Hosp. Sch., N. Y.	-	60	47	107
St. Luke's, N. Y.	218	121	74	413
St. Vincent's, N. Y.	83	102	59	244
St. Lawrence, Ogdensburg	35	19	-	54
Hartwick, Oneonta	49	59	22	130
Champlain Valley, Plattsburg	68	41	20	129
State Teachers, Plattsburg	74	112	71	257
Hudson River State, Poughkeepsie	22	9	8	39
St. Francis, Poughkeepsie	64	28	17	109
Vassar Brothers, Poughkeepsie	91	48	22	161
Creedmoor State, Queens Village	17	16	5	38
Genesee, Rochester	59	47	30	136
Highland, Rochester	41	36	25	102
Nazareth Coll., Rochester	12	29	21	62
Park Ave., Rochester	34	23	18	75

School & City	Fiscal Years			Total
	1943–1944	1944–1945	1945–1946	
Rochester Gen., Rochester	94	65	31	190
Rochester State, Rochester	25	-	-	25
St. Mary's, Rochester	181	78	38	297
✳c,e U. of Rochester, Strong Mem., Rochester	88	103	54	245
✳b Skidmore College, Saratoga Springs	9	19	-	28
Ellis, Schenectady	55	62	42	159
Craig Colony, Sonyea	4	7	-	11
Southampton, Southampton	35	15	7	57
✳b Wagner College, Staten Island	94	88	42	224
Crouse Irwing, Syracuse	2	36	47	85
General, Syracuse	-	22	9	31
✳b,c Syracuse Mem., Syracuse	62	1	4	67
✳ Syracuse U., Syracuse	151	122	78	351
Good Shepherd, Syracuse U., Syracuse	32	1	-	33
✳b Russell Sage, Albany Hosp., Troy	196	90	2	288
Samaritan, Troy	74	43	33	150
Utica State, Utica	19	11	7	37
Westchester, Valhalla	84	40	29	153
Good Sam., Watertown	67	-	-	67
Mercy, Watertown	69	42	16	127
Wyoming Co. Community, Warsaw	41	14	13	68
White Plains, White Plains	23	41	34	98
Harlem Valley St., Wingdale	19	7	-	26
St. John's Riverside, Yonkers	107	34	27	168
Yonkers Gen., Yonkers	34	-	-	34
Union Univ., Albany	-	-	35	35
State Total	7,906	5,143	2,906	15,955
NORTH CAROLINA				
Asheville Mission, Asheville	64	41	-	105
Grace, Banner Elk	31	7	7	45
Charlotte Mem., Charlotte	107	57	37	201
Mercy, Charlotte	41	40	27	108
✳ Presbyterian, Charlotte	24	65	27	116
Cabarrus County, Concord	53	46	16	115
✳ Duke U., Durham	157	119	57	333
Lincoln, Durham	50	16	42	108
Watts, Durham	130	64	31	225
Highsmith, Fayetteville	37	43	15	95
St. Leo's, Greensboro	20	91	30	141
Burrus Mem., High Point	40	20	15	75
Mem. Gen., Kingston	22	16	6	44
Thompson Mem., Lumberton	11	6	-	17
Grace, Morganton	49	29	10	88
Martin Mem., Mt. Airy	30	17	10	57
Dorothea Dix State Hosp., Raleigh	40	9	-	49

School & City	Fiscal Years			Total
	1943-1944	1944-1945	1945-1946	
Rex, Raleigh	118	45	25	188
St. Agnes, Raleigh	65	38	20	123
Park View, Rocky Mt.	29	20	11	60
Rocky Mt. San., Rocky Mt.	24	10	-	34
Rutherford, Rutherfordton	25	19	-	44
Rowan Mem., Salisbury	-	-	17	17
Shelby, Shelby	61	21	16	98
H. F. Long, Statesville	35	27	12	74
Community, Wilmington	39	23	20	82
Jas. Walker Mem., Wilmington	56	46	28	130
Carolina Gen., Wilson	39	10	12	61
Woodward Herring, Wilson	27	19	10	56
City Memorial, Winston Salem	36	39	23	98
Reynolds Mem., Winston Salem	60	14	10	84
N. C. Baptist, Winston Salem	115	71	38	224
State Total	1,635	1,088	572	3,295
NORTH DAKOTA				
Bismarck Ev., Bismarck	94	13	15	122
St. Alexius, Bismarck	101	37	16	154
St. Andrew's, Bottineau	23	4	1	28
Devil's Lake Gen., Devil's Lake	3	2	-	5
Mercy, Devil's Lake	22	12	9	43
St. John's, Fargo	141	66	46	253
St. Luke's, Fargo	105	62	38	205
Grafton Deaconess, Grafton	21	-	-	21
Grand Forks Deaconess, Grand Forks	95	49	12	156
St. Michael's, Grand Forks	56	46	32	134
Trinity, Jamestown	59	17	22	98
St. Joseph's, Minot	68	29	10	107
Good Samaritan, Rugby	29	24	4	57
Mercy, Valley City	43	23	6	72
Mercy, Williston	25	5	-	30
Trinity, Minot	125	42	28	195
State Total	1,010	431	239	1,680
OHIO				
City, Akron	227	77	26	330
Peoples, Akron	99	27	6	132
St. Thomas, Akron	109	45	8	162
Alliance City, Alliance	47	35	6	88
Samaritan, Ashland	-	19	9	28
Aultman, Canton	192	69	58	319
Mercy, Canton	186	56	-	242
Bethesda, Cincinnati	108	60	39	207
✳ Christ, Cincinnati	276	124	78	478
Deaconess, Cincinnati	76	90	-	166
✳ Good Samaritan, Cincinnati	224	106	81	411

School & City	Fiscal Years			Total
	1943-1944	1944-1945	1945-1946	
Jewish, Cincinnati	135	83	59	277
U. of Cincinnati, Cincinnati	75	79	41	195
City, Cleveland	154	75	60	289
Huron Road, Cleveland	140	77	41	258
Fairview Park, Cleveland	135	75	38	248
Glenville, Cleveland	-	34	-	34
Lutheran, Cleveland	81	34	33	148
Mt. Sinai, Cleveland	99	52	26	177
St. Alexis, Cleveland	83	69	42	194
St. John's, Cleveland	124	42	48	214
St. Luke's, Cleveland	199	89	44	332
St. Vincent Charity, Cleveland	130	50	28	208
Western Reserve, Cleveland	349	156	88	593
Grant, Columbus	121	85	45	251
Mt. Carmel, Columbus	161	102	41	304
Ohio State, Columbus	117	54	23	194
St. Francis, Columbus	35	37	24	96
White Cross, Columbus	151	70	60	281
Good Samaritan, Dayton	114	126	-	240
Miami Valley, Dayton	166	112	65	343
St. Elizabeth, Dayton	129	91	32	252
E. Liverpool City, E. Liverpool	30	14	16	60
Holzer, Gallipolis	66	37	22	125
Mercy, Hamilton	153	50	7	210
Lima Memorial, Lima	30	23	18	71
St. Rita's, Lima	62	24	32	118
Mansfield Gen., Mansfield	35	22	20	77
Martin's Ferry, Martin's Ferry	33	19	18	70
Massillon City, Massillon	91	46	2	139
Massillon State, Massillon	45	24	12	81
Middletown, Middletown	34	42	24	100
Newark, Newark	37	16	12	65
Mercy, Portsmouth	39	27	11	77
Salem City, Salem	7	11	10	28
Providence, Sandusky	22	29	3	54
Springfield City, Springfield	50	34	23	107
Ohio Valley, Steubenville	50	61	-	111
Flower, Toledo	94	60	20	174
Lucas Co., Toledo	81	40	10	131
Mercy, Toledo	148	71	33	252
Robinwood, Toledo	63	34	10	107
St. Vincent's, Toledo	239	63	19	321
Toledo, Toledo	119	59	43	221
Toledo State, Toledo	42	17	2	61
Women & Children, Toledo	33	22	21	76
Warren City, Warren	66	54	4	124
St. Elizabeth's, Youngstown	166	108	57	331
Youngstown Hosp. Assn., Youngstown	227	142	39	408

1525

School & City	Fiscal Years 1943-1944	1944-1945	1945-1946	Total
Bethesda, Zanesville	49	51	-	100
Good Samaritan, Zanesville	67	11	19	97
State Total	6,420	3,511	1,656	11,587
OKLAHOMA				
W. Okla. Charity, Clinton	42	37	12	91
Enid Gen., Enid	-	20	8	28
St. Mary's, Enid	3	12	6	21
University, Enid	-	29	-	29
Muskogee Gen., Muskogee	47	25	8	80
Okla. Baptist, Muskogee	42	16	6	64
Ok. City Gen., Ok. City	69	52	28	149
St. Anthony's, Okla. City	113	73	10	196
Wesley, Oklahoma City	122	46	8	176
Univ. of Okla., Oklahoma City	157	92	19	268
Ponca City, Ponca City	44	22	5	71
Hillcrest Mem., Tulsa	116	81	12	209
St. John's, Tulsa	150	67	21	238
State Total	905	572	143	1,620
OREGON				
St. Mary's, Astoria	19	27	18	64
St. Elizabeth, Baker	29	35	12	76
St. Anthony's, Pendleton	33	27	21	81
Emanuel, Portland	224	80	51	355
Good Samaritan, Portland	184	63	22	269
Providence, Portland	29	75	38	142
✳ U. of Oregon, Portland	159	132	21	312
The Dalles, The Dalles	71	33	28	132
Sacred Heart, Eugene	99	49	28	176
✳ U. of Portland, Portland	109	42	39	190
St. Vincent's, Portland	32	99	1	132
State Total	988	662	279	1,929
PENNSYLVANIA				
Abington Mem., Abington	131	62	62	255
Allentown, Allentown	157	78	36	276
Sacred Heart, Allentown	58	27	30	115
Altoona, Altoona	60	34	10	104
Mercy, Altoona	50	25	27	102
Ashland, Ashland	42	43	30	115
Providence, Beaver Falls	55	27	-	82
St. Luke's, Bethleham	100	62	61	223
Braddock Gen., Braddock	29	34	35	98
Bradford, Bradford	18	18	19	55
Brownsville Gen., Brownsville	62	28	15	105
Bryn Mawr, Bryn Mawr	59	61	30	150
Butler Co. Mem., Butler	46	61	53	160

School & City	Fiscal Years			Total
	1943-1944	1944-1945	1945-1946	
Cannonsburg Gen., Cannonsburg	13	17	19	49
St. Joseph's, Carbondale	48	18	24	90
Chester, Chester	83	26	21	130
Clearfield , Clearfield	50	42	18	110
Coatesville, Coatesville	32	15	15	62
Geisinger Mem., Danville	95	41	44	180
Easton, Easton	61	34	26	121
Hamot, Erie	93	52	48	183
St. Vincent's, Erie	52	45	37	134
Westmoreland, Greensburg	124	38	-	162
Harrisburg, Harrisburg	116	63	64	243
Harrisburg Polyclinic, Harrisburg	87	49	29	165
Homestead, Homestead	44	35	31	110
Indiana, Indiana	80	46	30	156
Conemaugh Valley Mem., Johnstown	150	65	48	263
Mercy, Johnstown	45	30	30	105
Nesbitt Mem., Kingston	55	30	35	120
Lancaster Gen., Lancaster	64	47	25	136
St. Joseph, Lancaster	31	46	34	111
Latrobe, Latrobe	39	26	25	90
Good Samaritan, Lebanon	22	10	11	43
Lewistown, Lewistown	35	8	14	57
McKeesport, McKeesport	116	52	40	208
Ohio Valley Gen., McKees Rocks	17	18	10	45
Meadville City, Meadville	80	26	-	106
Spencer, Meadville	52	19	21	92
Beaver Valley, New Brighton	20	9	14	43
Lockhaven, Lockhaven	10	12	12	34
Jameson Mem., New Castle	81	52	34	167
New Castle, New Castle	58	29	19	106
Citizens Gen., New Kensington	92	13	21	126
Montgomery, Norristown	59	34	30	123
Oil City, Oil City	47	14	19	80
Chestnut Hill, Philadelphia	44	29	15	88
Children's, Philadelphia	19	-	-	19
Frankford, Philadelphia	65	33	21	119
Germantown, Philadelphia	143	54	27	224
Hanhemann Hospital, Philadelphia	180	122	83	385
Jefferson, Philadelphia	160	95	68	323
Jewish, Philadelphia	138	68	39	245
Lankenau, Philadelphia	113	58	28	199
Mercy, Philadelphia	57	20	24	101
Methodist, Philadelphia	55	46	37	138
Mt. Sinai, Philadelphia	138	42	18	198
Northeastern, Philadelphia	45	18	15	78
Osteopathic, Philadelphia	45	30	28	103
Phila. Gen., Philadelphia	392	204	145	741
Pennsylvania, Philadelphia	122	54	45	221

School & City	Fiscal Years			Total
	1943-1944	1944-1945	1945-1946	
Presbyterian, Philadelphia	190	95	34	319
Prot. Episcopal, Phila.	218	84	39	341
St. Agnes, Phila.	29	69	48	146
St. Joseph's, Phila.	44	42	45	131
St. Luke's & Childrens, Phila.	112	52	23	187
Temple U., Phila.	252	133	88	473
✳ U. of Pa., Phila.	361	229	98	688
Woman's, Phila.	61	40	17	118
Woman's Med., Phila.	38	37	17	92
Woman's Homeopathic, Phila.	39	25	17	81
Philipsburg State, Philipsburg	65	37	29	131
Mercy, Pittsburgh	154	133	74	361
✳ Mercy, Duquesne, Pittsburgh	61	16	17	94
Montefiore, Pittsburgh	75	39	26	140
Pittsburgh, Pittsburgh	125	53	-	178
Presbyterian, Pittsburgh	201	101	61	363
✳ U. of Pittsburgh, Pittsburgh	108	60	22	190
Shadyside, Pittsburgh	160	71	41	272
Suburban Gen., Pittsburgh	54	28	18	100
Mt. Carmel, Pittsburgh	-	27	3	30
St. Francis, Pittsburgh	275	121	80	476
St. John's Gen., Pittsburgh	62	50	26	138
St. Joseph, Pittsburgh	37	26	29	92
St. Margaret's, Pittsburgh	32	25	17	74
South Side, Pittsburgh	37	28	21	86
✳ Western Pa., Pittsburgh	164	94	61	319
Pittston, Pittston	76	20	24	120
Pottstown, Pottstown	11	20	4	35
Pottsville Hosp., Pottsville	21	36	-	57
Reading, Reading	156	77	37	270
St. Joseph's, Reading	86	61	40	187
Rochester Gen., Rochester	22	15	11	48
Robert Packer, Sayre	125	52	51	228
Moses Taylor, Scranton	90	28	1	119
Hanhemann, Scranton	95	31	-	126
Mercy, Scranton	34	24	23	81
St. Mary's Mater Misericordiae, Scranton	40	19	20	79
Scranton State, Scranton	108	59	24	191
West Side, Scranton	30	17	13	60
Sewickley Valley, Sewickley	23	33	24	80
Miners, Spangler	61	10	14	85
Christian H. Buhl, Sharon	65	53	43	161
Allegheny Valley, Tarentum	-	38	-	38
Uniontown, Uniontown	69	29	29	157
Chester Co., West Chester	48	32	23	103
Mercy, Wilkes-Barre	144	63	31	238
Wilkes-Barre Gen., Wilkes-Barre	81	56	35	172

School & City	Fiscal Years			Total
	1943-1944	1944-1945	1945-1946	
Homeopathic, Wilkes-Barre	48	12	19	79
Columbia, Wilkinsburg	40	35	23	98
Williamsport, Williamsport	84	54	30	168
York, York	68	32	21	121
State Total	9,213	5,115	3,340	17,668
RHODE ISLAND				
St. Hosp. for Mental Diseases, Howard	7	-	-	7
Newport, Newport	38	52	26	116
Memorial, Pawtucket	114	54	26	194
Homeopathic, Providence	73	34	31	138
R. I. Hosp., Providence	270	146	61	477
St. Joseph, Providence	74	36	37	147
State Total	576	322	181	1,079
SOUTH CAROLINA				
Anderson Co., Anderson	73	45	-	118
Camden, Camden	32	17	5	54
Medical College, Charleston	172	74	21	267
St. Francis, Charleston	41	31	16	88
Columbia, Columbia	203	106	24	333
Good Samaritan- Waverly, Columbia	29	28	13	70
S. C. Baptist, Columbia	64	40	10	114
S. C. State, Columbia	16	2	-	18
McLeod Inf., Florence	96	65	27	188
Greenville, Greenville	136	98	27	261
Tri County, Orangeburg	82	36	9	127
York Co., Rock Hill	30	35	19	84
Spartanburg Gen., Spartanburg	163	63	32	258
Tuomey, Sumter	55	25	8	88
State Total	1,192	665	211	2,068
SOUTH DAKOTA				
Presentation, Aberdeen	491	148	85	724
Sprague, Huron	44	24	10	78
M. E. State, Mitchell	94	38	13	145
St. Mary's, Pierre	61	9	19	89
St. John's, McNamara, Rapid City	37	68	-	105
Sioux Valley, Sioux Falls	124	76	30	230
Bartron, Watertown	39	24	14	77
Luther, Watertown	39	17	-	56
Peabody, Webster	38	-	-	38
Sacred Heart, Yankton	51	25	18	94
State Total	1,018	429	189	1,636

School & City	Fiscal Years			Total
	1943-1944	1944-1945	1945-1946	
TENNESSEE				
Baroness Erlanger, Chattanooga	267	134	31	432
Appalachian, Johnson City	32	20	9	61
Fort Sanders, Knoxville	112	78	2	192
Knoxville Gen., Knoxville	105	57	19	181
St. Mary's, Knoxville	78	41	28	147
Baptist Mem., Memphis	275	143	42	460
Methodist, Memphis	208	107	33	348
St. Joseph, Memphis	89	92	13	194
U. of Tenn., Memphis	255	146	27	428
Meharry Med., Nashville	86	33	30	149
Nashville Gen., Nashville	127	66	23	216
Protestant, Nashville	37	28	21	86
St. Thomas, Nashville	101	61	42	204
Vanderbilt, Nashville	114	39	26	179
State Total	1,886	1,045	346	3,277
TEXAS				
Hendrick Mem., Abilene	72	56	22	150
N. W. Texas, Amarillo	108	36	-	144
St. Anthony's, Amarillo	76	44	16	136
Brackenridge, Austin	122	56	33	211
Seton, Austin	99	24	30	153
Hotel Dieu, Beaumont	77	19	25	121
Corpus Christi, Corpus Christi	49	30	-	79
Baylor U., Dallas	214	97	59	370
Methodist, Dallas	137	71	33	241
Parkland, Dallas	141	79	35	255
St. Paul's, Dallas	141	86	43	270
Hotel Dieu, El Paso	60	38	27	125
City-County, Ft. Worth	76	39	12	127
Harris Mem. Methodist Hosp., Ft. Worth	205	90	52	347
St. Joseph's, Ft. Worth	133	36	22	191
John Sealy, Galveston	228	85	62	375
St. Mary's, Galveston	60	24	10	94
Hermann, Houston	67	100	1	168
Jefferson Davis, Houston	159	92	30	281
Memorial, Houston	193	92	-	285
Methodist, Houston	78	40	9	127
St. Joseph's Inf., Houston	95	90	41	226
Lubbock Gen., Lubbock	64	41	19	124
W. Texas, Lubbock	69	37	27	133
McKinney City, McKinney	19	6	10	35
St. Mary's, Port Arthur	70	19	14	103
Shannon W. Tex. Mem., San Angelo	-	75	37	112
Medical & Surgical, San Antonio	93	71	49	213
Prairie View, Prairie View	-	41	-	41

School & City	Fiscal Years			Total
	1943-1944	1944-1945	1945-1946	
Shannon W. Texas., San Angelo	69	-	-	69
Physicians-Surgeons, San Antonio	56	49	-	105
Robt. B. Green, San Antonio	75	45	-	120
Santa Rosa, San Antonio	69	104	79	252
Wilson N. Jones, Sherman	57	35	-	92
King's Daughters, Temple	75	40	22	137
Hillcrest Mem., Waco	52	66	28	146
Providence, Waco	110	59	31	200
Wichita Gen., Wichita Falls	65	39	10	114
State Total	3,533	2,051	888	6,472
UTAH				
Wm. Budge Mem., Logan	23	15	3	41
Thomas D. Dee, Ogden	125	57	-	182
Latter Day Saints, Salt Lake City	262	120	-	382
Holy Cross, Salt Lake City	155	55	31	241
St. Mark's, Salt Lake City	135	59	1	195
Salt Lake Co. Gen., Salt Lake City	211	96	-	307
State Total	911	402	35	1,348
VERMONT				
Barre City, Barre	42	28	17	87
Bishop DeGoesbriand, Burlington	76	15	15	106
Mary Fletcher, Burlington	55	47	29	131
Heaton, Montpelier	35	35	9	79
Rutland, Rutland	40	34	13	87
St. Albans, St. Albans	26	21	13	60
Fanny Allen, Winooski	51	38	28	117
State Total	325	218	124	667
VIRGINIA				
Johnston Mem., Abingdon	45	13	8	66
Alexandria, Alexandria	34	41	17	92
U. of Virginia, Charlottesville	258	129	67	454
C & O, Clifton	77	42	33	152
Memorial, Danville	49	27	19	95
Dixie, Hampton	95	38	20	153
Hampton Inst., Hampton	6	-	-	6
Rockingham Mem., Harrisonburg	38	24	21	83
Lynchburg Gen., Lynchburg	52	31	9	92
Elizabeth Buxton, Newport News	70	32	28	130
Riverside, Newport News	52	16	6	74
Norfolk Gen., Norfolk	142	66	18	226
St. Vincent de Paul, Norfolk	122	32	36	190
Petersburg, Petersburg	19	17	14	50
King's Daughters, Portsmouth	68	53	18	139
Parrish Mem., Portsmouth	19	17	14	50
Radford Community, Radford	-	-	21	21

School & City	Fiscal Years			Total
	1943–1944	1944–1945	1945–1946	
Grace, Richmond	65	37	8	110
Johnston Willis, Richmond	46	66	29	141
✱ Medical College of Va., Richmond	139	91	49	279
St. Elizabeth's, Richmond	25	16	9	50
✱d St. Philip, Richmond	113	22	19	154
✱ Stuart Circle, Richmond	30	42	20	92
St. Luke's, Richmond	51	28	11	90
Jefferson, Roanoke	59	39	26	124
Lewis-Gale, Roanoke	84	67	38	189
Roanoke, Roanoke	35	37	14	86
Winchester Mem., Winchester	69	37	18	124
State Total	1,862	1,060	590	3,512
WASHINGTON				
St. Joseph's, Bellingham	53	37	10	100
St. Luke's, Bellingham	45	44	10	99
St. Ignatius, Colfax	33	11	-	44
Gen. Hosp., Everett	81	27	24	132
Providence, Everett	59	41	22	122
St. Peter's, Olympia	75	28	24	127
State College, Pullman	4	10	2	16
✱ Providence, Seattle	323	149	19	491
Columbus, Seattle	89	56	19	164
Swedish, Seattle	123	78	37	238
✱ U. of Wash., Seattle	119	85	28	232
Virginia Mason, Seattle	117	75	41	233
✱ Deaconess, Spokane	234	73	70	377
Sacred Heart, Spokane	179	110	60	349
St. Luke's, Spokane	156	70	30	256
St. Joseph's, Tacoma	108	53	18	179
✱ Tacoma Gen., Tacoma	134	50	45	229
St. Joseph, Vancouver	62	34	19	115
St. Mary's, Walla Walla	54	20	25	99
✱ Central Wash. Deaconess, *Wenatchee*	13	34	1	48
St. Anthony's, Wenatchee	44	16	5	65
St. Elizabeth, Yakima	69	58	25	152
State Total	2,174	1,159	534	3,867
WEST VIRGINIA				
Raleigh Gen., Beckley	-	34	9	43
Charleston Gen., Charleston	152	79	26	257
McMillan, Charleston	43	17	12	72
St. Francis, Charleston	60	28	31	119
St. Mary's, Clarksburg	139	40	-	179
Union Prot., Clarksburg	41	15	11	67
Davis Mem., Elkins	18	22	8	48
Fairmont Gen., Fairmont	75	14	18	107
Reynolds Mem., Glendale	35	16	3	54

School & City	Fiscal Years			
	1943-1944	1944-1945	1945-1946	Total
Huntington Mem., Huntington	62	25	14	101
St. Mary's, Huntington	114	84	50	248
Monogalia, Morgantown	41	34	-	75
Laird Mem., Montgomery	59	35	7	101
Camden-Clark Mem., Parkersburg	91	50	11	152
St. Joseph, Parkersburg	77	35	16	128
Ohio Valley Gen., Wheeling	112	67	47	226
Wheeling, Wheeling	122	62	49	233
State Total	1,241	657	312	2,210
WISCONSIN				
St. Joseph's, Ashland	83	13	11	107
Luther, Eau Claire	58	47	33	138
St. Agnes, Fond du Lac	178	77	25	280
Bellin Mem., Green Bay	55	31	19	105
St. Mary's, Green Bay	19	21	-	40
Mercy, Janesville	49	32	14	95
✳ St. Francis, La Crosse	67	52	32	151
Madison Gen., Madison	56	48	24	128
Methodist, Madison	48	23	26	97
St. Mary's, Madison	50	47	24	121
✳ U. of Wis., Madison	61	25	-	86
Holy Family, Manitowoc	13	17	8	38
St. Joseph's, Marshfield	42	16	20	78
Columbia, Milwaukee	54	45	28	127
Ev. Deaconess, Milwaukee	52	51	18	121
✳ Marquette U., Milwaukee	135	67	20	222
Misericordiae, Milwaukee	33	22	21	76
Mt. Sinai, Milwaukee	92	45	33	170
St. Mary's, Milwaukee	164	71	45	280
Mercy, Oshkosh	61	51	20	132
St. Luke's, Racine	112	39	22	173
St. Mary's, Wausaw	30	11	18	59
Milwaukee Co., Wauwatosa	185	143	33	361
State Total	1,697	994	494	3,785
WYOMING				
Memorial, Sheridan	43	23	9	75
Wyoming Gen., Rock Springs	20	15	8	43
State Total	63	38	17	118
PUERTO RICO				
District, Bayamon	-	93	37	130
Dr. Pila Hosp., Ponce	39	23	35	97
St. Luke's, Ponce	34	20	8	62
Santo Asilo de Damas, Ponce	-	48	30	78

1533

School & City	Fiscal Years			
	1943-1944	1944-1945	1945-1946	Total
Presbyterian, San Juan	83	34	21	138
Bishop Willinger, Ponce	42	5	-	47
Hospital Diaz Garcia, Santurce	-	-	15	15
State Total	178	223	146	567
GRAND TOTAL	95,346	55,551	28,427	179,294

Note* Code added by author.
*Schools of Nursing connected with a college or university.

a. Admits college graduates only
b. Offers new college program which, as a war emergency measure, grants the diploma in nursing at the end of three years and the baccalaureate degree at the end of an additional year.
c. Requires chemistry for entrance.
d. Admits Black students only.
e. Admits Black and White students.

Summary:

Total # College and University Programs 150
Total # College and University Programs
that participated in the Corps 144

Length of College and University program varied from
3 1/2 to 5 1/2 years.

Reference: National Council for War Service, September 1944.

Note* List of schools of nursing participating in the U. S. Cadet Nurse Corps obtained from the Office of the Historian, United States Public Health Service, Rockville, Maryland.

Edwards Brothers Malloy
Thorofare, NJ USA
April 14, 2014